Community Development for Soci

Community Development for Social Change provides a comprehensive introduction to the theory and practice of community development and associated activities, discusses best practice from global experience and links that to the UK context. The book integrates the realities of practice to key underpinning theories, human rights, values and a commitment to promoting social justice.

A range of practice models are described and analysed, including UK models, popular education and community organising, as well as a range of practice issues that need to be understood by community development workers. For example, strategies to promote individual and community empowerment, challenging discrimination, building and sustaining groups, and critical reflection on practice.

Finally, a range of case studies from the UK and overseas illustrates good practice in diverse contexts. These case studies are analysed with reference to the values of community development, the promotion of social justice and the underpinning theories. It is an essential text for those on community development courses as well as for a range of workers, including local government, national and local voluntary agencies, and community-based organisations.

Dave Beck manages the postgraduate programmes in Community Development at the University of Glasgow. With more than 20 years of Community Development experience, his research interests are rooted in participatory approaches to thinking about and doing empowering practice for social change. He is a member of the International Committee of the Community Development Society. Currently, he is co-editor of the *Radical Community Work Journal*.

Rod Purcell is a community development worker by profession. He also has an academic background, which includes Director of Community Engagement in the School of Education, and Head of the Department of Adult and Continuing Education at the University of Glasgow. He was a board member of the International Association for Community Development and Chair of the UK Federation for Community Development Learning. Rod is author of several books and many articles on community development. Currently, he is co-editor of the *Radical Community Work Journal*.

Community Development for Social Change

Dave Beck and Rod Purcell

Routledge
Taylor & Francis Group

NEW YORK AND LONDON

First published 2020
by Routledge
52 Vanderbilt Avenue, New York, NY 10017

and by Routledge
2 Park Square, Milton Park, Abingdon, Oxon, OX14 4RN

Routledge is an imprint of the Taylor & Francis Group, an informa business

© 2020 Taylor & Francis

The right of Dave Beck and Rod Purcell to be identified as authors of this work has been asserted by them in accordance with sections 77 and 78 of the Copyright, Designs and Patents Act 1988.

British Library Cataloguing-in-Publication Data
A catalogue record for this book is available from the British Library

Library of Congress Cataloging-in-Publication Data
Names: Beck, Dave, author. | Purcell, Rod, author.
Title: Community development for social change/Dave Beck and Rod Purcell.
Description: Abingdon, Oxon; New York, NY: Routledge, 2020. |
Includes bibliographical references and index.
Identifiers: LCCN 2019048047 (print) |
LCCN 2019048048 (ebook) | ISBN 9781138694149 (hbk) |
ISBN 9781138694156 (pbk) | ISBN 9781315528618 (ebk)
Subjects: LCSH: Community development–Great Britain–Case studies. |
Social justice–Great Britain–Case studies.
Classification: LCC HN49.C6 B384 2020 (print) | LCC HN49.C6 (ebook) |
DDC 307.1/4120941–dc23
LC record available at https://lccn.loc.gov/2019048047
LC ebook record available at https://lccn.loc.gov/2019048048

ISBN: 978-1-138-69414-9 (hbk)
ISBN: 978-1-138-69415-6 (pbk)
ISBN: 978-1-315-52861-8 (ebk)

Typeset in Sabon
by Newgen Publishing UK

Contents

About This Book

This book is premised on the idea that we live in an unequal world, where power and resources are primarily distributed in the interest of the rich and powerful. Our experience shows us that community development is one way of building engaged and democratic organisations to create personal, community and social change that helps to redress the balance.

To this end a number of themes run through the book: understanding power and how it can be gained by individuals and communities; that to make change we first have to understand the world and how it is socially constructed – to do this we need analytical tools based upon proven theories that help us see the relationship between global trends and everyday life in our communities; and that community development practice is most effective when it is a thought-through and planned process built upon theories and strategies that work.

We also need to recognise that although we are all subject to the effects of globalisation, how this works out locally is variable according to history, culture, political and social systems. Community development is a global activity with many commonalities. However, its local tradition and practice on the ground can vary significantly. For example, practice in the USA and the UK has developed from different traditions, ideological perspectives and significantly different social systems. This book is written from our perspective of working in the UK contexts and learning from other countries that share the same community development perspectives. We can, of course, and indeed must, draw on globalised experiences where this is helpful. In this book we apply lessons from the best of international ideas, North American practice, and the evolving practice models arising from Asian cities.

Structure of the Book

The content for this book is derived from a range of sources. The starting point was the reworking of university-level community development and social theory teaching material that had been tried and tested with many cohorts of undergraduate and postgraduate students. We also made significant use of, and developed discussions from, our previous publications that explored some of the underpinning ideas and practice of community development (Beck and Purcell, 2010, 2013; Purcell, 2005; various journal articles).

The majority of the material though, comes from extensive use of the wider litera-ture and research around social theory, concepts of power and community, community development models and practice from the UK, South America, Africa, Asia and the USA. In addition, we have commissioned 12 UK and international practice case studies for this book.

The book is divided into six thematic sections. Each section is comprised of chapters that take us sequentially through the key elements of the section theme. At the end of each chapter is a summary of key ideas, learning tasks for the reader and key references.

Section 1, The Context of Community Development Work, explores the various contexts of community development practice. This includes the underpinning Values and Purposes of community development, Human Rights, Inequality, an overview of Globalisation and Neo-Liberalism, and an introduction to community development in the UK.

Section 2, Underpinning Theories, is an introduction to key practice theories that are essential to understanding the main elements of working in the community. We discuss Gramsci and his ideas around Power and Hegemony. This is followed by an introduction to the ideas of Paulo Freire. We then explore what we understand the idea of 'Community' to mean, and finally discuss the notion of 'Everyday Life' in communities.

Section 3, Models of Practice, discusses various models of community development prac-tice. We start with an overview of how practice is currently structured, why this is so, and its benefits and drawbacks. This is followed by considering Direct Action, which sits alongside various concepts of community development. We then discuss the US-derived model of Community Organising, the innovative model created by the Slum Dwellers International network, understanding the idea and usefulness of mapping and utilising local Assets. Finally, we offer an overview of how these apparently contradictory models can be integrated into an overarching concept of practice.

Section 4, Practice Issues for Community Development Work, looks at key practice issues around community development. We consider some ways of understanding the commu-nity, how to promote and facilitate Personal and Collective Empowerment, the idea of

Capacity Building and Capability, how to build Community Resilience, ideas and models of local Leadership, inclusive and developmental Group Work and, finally, how to Evaluate Practice.

Section 5, Case Studies of Practice, is comprised of 12 case studies. Each study discusses an area of practice, looking at what was done, why it was done and what it achieved. The purpose of the studies is to provide a sense of how diverse practice can be, both in terms of areas of work, issues being explored, and models of intervention. Each case study has a commentary that links the study to key parts of the book.

Section 6, Summing Up, brings the book to its conclusion. Here we sum up what community development can achieve, where community development is going, and how this might help us all achieve a better future.

Contributors

Dave Beck manages the postgraduate programmes in Community Development at the University of Glasgow. With more than 20 years of Community Development experience, his research interests are rooted in participatory approaches to thinking about and doing empowering practice for social change. He is a member of the International Committee of the Community Development Society. Currently, he is co-editor of the *Radical Community Work Journal*.

Rod Purcell is a community development worker by profession. He also has an academic background, which includes Director of Community Engagement in the School of Education, and Head of the Department of Adult and Continuing Education at the University of Glasgow. He was a board member of the International Association for Community Development and Chair of the UK Federation for Community Development Learning. He is author of several books and many articles on community development. Currently, he is co-editor of the *Radical Community Work Journal*.

Case Study Authors:

Mike Barclay has a background in staffed play provision and out of school childcare but for more than a decade was the play sufficiency lead for Wrexham Council. Here he led on the completion of the Local Authority's play sufficiency assessments and implementation of associated action plans. With Ben Tawil, Mike formed Ludicology in 2013 to provide advice, research and training services to all those concerned with children's play. Working closely with the maintained and non-maintained sector, their work includes participatory research with children; research with adults; co-ordinating partnership working in support of children's play; developing play-centred policies and practices; and providing advice and guidance on how to create the physical and attitudinal conditions necessary to support children to exercise their right and need to play.

Rehana Begum is a British born, Bangladeshi woman, currently working as a Chief Officer and Company Secretary for Diversity Matters North West. She has served the local community for over 15 years in various capacities and has a passion for supporting and empowering others to achieve their full potential.

Luke Campbell is an experienced community practitioner with significant experience in anti-racism education, challenging youth homelessness, and promoting social inclusion. At present he works as an Associate Lecturer (University of the West of Scotland), as an Associate Tutor (University of Glasgow), and is undertaking a PhD in Social Work, researching community resistance movements (University of Edinburgh).

Trudi Cooper was a youth worker for ten years in the UK, before becoming a youth and community work lecturer. Since 1991 she has led the Youth Work degree programme at Edith Cowan University, in Perth, Western Australia, and is director of the Social Program Innovation Research and Evaluation (SPIRE) group. As part of this research, she evaluated the social impact of an Art centre that was established with funding from the state government of Western Australia to facilitate commercial production and sales of Indigenous Australian Art. She also led a national team funded by the Office of Learning and Teaching to renew the youth work curriculum for Australian higher education. She received local and national awards for her outstanding contribution to learning and teaching, and in 2016 became an Australian Learning and Teaching Fellow.

Yvonne Field has more than 40 years' experience of working with organisations, groups and individuals in grass-roots community organisations, front-line staff, senior management, policymakers and planners in local, national and international government, civil society organisations and the corporate sector. Her strategic interventions and sphere of influence has been across the UK, mainland Europe, the English-speaking Caribbean region and South Africa. In 2014, she established a unique national African Diaspora-led social enterprise which creates community spaces which support intergenerational leadership development, community enterprise and social change. She teaches on the BA degree in Applied Social Sciences, Community and Youth at Goldsmiths, University of London.

Danny Gregory was a student just finishing his final year of his Clinical Psychology BSc (Hons) Degree at the University of Worcester at the time of this research. He has an interest in the well-being and support for staff working in caring positions.

Rick Gwilt is a highly experienced freelance consultant and writer, specialising in planning, governance and bid-writing. During the period of his case study he was working as the Charity's Interim Chief Officer.

Nicola Hay has worked with several Third Sector organisations. She served as Campaigns Manager for Show Racism the Red Card Scotland for three years. Now an Associate Lecturer at the University of the West of Scotland, her PhD research investigates 'Who is talking to Roma, Gypsy, Traveller people about careers?'

Frances Howard is a Lecturer in Youth Studies. She has recently completed her PhD investigating 'dis-engaged' young people's experience of Arts Award programmes. Her research interests focus on young people and the arts and her current research includes socially engaged arts programmes, young people's music making and well-being. She has previously worked in arts education and as a Youth Worker, continuing to volunteer for Nottinghamshire YMCA's Young Creatives project.

P. J. Humphreys is Community Development Worker at Community Plus+, and Member, Community Praxis Co-operative.

Ruth Jones is a Principal Lecturer at the University of Worcester and founding Director of the National Centre for the Study and Prevention of Violence and Abuse (NCSPVA). She specialises in gender issues and all aspects of gender-based violence and abuse. She has worked for organisations such as Women's Aid, Relate, the Sandwell Against Domestic Violence Project and Asha Women's Centre. She has worked at the University of Worcester since 2001 where she has developed and delivered innovative and award-winning courses. She also designs and delivers training for professionals from statutory agencies, voluntary organisations, educational establishments and the corporate sector and is consultant to many projects locally, nationally and internationally. She has worked in the UK, India, Pakistan, the US, Fiji, India, Russia, Amsterdam, Cambodia, Malta, Bulgaria, Sweden and many other countries and has contributed to media articles and radio/TV programmes, most notably a Panorama documentary on domestic abuse.

Joanne Lewis is a Senior Lecturer at the University of Worcester and Course Leader for the Youth and Community Work. She specialises in work with young people who have learning disabilities. She has worked for Local Authority Youth Service provision and 3rd Sector Organisations in County Durham, West Sussex and Worcestershire. She has worked as a university lecturer since 2007 in the School of Allied Health and Community at University of Worcester. Her interest areas and research include the pedagogy of teaching reflective practice, adaptive working within challenging landscapes for youth and community workers and broadening horizons for young people with learning disabilities.

Martin Purcell is a Senior Lecturer at the University of Huddersfield. Having taught at various institutions in the North of England, he has been the Youth & Community Work Course Leader at Huddersfield for the past three years. He worked for ten years at the Policy Research Institute, Leeds Beckett University, where he evaluated a number of government-funded initiatives around community engagement, neighbourhood management and regeneration; his focus here was on the translation of professional values into community development practice. Martin has worked in community development in some of the most marginalised communities in Wales, Scotland and the north of England for the past 30 years, and remains active in his local community.

Tina Salter is HE Programmes Director at the YMCA George Williams College in London, a specialist youth and community training College. She is a qualified youth and community worker and has also trained and specialised in mentoring and coaching programmes for young people. In addition to lecturing and tutors, she also carried out evaluative research projects on behalf of youth and community organisations. She is also on the editorial board for Youth and Policy, an open-access online journal for youth and community workers.

Clive Sealey is a Senior Lecturer in Social Policy and Theory at the University of Worcester. He is the author of Social Policy Simplified. His research interests are poverty and social exclusion, and issues related to ideology and social policy. Prior to working as an academic, he worked as a community worker in a variety of settings, including posts overseas. His current specific interest is in ensuring engagement in social policy as a topic.

John Stansfield is a serial social entrepreneur and Senior Lecturer in Community Development at Unitec Institute of Technology in Auckland, New Zealand. He has worked extensively in the NGO sector in advocacy and leadership positions and has campaigned on sustainable development issues for several decades. He is currently Chair of the International Association for Community Development, Education Subcommittee, and is the President of the Aotearoa Community Development Association. He is Deputy Editor of *Whanake, The Pacific Journal of Community Development*. He holds a Master's in International and Intercultural Management from SIT Vermont, USA, with a major in sustainable development; a Postgraduate Diploma in NGO Management and Leadership from SIT, BRAC Bangladesh, and a Bachelor of Social Work and Social Policy from Massey University, Palmerston North, New Zealand.

Ben Tawil has worked in early years settings, in management positions at two adventure playgrounds, as National Play Development Officer for Play Wales as well as lecturing in the subject fields of childhood studies, play and playwork in both Higher and Further Education.

Andy Turner is a community development worker with over 30 years' experience in Manchester and Hackney, East London, where he lives and works. He is a trustee involved in numerous civil society organisations and has facilitated Voice 4 Deptford meetings since 2014. He is a lecturer on the BA Applied Social Science Community and Youth Work and MA Applied Anthropology and Community and Youth Work courses, is a researcher at the Centre for Community Engagement Research and is currently completing his PhD at the Faith and Civil Society Unit – all at Goldsmiths, University of London.

Peter Westoby is an Associate Professor in Social Science and Community Development at Queensland University of Technology, Australia (School of Public Health & Social Work); and a Visiting Professor at the Centre for Development Support, University of the Free State, South Africa.

Acknowledgements

We would like to thank the hundreds of students who we have worked with over the past 20 years. Together we have debated, discussed and honed the ideas found in this book. Our understanding of the theory and practice of Community Development would have been greatly diminished without those co-learners.

We would like also like to thank all of the colleagues, community groups and projects that have helped us to see new ideas, shared amazing practice and shown us that community development works. We especially acknowledge the input and support of our friend and colleague Lynette Jordan who has been part of the team from the start.

Finally, we acknowledge the contribution of Paula Allman who inspired a generation of radical educators and greatly influenced our thinking and practice.

Section 1

The Context of Community Development Work

In this section we explore the underpinning values of community development practice. We begin with (in the UK) the professional values for practice. The discussion then broadens out to explore ideas of Social Change and Human Rights. We then discuss how the belief in human rights operates at a micro level through Anti Oppressive practice. The discussion then opens out to explore current debates about the impact of Globalisation and neo-Liberalism. Finally, we set the scene for the next section through analysing the development of community development in the UK.

1.1 Values and Purpose of Community Development

Introduction

The purpose of Community Development is to work alongside people to establish a new social settlement; in other words, a world in which people, the economy and the state interact with each other in radically different ways. The New Economics Foundation (Coote, 2015) proposes the following goals of this new settlement.

Social justice – every individual has an equal chance to enjoy the essentials of a good life, to fulfil their potential, and to participate in society. Where well-being, equality, and satisfaction of needs are central to that understanding.

Environmental sustainability – living within environmental limits and respecting planetary boundaries, ensuring that the natural resources that are needed for life to flourish are unimpaired for present and future generations.

A more equal distribution of power – the formal and informal means by which people participate in, and influence, decisions and actions at local and national levels, and to challenge the inequalities of power between groups caused by combinations of economic, social, and cultural factors.

Community Development has a pivotal role in the establishment of such a new settlement. However, abstracted from a clearly understood framework of values and principles, Community Development is reduced to a set of practices that have as much potential to manipulate and exploit communities as it has to support its empowerment. In order to avoid this negative outcome, practitioners must develop a set of values and principles that ensures that their work helps people harness their individual and collective power in ways that make the world a more human, creative and equitable place.

It is important at this stage to make it clear that throughout the book when we discuss Community Development we refer to the various forms of practice found under this broad umbrella term. It therefore includes youth work, community-based adult education and other forms of practice that are participatory in their nature and have a goal of social change.

The centrality of values and principles is clearly reflected in the various definitions of Community Development that cover the many forms of practice described above. For example, the national occupational standards for community development in the UK describe community development as, a long-term value-based process which aims to address imbalances in power and bring about change founded on social justice, equality and inclusion (Lifelong Learning UK, 2010). They go on to identify the core values of community development as:

- Social justice and equality
- Anti-discrimination
- Community empowerment
- Collective action
- Working and learning together

The International Association for Community Development (Craig, 2004) facilitated a process whereby more than a hundred community workers, researchers, donors and policymakers, and representatives from government, civil society organisations and community groups, from 33 countries across the European Union and beyond, produced the Budapest declaration which outlines the importance of community development processes in the building of international co-operation and cohesiveness. Within that they define community development as, 'a way of strengthening civil society by prioritising the actions of communities, and their perspectives in the development of social, economic and environmental policy. Within this declaration there is also a set of core values/social principles covering human rights, social inclusion, equality and respect for diversity; and a specific skills and knowledge base.'

These, and many other, statements of values lead to a set of beliefs that are held about the processes and impacts of community development. Phillips and Pittman (2008: 60) define those beliefs in the following terms:

1   People have the right to participate in decisions that affect them.
2   People have the right to strive to create the environment they desire.
3   People have the right to make informed decisions and reject or modify externally imposed conditions.
4   Participatory democracy is the best method of conducting community business.
5   Maximising human interaction in a community will increase the potential for positive development.
6   Creating a community dialogue and interaction amongst citizens will motivate citizens to work on behalf of their community.
7   Ownership of the process and commitment for action is created when people interact to create a strategic community development plan.
8   The focus of Community Development is cultivating people's ability to independently and effectively deal with the critical issues in their community.

The above statements and the values and beliefs that they represent lead to a set of practices which operationalise them. For example, the Community Development Society (CDS) outlines those practices as follows:

- 'Promote active and representative participation toward enabling all community members to meaningfully influence the decisions that affect their lives.
- Engage community members in learning about and understanding community issues, and the economic, social, environmental, political, psychological, and other impacts associated with alternative courses of action.
- Incorporate the diverse interests and cultures of the community in the community development process; and disengage from support of any effort that is likely to adversely affect the disadvantaged members of a community.
- Work actively to enhance the leadership capacity of community members, leaders, and groups within the community.
- Be open to using the full range of action strategies to work toward the long-term sustainability and wellbeing of the community.'

(CDS, n.d.)

However, it has long been recognised that community development happens in conflictual spaces (London Edinburgh Weekend Return Group, 1980). Currently this situation is exacerbated by an increasing typification of the people we work with in communities in purely economic terms. In the context of increasing pressure on practitioners to follow agendas around employability and other prescribed agendas, it is vital that as a profession we have a clear sense of ourselves and that we are able to articulate clearly our values, principles and professional commitments.

However, our commitment to clarifying and adhering to a clear set of principles and values that are specific to our field of endeavour must not undermine our epistemological openness. As individuals and as a profession we need to recognise and celebrate different ways of knowing the complementary values and principles found in other forms of practice. The process of deconstructing or crossing those professional borders involves working within, and outside of, current discourse to create new ideas or alternative forms of knowledge (Giroux, 2005). This opens up the possibility for *us* to learn from different perspectives. It also opens up the possibility for productive partnerships and practice. Some examples of values statements that are complementary to those of community development are seen below.

The Scottish General Teaching Council in its Standards for Registration: Mandatory Requirements for Registration with the General Teaching Council for Scotland (GTC Scotland, 2012) outlines its commitment to social justice within the teaching profession. They define social justice as:

- Embracing locally and globally the educational and social values of sustainability, equality and justice and recognising the rights and responsibilities of future as well as current generations.
- Committing to the principles of democracy and social justice through fair, transparent, inclusive and sustainable policies and practices in relation to: age, disability, gender and gender identity, race, ethnicity, religion and belief, and sexual orientation.
- Valuing as well as respecting social, cultural and ecological diversity and promoting the principles and practices of local and global citizenship for all learners.
- Demonstrating a commitment to engaging learners in real-world issues to enhance learning experiences and outcomes, and to encourage learning our way to a better future.
- Respecting the rights of all learners as outlined in the United Nations Convention on the Rights of the Child (Gov.UK, 2010) and their entitlement to be included in decisions regarding their learning experiences and to have all aspects of their well-being developed and supported.

It is clear to see the commonality of the expressed position of the teaching profession and that of community development. This reveals the potential for community development to bridge the gap between schools and communities in ways that are beneficial to schools, the families that use them and the wider community; this is a potential which, as yet, is generally underdeveloped.

Similarly, we might find resonance in these statements from the Joint Statement of Professional Values from the Nursing and Midwifery Council and General Medical Council in the UK, where they state that Doctors and Nurses should:

- Listen to, and work in partnership with, those for whom they provide care.
- Work constructively with colleagues to provide patient-centred care, recognising that multi-disciplinary teamwork, encouraging constructive challenge from all team members, safety-focused leadership and a culture based on openness and learning when things go wrong are fundamental to achieve high quality care.

(Nursing and Midwifery Council, 2012)

Again, we can see that there are some cultural similarities across these professions. Given that health and well-being scholars and practitioners are seeing the advantages of community development approaches and processes in the creation of individual and community well-being, there are great opportunities for creative partnerships that impact fundamental issues in people's lives.

Of course, it is not only health and education that yields opportunities for collaborative work. An example of the kind of cross-fertilisation that we can experience as we work across professional borders can be seen in the work of the Detroit Collaborative Design Centre (DCDC), a multi-disciplinary, non-profit architecture and urban design firm at the University of Detroit, Mercy School of Architecture, dedicated to creating sustainable spaces and communities through quality design and the collaborative process. They work with community-based development organisations, local government, residents, private developers, students, and local design professionals to enhance local leadership capacity and to promote quality design. Using community development approaches, they respond to locally defined concerns whilst empowering residents and stakeholders to facilitate their own process of community planning, development, and building design (University of Detroit Mercy School of Architecture, n.d.).

'There is no such thing as a perfect community engagement process,' reminds Christina Heximer. 'You have to be very nimble. It is always changing, and there are always going to be different theories of planning and design. But at our core, what we try to do is facilitate conversations with the community. We try to be the "pencil" for ideas to help shape a community's vision for itself, so that decisions are less "top down". And in the end, it's way more exciting.'

'From access to services, processes and visioning sessions to actual construction, DCDC builds capacity in community by valuing its partnership with community,' says O'Leary.

Finally, we need to consider the tensions that exist between the values that we hold and the values that may exist within different aspects of the communities we work with. There continues to be discussion within the community development literature about the need to be both non-directive and non-judgemental (Drake and Simmons, 2014). Whilst we understand the impetus for such an assertion we remain unconvinced about the reality or even the desirability of such a position. If we have our own personal and professional values position, then we are bound to both direct and make judgements. For example, in a situation where one group of people is oppressing another group, it seems to us only right and proper that a professional worker would make a judgement in that situation and try to influence something more equitable. In any case, as Foucault and Sherridan (1979) outline, we are constructed within a system of normative judgements whereby how we see ourselves and others is shaped by power. It would be very arrogant of us to believe that we are somehow immune to that process, particularly those of us who have undergone extensive processes of education. It is therefore incumbent upon us to be reflexive in order to be clear about what values are and what impact they have on our interactions with people.

Key Learning Points

- Community Development is a value-based practice
- Its ultimate purpose is personal and social transformation
- Values clarify our roles and help us define how we work with people
- Common values offer us the basis to work across professional boundaries
- Clashes of values can cause tension and bring us into conflict

Learning Tasks

Helping to clarify values in a group:

- In small groups, brainstorm the character traits or values you believe are essential to our democratic society. Using post-it-notes, list each value on a separate sheet
- Working in small groups, each group member in turn will present one value/character trait they feel is essential to our democratic society. The group will place the value/character trait into one of three categories
- Yes, we all agree this is important and that Community Development has a responsibility in promoting it (agreement)
- One or more individuals do not believe it is important from their perspective, or they do not believe that Community Development has a responsibility in promoting it but could live with it (lukewarm/moderate)
- One or more individuals do not believe it is important, and/or disagree that Community Development has a responsibility in promoting it (opposition/no agreement)
- The characters/values in each category are grouped based on their similarity. After groups are formed, each is given a name that summarises the traits/values included in that group. (Example: honesty, trust, integrity, truthfulness might all fit under the name integrity)
- After naming, the group will define and provide a short rationale as to why this value is important for everyone
- Each small group will feed back a definition of one value/trait they feel is essential for Community Development to promote. (The activity requires the groups to focus on what they agree on and not on areas of disagreement)

Key Reading

Craig, G. (2011) *The Community Development Reader: History, Themes and Issues*. Bristol: The Policy Press.

References

CDS (Community Development Society) (n.d.) 'Principles of Good Practice'. Available at: www.comm-dev.org/about/principles-of-good-practice.

Coote, A. (2015) 'People, Planet, Power: Toward a New Social Settlement', *The International Journal of Social Quality*, 5(1), 8–34.

Craig, G. (2004) 'The Budapest Declaration: Building European Civil Society through Community Development', *Community Development Journal*, 39(4), 423–429.

Drake, H. and Simmons, K. (2014) 'Building Communities Collaboratively: The Milton Keynes Community Mobiliser Service', *Community Development Journal*, 49(2), 311–326.

Foucault, M. and Sheridan, A. (1979) *Discipline and Punish: The Birth of the Prison*. London: Penguin Books.

Giroux, H.A. (2005) *Border Crossings: Cultural Workers and the Politics of Education*. New York: Routledge.

Gov.uk (2010) United Nations Convention on the Rights of the Child (UNCRC): How Legislation Underpins Implementation in England – Publications – GOV.UK. [online]. Available at: www.gov.uk/government/publications/united-nations-convention-on-the-rights-of-the-child-uncrc-how-legislation-underpins-implementation-in-england, accessed 19 March 2015.

GTC Scotland (2012) *The Standards for Registration: Mandatory Requirements for Registration with the General Teaching Council for Scotland*. Edinburgh: GTC Scotland.

Lifelong Learning UK (2010) *National Occupational Standards for Community Development*. London: Lifelong Learning UK.

London Edinburgh Weekend Return Group (1980) *In and Against the State*. London: Pluto Press.

Nursing and Midwifery Council (2012) 'Joint Statement on Professional Values'. Available at: www.nmc.org.uk/news/news-and-updates/nmc-and-gmc-release-joint-statement-on-professional-values/, accessed 12 September 2019.

Phillips, R. and Pittman, R.H. (2008) *An Introduction to Community Development*. New York: Taylor & Francis Ltd – M.U.A.

University of Detroit Mercy School of Architecture (n.d.) Detroit Collaborative Design Centre. Available at: www.dcdc-udm.org/about/, accessed 15 April 2016.

1.2 Social Change

Introduction

Social change refers to significant changes in the ways that individuals and groups interact with each other and the culture within which those interactions take place. It includes the ways that things are done and it also encompasses changes in the norms, values and beliefs that are held within society (Weinstein and MyiLibrary, 2010). Social change can arise from a variety of sources including technological changes, such as the developments that led to the industrial revolution. It can also be caused by major changes in populations, including the rise of urbanisation: in 1950 only 30 per cent of the world's population lived in urban areas, today it is 55 per cent and it is expected to increase to 68 per cent by 2050 (UN, 2018). The social conflict and wars we are witnessing in the early twenty-first century are producing massive social change both in conflict zones and globally, through immigration and other issues. Finally, social movements produce social change; for example, the impact that the feminist movement has had in terms of democracy, reproductive rights and employment (Hannam, 2016).

Not all social change is planned, neither is it always positive, but one thing is clear, social change is an inevitable feature of our lives. 'The world is not finished. It is always in the process of becoming' (Freire, 1998: 72) This process of becoming is a social one, relying on the individual and collective agency of people to shape and reshape culture, practices and structures; it is not some abstract force that happens to us as individuals and communities – although it may feel like that at times. As agents of grass-roots social change, our challenge is to work with individuals to create a sense of personal power and agency, to bring people and organisations together around common interests and to build people power which can both create impetus for positive social change and act as a force to resist negative social change.

How we theorise social change will inevitably influence how we practise, and much of our theorising will rest on how we conceptualise power. In addition to Freire and Gramsci's insights on power and social change discussed below, it is useful to consider Foucault's insights (1980, 1982) that power is distributed in more complex and contradictory ways than the traditional materialist paradigm acknowledges. Perhaps we need to understand the oppressor/oppressed dialectic that Freire discusses as more of a shifting set of relationships that is played out in the world, rather than a fixed position of certain individuals and groups. This allows us to understand the complexity of our current age and the real experience that people have of being powerful and powerless, the oppressed and the oppressor in different circumstance or different times. This complex dynamic also opens up a space for us to think about Foucault's second insight, that every site where power is exercised contains potential for resistance. It takes us away from thinking that only global change or the overthrowing of capitalism is valid in terms of achieving social change and helps us recognise the importance and the contribution that much more modest changes make to fundamental and sustainable social change.

We suggest that the practice of supporting social change rests on two complementary foundations: First, the symbolic reconstruction of people's narratives (Ezzy, 1998). This involves a critical reflection on people's lived experience, uncovering both its history, the impact of that history and the processes that maintain present circumstances. It is from a place of new insights that a vision for a transformed self and a transformed future arise. Drawing from both Ezzy (1998) and Freire, this is an intersubjective process, that is, both the analysis, and the agency that arise from it, are collective processes. However, analysis, transformed personal and collective narratives and a new sense of identity, positive though all that is, do not go far enough. Material changes in the processes and structures of the world, locally and globally, must match those symbolic changes. The development of a more empowered people must similarly be matched by the development of more receptive organisations and agencies.

Having explored some of the thinking around social change, we now consider some of the themes and potential areas of focus within which practice can operate.

Thin (2002) explores four themes of social change that allow the worker to analyse their practice in terms of social change. They are:

- Social justice – equal opportunity and the achievement of all human rights
- Solidarity – cohesion, empathy, co-operation and associational life
- Participation – opportunities for everyone to play a meaningful part in development
- Security – livelihood security and safety from physical threats

Any youth and community work practice which claims to be working for social change should be able to demonstrate specific impacts in some or all of the themes identified above. This typology gives a useful checklist by which you can assess the impact of your work. Not every project will achieve in all four areas but if it is not achieving in any, can it still be considered to be effecting meaningful social change?

Three Foci of Social Change

In order to deepen our analysis of social change we must consider, not just a general sense of things getting better, but identify the distinct arenas of social experience where intentional change for good can occur.

Legal Change

One area of focus for youth and community work is in influencing law and social policy. There is a long tradition of community campaigning to change the law stretching back to the 1960s with the Campaign for Nuclear Disarmament (CND) and others. In recent years, community-based campaigns around environmental issues, equality in marriage for same sex couples, anti-discrimination, human rights, changes in law and policy around asylum seekers have been to the fore.

An example of this type of change is the Community Empowerment Act (Scotland) 2015, which came about partly as a result of the campaigning of land reform activists (Braunholtz-Speight, 2015) and was shaped by lengthy consultations between government and a wide range of community organisations and other agencies. It aims to give more power to Scotland's communities to have their voices heard in decisions that matter to them, and to take action for themselves.

Although the stated intention of the legislation seems to support the social justice dimension of social change discussed above, it must be understood in its wider context and its application in practice. It could be argued that these legal changes are a reflection of a broader shift from a welfare to an enabling model of state, which is seen by some, not as an empowering model at all but as a money-saving process within which the state relinquishes its responsibilities and delegates to other segments of the market and society (Markantoni et al., 2008).

It could be similarly argued that legal changes are only effective when people have the power to enforce them. However, O'Connor and Steiner (2018) note in their early evaluation of the process in regards to Participation Requests that marginalised groups are not well supported in the process, meaning that they are less likely to benefit from the opportunities to have influence that are afforded by the Act.

And so, whilst focusing on legislative change remains a valid focus for social change, it is problematic and cannot be expected to succeed on its own; parallel developments in both awareness raising in the wider community and the development of power structures within communities experiencing injustice, which can then ensure that legislation is enforced, is also required.

It could also be argued that certain forms of government or constitutions will result in social change. In situations where there are authoritarian states the focus of social change could be the establishing of more democratic forms of power. Within the UK a legitimate focus for social change that youth and community workers could be involved in is the development of more participative forms of democracy rather than representational ones. Much of the work around community planning, for example, would fall into this category and would seek to fulfil the social change aim of developing participation and solidarity.

The role of community development is crucial in this arena where social policy is outworked in practice, since social policy often suffers from the distance between decision and implementation. I am sure we can all think of laws or policies which are good at the point of decision but the implementation is carried out by people and organisations who were neither involved in the decision nor support its aims. They are able to amend it, ignore it or fudge it sufficiently to rob it of any effectiveness. Youth and community workers are in a strong position to both work with the community to understand their rights and responsibilities and to support them to organise to exercise control of the social realm, work with agencies and policymakers, and ensure that what was planned happens.

Economic Change

The second area where youth and community workers can focus their efforts in achieving social change is what is broadly termed the economic sphere. These models of change are based on increasing economic resources in terms of actual money and free or subsidised housing, health, education and childcare etc. with a view to moving groups and individuals from a position of low resource and dependence to high resource and independence.

Micro finance initiatives give access to credit to the world's poorest people, which they then use to establish businesses, take part in education or improve their homes and neighbourhoods. We can see from these examples that much can be achieved in terms of Social Justice, Solidarity, Participation and Security. However, the results of this approach are not always guaranteed. It is suggested that individuals, communities or countries will be able to make use of these additional economic resources only if they have pre-existing 'productive potential' (Coleman, 1971: 67). This is why the Grameen Bank focuses almost exclusively on working with women, since it is claimed that:

> Women make better use of small loans than men
> Women have a better track record when it comes to repayment
> Women are a huge untapped labour pool
> Women have the right to access capital
> Women who receive loans adopt healthier lifestyles and are empowered
>
> (Esty, 2014)

Coin Street Community Builders, a not-for-profit development trust which since 1984, has had the responsibility for regenerating 13 acres of prime real estate on London's South Bank, formed as a response to the Greater London Council's development plan for the area in the 1970s. Over the years they have taken control of redevelopment and created affordable housing, recreational space, workspace, shopping and leisure facilities for the use of the whole community. The project demonstrates, that 'there is another way'. All of what they achieved happened because of the coming together of interconnected elements. First, there were changed attitudes to authority within the area and the country, exemplified by the rise of the consumer movement, CND and others. At the same time there were changes in planning legislation, which ensured that the public had to be consulted as part of the planning process. Finally, there was the social mix of the people involved in the campaign; these included local people, councillors, priests, planners and community workers. The confluence of societal attitudes, changes in legislation and the availability of, and connections between, groups of people resulted in the community being able to take advantage of the situation that was there, however, not all situations are as favourable as this one.

In conclusion, it seems that the immense possibilities for social change afforded by this approach can only be realised when they are based on a foundation of both the opportune moment and the mix of skills, experience and networks within the organisation taking up the challenge. The challenge for the youth and community worker is to be able to both read the signs of the times and assess the capacity for groups and individuals to act in any given situation. To paraphrase Alinsky (1989) only take on the battles you know you have a chance of winning.

Changes in Individuals

Social change based on work that is directed at individuals is the final area to be considered. These are models based on the idea that social change is achieved by the aggregation of individual changes in beliefs, personality or lifestyle. These approaches can be broken down into two broad categories – individualist and revolutionary.

Individualist theories could be typified by an orientation towards achievement and a prioritising of the individual over the group, family and community. Social change is then affected by the aggregation of increases in individuals' human capital in the context of freedom from social constraint and requires a stable market within which to operate.

Youth and community work approaches under this model would be typified by those focusing on the development of human capital and would include confidence building, training and skills development. The logic of this approach is that the development of skill and confidence can overcome the culture of communities which might be typified by a lack of aspiration and limited expectation of meaningful employment. Increases in skills and qualifications would then lead to increased employment levels and more affluent communities. As a result of this, related issues of crime, drug-taking and poor health would be improved.

A criticism that could be levelled at this approach is that, if the intention is social change in a neighbourhood, often what happens in reality is that individuals develop their confidence, skills and qualifications and leave the neighbourhood for a more affluent one. The result for a neighbourhood is detrimental because inevitably it is the more able members of communities who are able to make best use of these provisions. This is not to say that community-based education and training programmes are not valuable; clearly the impact of such programmes can be life changing for the individuals involved. The problem does remain that on its own, it may not achieve a collective change within the community. The challenge is therefore to consider what parallel interventions may lead to change on a community scale.

Perhaps it is useful to consider aspects of the other model of individual approaches, which may add an important dimension to practice. Revolutionary theories posit change within individuals through taking part in the revolutionary act, this could include community action and activism – it is the action itself that brings about the change. In contrast to the individualist view, it is commitment to the movement rather than individual development that is foregrounded, and so social change is brought about by the collective force of the revolutionary (community) group. Whilst not a revolutionary project as such, youth and community work approaches that have a strong campaigning focus can have some similar characteristics. Within these groups, members reconceptualise individual issues as collective issues, they are united in a common cause to effect change within society and their personal agendas are subsumed within the overall cause.

Gittell et al. (2000), in their study of women's Community Development Organisations, indicate the potential of participation in collective action to achieve individual and social change.

> The participatory structure of most of the CDOs in our study and the way the organizations built participation into their programs created a democratic space where community residents could both form ties with each other and develop as individuals while collectively working for the betterment of the whole community.
>
> (2009: 125)

There is perhaps an inherent instability within this approach because of the special conditions required to maintain the collective identity of the community group. For example, an organisation may be formed to campaign for improvement in housing conditions within a neighbourhood. This will result in a variety of collective and individual actions which will precipitate individual and social change; however, when the particular issue is resolved, the group will either shrink dramatically in size or cease to exist.

Challenges and Tensions of Social Change

The work of Antonio Gramsci (1971), particularly in his concept of hegemony, by which he means the political and moral leadership exercised by one group over another, points to an essential inertia that must be faced up to by those seeking to effect social change.

> Dominant groups in society, including fundamentally but not exclusively the ruling class, maintain their dominance by securing the 'spontaneous consent' of subordinate groups, including the working class, through the negotiated construction of a political and ideological consensus which incorporates both dominant and dominated groups.
>
> (Strinati, 1995: 165)

In this state people accept the prevailing order because they are compelled by current apparatus of state and economy to devote their time to making a living and because they cannot conceive another way of organising society, since they have internalised the vision and culture of their oppressor (Freire, 1972). They therefore fatalistically accept the world as it is, thereby rendering meaningful social change difficult. Social change in this context is therefore counter-hegemonic. It is not change for its own sake; rather it seeks to replace an oppressive and dehumanising social order with a just one. Counter-hegemony suggests much more than merely improvement of material conditions, it must also contain elements of critical education (Allman, 2001) and the building up of networks of alliances between social minorities in order to develop a different consensus of what society could be.

> *The revolutionary forces have to take civil society before they take the state, and therefore have to build a coalition of oppositional groups united under a hegemonic banner which usurps the dominant or prevailing hegemony.*
>
> (Strinati, 1995: 169)

Within this collective process of social change, there is a role for exceptional individuals described by Gramsci as Organic Intellectuals.

> *The mode of being of the new intellectual can no longer consist in eloquence ... but in active participation in practical life, as constructor, organiser, permanent persuader and not just a simple orator.*
>
> (1971: 10)

Brookfield (2005) argues that only indigenous leaders can truly fulfil this function since they alone can understand the people, feel their passions and therefore represent their interests. However, I would suggest that youth and community workers by virtue of their organic connections with groups and individuals within communities have an important role in developing critical thinking and collective action in the pursuit of social change. They bring an understanding of processes of organising and change, and theoretical ways of understanding social phenomena, which can prove invaluable in enabling community groups to critically reflect on their lives and to plan, execute and reflect on action to change. I would argue that action which brings together local knowledge, global perspectives and clear theory and analysis will have a greater chance of achieving positive outcomes.

Even when a degree of success has been achieved, the battle is not over. Carroll and Ratner (2001) suggest that there are two challenges to maintaining counter-hegemonic activity. These come in the form of colonising and marginalising moves by both capital and state. Often organisations that cause trouble will have their funding cut, will not be allowed representation on committees and will be generally marginalised. If this tactic does not work, colonising and incorporation is attempted. Many movements that start with radical intentions end up being drawn into 'the system' by being given buildings to run, staff to manage and service level agreements to meet – thereby diverting them from their original mission and robbing them of their power to challenge the status quo.

In response to this, social action organisations must provide an ongoing basis for alternative formations of identity and community through a process of politicising their constituents and transforming received identity scripts. They must also provide an ongoing basis for alternative modes of satisfying the needs and nurturing the capacity of their community. Finally, they must develop a repertoire of collective action that actively and visibly contests hegemonic relations and practices.

In conclusion, genuine social change is change that reshapes the balance of social power away from ruling elites into the hands of people who are marginalised in the current social order. It comes about through a process of critical thinking and collective action, which produces people with a new vision of themselves and their society and new organisations which provide an abbreviated experience of transformed relationships and a power base for political change.

Ethical Issues

Kelman and Warwick suggest that ethical issues must be considered in any social intervention, which they describe as: 'any act planned or unplanned that alters the characteristics of an individual or the pattern of relationships between individuals' (Kelman and Warwick, 1978: 3). They suggest four areas which must be considered: the ends served by the change, the targets at which it is directed, the means of implementation and the assessment of the intended or unintended consequences. In each of these areas the worker must recognise the imbalance of power that could potentially result in their values and agendas being imposed on the community. As such this would be an act of cultural invasion (Freire, 1972) rather than an act of empowerment.

There is a difficult balance to be struck between a non-directive approach, whereby the worker might as well not be there, to one where the community group serve to act on the worker's pet projects. Neither of these extremes is desirable. Rather, problem-posing approaches which allow both the worker and the community group to enter into dialogue about the nature of the problem, its causes and solutions and appropriate ways to act to counter them must be sought. This process of co-investigation and collective action and reflection form the basis of an ethical and democratic approach to supporting social change. These are the approaches that this book explores.

Key Learning Points

- Social change is the key aim of Community Development
- Social Change involves:
    - Social justice – equal opportunity and the achievement of all human rights
    - Solidarity – cohesion, empathy, co-operation and associational life
    - Participation – opportunities for everyone to play a meaningful part in development
    - Security – livelihood security and safety from physical threats
- Social change can focus on legal change, economic change and change within individuals
- There are several tensions and ethical issues which arise whilst acting as an agent of social change

Learning Tasks

Micro-finance, as seen in the work of the Grameen Bank (https://grameenfoundation.org/what-we-do), is arguably one way of achieving social change.

- To what extent does this approach achieve social change?
- Are there any gaps?
- What can community development learn from this approach?

Key Reading

Coburn, A. and Gormally, S. (2017) *Communities for Social Change: Practicing Equality and Social Justice in Youth and Community Work*. New York: Peter Lang.

References

Alinsky, S.D. (1989) *Rules for Radicals: A Practical Primer for Realistic Radicals*. New York: Vintage Books.

Allman, P. (2001) *Critical Education against Global Capitalism: Karl Marx and Revolutionary Critical Education*. London and Westport, CT: Bergin & Garvey.

Braunholtz-Speight, T. (2015) 'Scottish Community Land Initiatives: Going Beyond the Locality to Enable Local Empowerment', *People, Place and Policy*, 9/2, 123–138.

Brookfield, S. (2005) *The Power of Critical Theory for Adult Learning and Teaching*. Maidenhead: Open University Press.

Carroll, W. and Ratner, R. (2001) 'Sustaining Oppositional Cultures in "Post-socialist times": A Comparative Study of Three Social Movement Organisations', *Sociology*, 35(3), 605–629.

Coleman, J.S. (1971) 'Conflicting Theories of Social Change', *American Behavioural Scientist*, 14, 633–650.

Esty, K. (2014) '5 Reasons Why Muhammad Yunus Focuses on Lending to Women'. Available at: www.impatientoptimists.org/Posts/2014/01/5-Reasons-Why-Muhammad-Yunus-Focuses-on-Lending-to-Women, accessed 12 September 2019.

Ezzy, D. (1998) 'Theorizing Narrative Identity: Symbolic Interactionism and Hermeneutics', *The Sociological Quarterly*, 39(2), 239–252. doi: 10.1111/j.1533–8525.1998.tb00502.x.

Foucault, M. (1980) *Power/Knowledge: Selected Interviews and Other Writings 1972–77*. New York: Harvester Wheatsheaf.

Foucault, M. (1982) 'The Subject and Power', in H.L. Dreyfus and P. Rabinow (eds), *Michel Foucault: Beyond Structuralism and Hermeneutics*. Brighton: Harvester Press, 208–228.

Freire, P. (1972) *Pedagogy of the Oppressed*. London: Penguin.

Gittell, M., Ortega-Bustamante, I., and Steffy, T. (2000) 'Social Capital and Social Change: Women's Community Activism', *Urban Affairs Review*, 36, 123–147.

Gramsci, A. (1971) *Selections from Prison Notebooks*. New York: International Publishers.

Hannam, J. (2016). *Feminism*. Abingdon: Routledge.

Kelman, H.C. and Warwick, D.P. (1978) 'The Ethics of Social Intervention: Goals, Means, and Consequences', in G. Bermant, H.C. Kelman, and D.P. Warwick (eds), *The Ethics of Social Intervention*. Washington, DC: Hemisphere.

Markantoni, M., Steiner, A., Elliot Meador, J., and Farmer, J. (2008) 'Do Community Empowerment and Enabling State Policies Work in Practice? Insights from a Community Development Intervention in Rural Scotland', *Geoforum*, 97, 142–154.

O'Connor, C.H. and Steiner, A. (2018) *Review of Participation Requests Annual Reports: Summary*. Glasgow: Glasgow Caledonian University.

Strinati, D. (1995) *An Introduction to Theories of Popular Culture*. Routledge: London.

Thin, N. (2002) *Social Progress and Sustainable Development*. London: ITDG Publishing.

United Nations (2018) 'Population Facts'. Available at: https://population.un.org/wup/Publications/Files/WUP2018-PopFacts_2018-1.pdf.

Weinstein, J.A. and MyiLibrary (2010) *Social Change*, 3rd edn. Lanham, MD: Rowman & Littlefield Publishers.

1.3   Human Rights

A Framework for Action

Introduction

There is a long-established connection between Community Development and Human Rights. In the 1940s, Saul Alinsky (1989) understood his practice as a way to enable people to achieve what can broadly be understood as their basic human rights, 'they will have the power and opportunity to best meet each unforeseeable future crisis as they move ahead in their eternal search for those values of equality, justice, freedom, peace, a deep concern for the preciousness of human life' (Alinsky, 1989: 28). Sen (2004) reminds us that the ethical demands placed on us to uphold the freedoms that human rights discourse point to generate powerful reasons for action for us in what can be broadly described as the helping professions; whereas in some quarters there is the perception that human rights mobilisation is best achieved by lawyers or professional policy advocates (Reichert, 2006).

Ife (2010) argues that, for a society to truly respect and value human rights, people must be encouraged to both exercise those rights, and accept their responsibility to act. This posits a vision of society where citizens are supported to be active contributors to civic life rather than passive consumers. It is within this understanding of human rights that we see a clear role for community development that has ideals of participatory practice at its heart. If we are to achieve this active citizenship and begin to realise human rights and social justice, community development workers, youth workers and others must engage in consciousness-raising and social mobilisation at the local level (Libal and Harding, 2015).

Human rights practice is carried out locally, nationally, and internationally, whilst standards are set at regional and international levels. This gives rise to the question of which standards we choose to accept and apply. Statements on Human Rights go back as far as The Declaration of the Rights of Man and of the Citizen, a foundational statement from the French revolution adopted in August 1789. More contemporary examples are: The American Declaration of the Rights and Duties of Man, adopted by the Ninth International Conference of American States, Bogota, Colombia, 1948; on 10 December 1948, the General Assembly of the United Nations adopted and proclaimed the Universal Declaration of Human Rights; on 4 November 1950 the Council of Europe adopted the European Convention on Human Rights; and the African (Banjul) Charter on Human and Peoples' Rights was adopted 27 June 1981. Not all of these can be considered universal – applying to all cultures at all times – since, though these various pronouncements have similarities, they also have many fundamental differences. Given these competing claims for moral and political authority we must have ways of ascertaining their validity within the historical and cultural context within which we work.

Human Rights both as a theory and as a social movement has been widely criticised. Marie-Bénédicte Dembour (2006: 4) highlights five strands of critique of Human Rights theory:

- **Realists** intimate that human rights cannot be 'above' or 'beyond' the state but necessarily originate from, and are enmeshed within, the state; they reject the idea that human rights are natural, existing outside of social recognition.
- **Utilitarians** oppose the granting of individual rights regardless of the consequences for the common good; nor do they think it is possible for human rights to be absolute and/or inalienable.
- **Marxists** view rights as sustaining the bourgeois order and thus feeding oppression by privileging a particular class to the detriment of the oppressed majority.
- **Particularists** object to the idea that moral judgements can be made which hold true across cultures; they call for tolerance of practices that are not comprehensible within the dominant perspective and denounce what they see as the inherent imperialism of human rights that are not universal but the product of the society which has created them.
- **Feminists,** finally, attack human rights' pretence of equity and neutrality by observing that rights, which have generally been defined by men, largely bypass the interests and concerns of women.

A further critique would be that the roots of human rights thinking and practice is that it is rooted in Western thought and that it therefore establishes Eurocentric political, economic, and cultural norms which it then seeks to impose on non-Western societies (Mutua, 2002). This gives rise to many concerns about the mismatch between competing cultural assumptions, a primary example being the centrality of the individual within the Western paradigm which is at odds with a more collective starting point in, for example, African and Asian traditions; the implications of this are explored in our discussion of rights and responsibilities below.

Ife (2016) identifies three traditions of Human Rights thinking and practice (see table below) and suggests Constructed Rights, which he contrasts to both Natural Rights and State Obligations, as being one closely aligned with Community Development practice.

Natural Rights are in line with what Thomas Hobbes (2008) discusses as the *right of nature* where each man (sic) has the right to preserve his own life by any means, which, in his own judgment and reason, is most apt. Developing from that, John Locke (2002) posits that the law of nature and reason demands that all are equal and independent and that no one ought to harm another in his life, health, liberty or possessions. This position is perhaps best expressed by Thomas Jefferson (1776), in the 'Declaration of Independence' where he presents this statement of human rights:

> We hold these Truths to be self-evident, that all Men are created equal, that they are endowed by their Creator with certain unalienable Rights, that among these are Life, Liberty, and the Pursuit of Happiness – That to secure these Rights, Governments are instituted among Men, deriving their just Powers from the Consent of the Governed, that whenever any Form of Government becomes destructive of these Ends, it is the Right of the People to alter or to abolish it, and to institute new Government, laying its Foundation on such Principles, and organizing its Powers in such Form, as to them shall seem most likely to affect their Safety and Happiness.

A State Obligations approach to human rights is one where the role of the state is seen as the central driver for defining and upholding the human rights of the citizen. Examples of this can be seen in discourses around human rights approaches to international development (Hamm, 2001). The weakness of this approach lies in the state's inability or unwillingness to adequately ensure the rights of groups and individuals at a local level. It is similarly ineffective where the relationship between the state and the individual is an ambiguous one, that is, where people are considered non-citizens such as refugees and migrants. Finally, it puts the business of human rights in the hands of lawyers and other experts, thereby disempowering ordinary citizens. This leads us to consider the notion of Constructed Rights.

Within the conception of Constructed Rights, human rights can be seen as something which is being constantly redefined, contested and adjusted at all levels of society. Rather than being understood as a set of fixed and universal ideas, human rights are produced through our shifting understanding of what it means to be human and how we as human beings want to interact with each other. 'From this perspective, it is developing a culture of human rights that is important in human rights work, not just the passing of legislation and strengthening of legal mechanisms and forms of accountability' (Ife, 2016: 76).

Three Traditions of Human Rights

	Natural rights	*State obligations*	*Constructed rights*
Justification	human nature, God-given	the nation-state and the UN	people's lived experience
How it is studied	philosophy and theology	law and political science	anthropology and sociology
Universality	universal	subject to jurisdictions	contextual
Practice	education and activism	law, policy development and advocacy	community development

Source: Adapted from Ife (2016: 77).

Rights and Responsibilities

Drawing on the tradition of Constructed Rights, we see that thinking about, and practice around, human rights is something which all citizens can and should be involved in and that, as community development workers and youth workers, we are well placed to encourage and support both of those activities. We also see that passivity is not an option. Human rights are not something that are given, either by nature or the state, but they are the result of human agency. Therefore, both individually and collectively, we have both rights and responsibilities in this area. A society that respects and values human rights is one where people are encouraged to exercise their rights, and accept a responsibility to do so where they can. This is an active participatory society, on which requires citizens to be active contributors rather than passive consumers; and the promotion of such a participatory society has long been on the agenda of community development (Ife, 2016: 4).

As mentioned above, the Western view of human rights invites us to consider those rights purely as the domain of the individual. However, Human Rights operates in that messy interaction between individuals and the communities of which they find themselves a part; the rights of the community impose certain responsibilities on the individual and the rights of the individual cannot operate without others external to the individual exercising their responsibilities.

This discussion about the relationship between rights and responsibilities is something that has been central to politics on both sides of the Atlantic. The reconstruction of the UK's Labour Party in the late 1990s, dubbed the third way, had a number of central concerns. First, it sought to develop alternatives to state provision and government control. This is reflected more recently in the Conservative government's policy 'Big Society', launched under David Cameron. Second, it sought to promote wealth creation by being fiscally 'prudent'; this neo-liberal agenda has continued through successive governments. Finally, it sought to rebalance the tension between rights and responsibilities, where a model of joint responsibility between state and citizen was envisaged, thereby fostering a culture of duty within strong communities (Driver and Martell, 2000). The Third Way has been widely critiqued (Jordan, 2010) for the establishment of a culture of individualism which makes people unable to recognise opportunities to act together, suggesting that this fragmentation will favour the better-off and more experienced and therefore contribute to greater inequalities of resources and power.

What then is our response to Human Rights in the face of the confusing and contradictory picture outlined above? First, in keeping with Community Development values we must see human rights as a collective issue.

> Human rights become not so much a claim made by an individual or individuals, but a process and a structure for human community. From this perspective all humans share a moral order and are subject to moral law.
>
> (Gandhi, 2007; Parel, 1997)

> Human rights then, are collectively constructed, collectively understood and collectively experienced. I cannot have 'my' rights if you do not have 'yours', and hence they become 'our' rights.
>
> (Ife and Fiske, 2006: 303)

Second, also in keeping with Community Development values, we must see Human Rights as a bottom-up issue. This means that, rather than accepting an imposed set of standards devised outside the local community with its own values, culture and history, any statement of Human Rights becomes a starting point for critical reflection and action. Finally, we must see Human Rights as Praxis; not simple an idea to be considered or a set of actions to be undertaken by the powerful on behalf of the weak but the site for combined critical reflection and action, which has its starting point as the experience of those who are robbed of their rights. As Jan Hancock puts it: 'Moreover, the ideological pigeonholing of human rights as a hegemonic instrument rather than an arena of political struggle overlooks an important aspect of human rights as praxis; that is as an instrument to challenge social power relations' (Hancock, 2006: 2), and so if we are to understand human rights as praxis, we must rethink and remake that practice in the light of our current historical material conditions.

Some of the newer tactics which are emerging include: engaging in rights-based impact assessments of policy, conducting budgetary analysis, and developing human rights indicators and benchmarks to measure the extent of effort a government expends to realise a given right (Libal and Harding, 2015).

> Increasingly there has been a focus on intergenerational rights, recognising that human rights violations that happened in the past have an impact on the present generation and in turn the present generation has a responsibility for human rights of generations

to come. This can be seen in many areas but perhaps most clearly in the relationship between human rights and the environment.

Key Learning Points

- Human Rights potentially offers a foundation for Community Development practice
- It provides a framework to discuss rights and responsibilities
- A participative model of bottom-up human rights offers rich opportunities for us to shape practice that supports social change

Learning Tasks

- What are the advantages and challenges of using human rights as a foundation for community development practice?
- From what you have read, can you envisage any ambiguity or conflict arising out of using Human Rights as a foundation for local practice?
- What could you foresee as your role in this?

Key Reading

Ife, J. (2010) *Human Rights from Below: Achieving Rights through Community Development*. Cambridge: Cambridge University Press.

References

Alinsky, S.D. (1989) *Rules for Radicals: A Practical Primer for Realistic Radicals*. New York: Vintage Books.

Dembour, M. (2006) *Who Believes in Human Rights? Reflections on the European Convention*. Cambridge: Cambridge University Press.

Driver, S. and Martell, L. (2000) 'Left, Right and the Third Way', *Policy & Politics*, 28(2), 147–161.

Gandhi, M. (2007) *An Autobiography: Or the Story of My Experiments with Truth*. London: Penguin.

Hamm, B.I. (2001) 'A Human Rights Approach to Development', *Human Rights Quarterly*, 23(4), 1005–1031. doi: 10.1353/hrq.2001.0055.

Hancock, J.M. (2006) *Universal Human Rights: Claims by the Ogoni People of Nigeria and the Paradox of Cultural Relativism*. San Diego, CA: Annual meeting of the International Studies Association. Available at: www.allacademic.com/meta/p. 100631_index.html.

Hobbes, T. (2008) *Leviathan*. London: Longman.

Ife, J. (2010) *Human Rights from Below: Achieving Rights through Community Development*. Cambridge: Cambridge University Press.

Ife, J. (2016) *Community Development in an Uncertain World: Vision, Analysis and Practice*, 2nd edn. Port Melbourne, VIC, Australia: Cambridge University Press.

Ife, J. and Fiske, L. (2006) 'Human Rights and Community Work: Complementary Theories and Practices', *International Social Work*, 49(3), 297–308.

Jefferson, T. (1776) 'The Declaration of Independence', *Historic American Documents*, Lit2Go Edition. Available at: http://etc.usf.edu/lit2go/133/historic-american-documents/4957/the-declaration-of-independence/, accessed 14 September 2016.

Jordan, B. (2010) *Why the Third Way Failed: Economics, Morality and the Origins of the 'Big Society'*. Bristol: The Policy Press.

Libal, K.R. and Harding, S. (2015) *Human Rights-Based Community Practice in the United States*. Cham: Springer.

Locke, J. (2002) *The Second Treatise of Government and a Letter Concerning Toleration*. New York: Dover Publications.

Mutua, M. (2002) *Human Rights: A Political and Cultural Critique*. Philadelphia, PA: University of Pennsylvania Press. Available at: www.jstor.org/stable/j.ctt3fhtq0.

Parel, A.J. (1997) *Gandhi: 'Hind Swaraj' and Other Writings*. Cambridge: Cambridge University Press.

Reichert, E. (2006) *Understanding Human Rights: An Exercise Book*. London: Sage.

Sen, A. (2004) 'Elements of a Theory of Human Rights', *Philosophy and Public Affairs*, 32(4, Fall), Research Library Core, 315.

1.4   Anti-Oppressive Practice

Introduction

Anti-oppressive practice is a key area of work for both community workers and youth workers, recognising as it does the essentially unequal nature of society; it is the operationalising of the worker's commitment to the value of social justice. To understand the individual acts of prejudice and discrimination, and the cultures and societal structures that make space for those acts, we must see them as a manifestation of hegemony as discussed above. We must recognise prejudice and discrimination, not only in terms of individual pathology, but also as socially produced phenomena which help to maintain the status quo of our unequal world. If that is true, then the locus of our interventions must not only be with the individual (as is the case with many forms of practice) but we must also seek to have an impact at the cultural and structural level. We will discuss this in more detail below.

> Challenging inequality and transforming social relations is an integral part of anti-oppressive practice. Knowing oneself better equips an individual for undertaking this task. Self-knowledge is a central component of the repertoire of skills held by a reflective practitioner … Moreover, reflexivity and social change form the bedrock upon which anti-oppressive practitioners build their interventions.
>
> (Dominelli, 2002: 9)

To quote the song from the musical Avenue Q, 'everyone's a little bit racist' (Lopez and Marx, 2003) and part of our reflexivity as practitioners is to recognise that – and all the other forms of prejudice and discrimination that we are vulnerable to as human beings. This is an important first step in the process of helping other people to challenge their discriminatory and oppressive attitudes and behaviours. This area of work is challenging and difficult for people and it is easy to make people feel judged, and put them on the defensive. They might then alter their inappropriate use of language and other practices only when they are in your presence. The result of this is an inability to authentically engage with the values and beliefs that people hold and perhaps to get them to think about them in a different way.

What we must do is create social spaces where people feel safe enough to honestly explore all aspects of who they are, including the ones that either they are uncomfortable with or that they recognise other people may be uncomfortable with. It seems to us that we live in an age where those spaces are very difficult to find. This has been exemplified in the UK during the referendum to leave the European Union in 2016. There was an unhelpful polarisation of positions whereby people who wanted to vote to leave the EU were caricatured as being racist. This obstructive stereotyping closed down much of the possibility for meaningful debate amongst people with different positions. The upshot of this was that people were unable to discuss their ideas and concerns; for example, issues around immigration and its impact on jobs, housing, education and health provision. In situations where people feel that they have no voice within mainstream politics, they feel forced towards more extreme positions. It could be argued that similar phenomena were seen within the US elections also in 2016.

Community development is well placed to foster creative engagement around difficult issues since it builds on the relationships and trust that have built up through practice. This will only be possible if we are both open about our own individual struggle, and allow people to honestly explore what they think and feel. Within this dialogical safe space, we can coinvestigate the phenomena of discrimination, how we are constructed by, implicated in and are resisting it and then explore how we might work together on ourselves and our world to eradicate it.

A first step for us to become skilled practitioners in this area is for us to develop a clear set of definitions for the terms that we use within, since, as with many areas of practice, the terms used are contested ones. Not that we will develop final definitive definitions; rather, definitions are constructs of convenience designed to sharpen one's thinking observation (Gravells and Simpson, 2012).

Let us start with prejudice, which is the basis for much that is oppressive within our society. Prejudice has been defined as an attitude based on judgement or evaluation, directed at a specific social group or its members and involving negativity, hostility, or dislike (Herek, 2004). Jackson (2011) takes this discussion further by suggesting that prejudice can be obvious or subtle, clear or ambivalent, passionate or dispassionate and that involves stereotyping, is emotional, involves people's values and beliefs and rationalises inequality. In the end, she defines it as a disrespectful attitude towards or negative evaluative response to groups as a whole or towards individuals on the basis of their group membership.

A term that is related to, and builds on, prejudice is Discrimination. Since the 1970s discrimination has been discussed as prejudice plus power (Bidol, 1972). Of course, we understand that everyone has some form of power at different times and since we also have prejudices, it follows that everyone at some point is discriminatory in their actions. This does not always happen on a conscious level but because prejudice is woven into the fabric of who we are, we act on the stereotypes and assumptions that we hold. For example:

> If you have a strongly pro-white pattern of associations ... there is evidence that that will affect the way you behave in the presence of a black person ... In all likelihood, you won't be aware that you are behaving any differently than you would around a white person. But chances are you'll lean forward a little less, turn away slightly from him or her, close your body a bit, be a bit less expressive, maintain less eye contact, stand a little farther away, smile a lot less, hesitate and stumble over your words a bit more, laugh at jokes a bit less. Does that matter? Of course, it does.
>
> (Gladwell, 2006: 85–86)

People often act out of unconscious bias rather than deliberately discriminating against people. This phenomenon is explored by Moule (2009) in the context of recruitment practices. She identifies that this process of unconscious bias was in play even in people whose conscious intention was to increase the number of qualified minority employees that they employed in their organisation. She observed that they were unconsciously rating the résumés from people with black-sounding names as less qualified. With other factors held constant, white-sounding names at the top of résumés resulted in 50 per cent more calls for interview than African-American-sounding names. In similar studies, the human resources managers who were involved in these processes were shocked that the results were contrary to their intentions (Bertrand and Mullainathan, 2004). And so, we can see that explicit bias can occur not only without the intent to discriminate, but also despite explicit desires to create a more just environment.

Finally, we turn to the broader term of oppression. If discrimination is the process of treating individuals unfairly based on prejudice and stereotype, oppression takes account not only of the sum of direct and indirect acts of discrimination, but also of the structural dimensions of power and the way in which these are reproduced through daily social interaction. Central to this is the concept of identity. Identity is fluid rather than static, so that most people are likely to be both oppressors and oppressed, dependent on their circumstances or the context. Evelyn Veronica Almeida Garcia (2017) explores this duality:

> My reality is that I am a mestizo from Ecuador, and in Ecuador mestizo is the dominant and 'preferred' ethnicity. This duality makes me a person with unique characteristics. Characteristics that on occasion make me privileged and a person who commonly oppresses, exploits, and rules others with economic and social force. On the other hand, other situations make me a colonised person who is characterised by being self-depreciated, dependent, and masochist when I am in the position of Latino woman in the United States.
>
> (2017: 80)

It is not helpful to think in terms of a hierarchy of oppressions, for example that to be black necessarily involves worse oppression than to be old. People have multiple identities: one person may be black, female, old, disabled, lesbian and have many other attributes. Any one of these may predominate in a particular interaction. All the various forms of oppression can be viewed as interlinked.

Having laid that conceptual foundation, let us now consider what Anti-discriminatory practice is, and how it responds to those issues. Anti-discriminatory practice is foregrounded in the national occupational standards for community development in the UK (Lifelong Learning UK, 2015). It seeks to strike a balance between celebrating the rich diversity of culture, race and other varied aspects of our society with the need to challenge policies, practices and behaviours, which are inherently oppressive. They set a standard for practice where workers respect, value, support and promote difference and diversity whilst rejecting and challenging any form of discrimination. Drawing attention to the informal educative nature of anti-oppressive practice, they encourage workers to support others to explore and challenge all forms of discrimination. It is appropriate that this takes place on a community level rather than abstracting the locus of defining discrimination and creating strategies for its eradication to agencies, external to the community. Only when this process is owned individually and within the culture of the community is there a real possibility of lasting change. Similarly, it is appropriate for this process to happen, not only with community members but also with other workers and agencies, recognising the reality of the personal and institutional discrimination that has an impact on services and the communities that receive them. The national occupational standards also enshrine a multilevel analysis, encouraging workers to recognise that discrimination works at individual, community, organisational/institutional and societal levels. An implication of this is that, in addition to the individual and group work that community and youth workers regularly engage in, workers must find ways in which local people can engage in the development of policies and practices which actively support and value diversity.

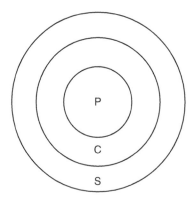

Figure 1.1 Thompson's PCS Model

This analysis of practice draws on the influential work of Neil Thompson (2012). He analyses the impact of discrimination at the personal, cultural and structural levels.

Personal (P) Level

This is normally concerned with an individual's views, particularly in the case of a prejudice against a certain group of people. For example, this could relate to a young person who makes racist comments. It is purely related to individual actions and you are likely to come into contact with this in practice. The 'P' is located in the middle of Figure 1.1, because that individual has his beliefs and ideas supported through two other levels...

Cultural (C) Level

This analysis relates to the 'shared values' or 'commonalties'. For example, shared beliefs about what is right and wrong, good or bad, can form a consensus.

Structural (S) Level

This analysis demonstrates how oppression is 'sewn into the fabric' of society through institutions that support both cultural norms and personal beliefs. Some institutions, such as sections of the media, religion and the government can cement these beliefs.

Anti-oppressive practice that operates on the level of the personal, would draw on Freirean approaches. As discussed above, the creation of safe, non-judgemental spaces are essential if people are to honestly engage in these difficult issues. The use of images, videos and songs, for example, enable people to have these discussions mediated by objects. This then enables people to develop a critical distance between themselves and the issues they are looking at; in a sense it de-personalises their personal prejudices, enabling them to analyse and potentially change them.

At the cultural level, a process of building bridging social capital (Field and Dawson Books, 2008) could be utilised as anti-oppressive practice. This is a process whereby groups of people with different beliefs, different experiences and different cultures develop trust, norms of reciprocity and a sense of relationship. This is most effectively achieved where bonding social capital is high. In other words, people must be secure in their own sense of identity, their history and their place in the world. In some cases that bonding social capital needs to be built before the work of developing bridging social capital can be undertaken. There are many examples of this practice found in the work done by youth workers and others in post-conflict Northern Ireland (Church et al., 2004; Jones, 2004). In this situation the divide experienced by Catholic and Protestant communities was so deeply ingrained, that an extensive process of single identity work had to be undertaken before people had the confidence to go beyond their own community.

At the structural level a process of establishing a counter-hegemonic bloc is ultimately the only solution to structural inequality. The development of a new common sense, and a new understanding of how society functions, is the grand vision that we hold. Community workers are well placed to be involved in this project at a local level. Through the development of new technologies, at any point in history developing networks both locally and globally has never been easier.

Into this context we are seeing the emergence of a potential counter-hegemonic bloc in the form of the World Social Forum, which represents today, in organisational terms, the most consistent manifestation of counter-hegemonic globalisation that conceives itself as a struggle against neo-liberal globalisation (De Sousa Santos, 2008). Started in 2001, it takes the form of an annual international gathering of activists, NGOs, social movements and others, organised as a cumulative process that seeks to identify convergences amongst the movements and explore the possibilities of communal actions and alternatives. The World Social Forum is an open meeting space for reflective thinking, democratic debate of ideas, formulation of proposals, free exchange of experiences and interlinking for effective action, by groups and movements of civil society that are opposed to neo-liberalism and domination of the world by capital and any form of imperialism, and are committed to building a planetary society directed towards fruitful relationships amongst Humankind and between it and the Earth. Judith A. Hitchman (2011) describes the World Social Forum as one that 'continues to provide a space for developing connections and dialogue across borders and differences. It may not be a space for action per se, but it does provide the basis for developing actions that reach beyond the few days of the Forum.'

The Forum takes a broad holistic approach to global issues, as demonstrated in the themes of their recent gathering in Montreal.

- Democratisation of knowledge and the right to communication
- Culture of peace and the combat for justice and demilitarisation
- Decolonisation and self-determination of peoples
- Defense of the rights of nature and environmental justice
- Global combats and international solidarity
- Human and social rights, dignity and the combat against inequality
- Combating racism, xenophobia, the patriarchy and fundamentalism
- Combating the dictatorship of finance and support for resource sharing
- Migration and citizenship without borders
- Democracy, social and citizen movements
- The working world faced with neo-liberalism

Another example of encouraging practice that is facilitated by communications technology and supports counter-hegemonic practice is Beautiful Trouble (https://beautifultrouble.org/). They say that Beautiful Trouble exists to make non-violent revolution irresistible by providing an ever-growing suite of strategic tools and trainings that inspire movements for a more just, healthy, and equitable world.

In conclusion, not all anti-oppressive practice will address all three dimensions discussed above but good practice recognises the interdependence of each of them if we hope to achieve lasting change.

Key Learning Points

- Anti-oppressive practice operationalises the worker's commitment to the value of social justice
- It both celebrates diversity and challenges behaviour and structural injustice
- Prejudice and discrimination consciously and unconsciously oppress people
- Anti-oppressive practice operates at the personal, cultural and structural levels

Learning Tasks

Oppression Awareness, Group Exercise

- Go around the group – when did you first experience or witness some form of oppression (racism, patriarchy, heterosexism, etc.)?
- Using a strict time limit, tell your story
- Discussion – ask questions, not challenge
- Go around again: what is one thing you could do differently to have a more liberating outcome?

Key Reading

Thompson, N. (2012) *Anti-Discriminatory Practice: Equality, Diversity and Social Justice.* Basingstoke: Palgrave Macmillan.

References

Bertrand, M. and Mullainathan, S. (2004) 'Are Emily and Greg More Employable Than Lakisha and Jamal?', *American Economic Review*, 94, 991–1013.

Bidol, P. (1972) *Developing New Perspectives on Race: An Innovative Multi-media Social Studies Curriculum in Racism Awareness for the Secondary Level.* Detroit, MI: New Perspectives on Race.

Church, C., Visser, A. and Johnson, L.S. (2004) 'A Path to Peace or Persistence? The "Single Identity" Approach to Conflict Resolution in Northern Ireland', *Conflict Resolution Quarterly*, 21, 273–293. doi:10.1002/crq.63.

De Sousa Santos, B. (2008) 'The World Social Forum and the Global Left', *Politics & Society*, 36(2), 247–270. doi: 10.1177/0032329208316571.

Dominelli, L. (2002) *Anti Oppressive Social Work Theory and Practice.* Basingstoke: Palgrave Macmillan.

Field, J. and Dawson Books (2008) *Social Capital*, 2nd edn. Abingdon: Routledge.

Garcia, E.V.A. (2017) 'The Duality of Being both Oppressor and Oppressed in Different Places', *INNOVA Research Journal*, 2(3), 80–90.

Gladwell, M. (2006) *Blink: The Power of Thinking Without Thinking.* London: Penguin.

Gravells, A. and Simpson, S. (2012) *Equality and Diversity in the Lifelong Learning Sector*, 2nd edn. London: SAGE/Learning Matters.

Herek, G.M. (2004) 'Beyond "Homophobia": Thinking about Sexual Prejudice and Stigma in the Twenty-first Century', *Sexuality Research & Social Policy*, 1(2), 6–24.

Hitchman, J. (2011) 'The Social Forum Movement in Africa'. Available at: www.ciranda.net/The-Social-Forum-movement-in?lang=pt_br.

Jackson, L.M. (2011) *'Defining Prejudice'. The Psychology of Prejudice: From Attitudes to Social Action.* Washington, DC: American Psychological Association PsycBOOKS, EBSCOhost, 7–28.

Jones, T.S. (2004) 'Enhancing Collaborative Tendencies: Extending the Single Identity Model for Youth Conflict Education', *New Directions for Youth Development*, 102, 11–34. doi:10.1002/ yd.79.

Lifelong Learning UK (2015) *National Occupational Standards for Community Development*. London: Lifelong Learning UK.

Lopez, R. and Marx, J. (2003) 'Everyone's a Little Bit Racist'. *On Avenue Q the musical: Original Broadway cast recording [CD]*. New York: Max Merchandising, LLC.

Moule, J. (2009) 'Understanding Unconscious Bias and Unintentional Racism: Acknowledging our Possible Biases and Working Together Openly is Essential for Developing Community in our Schools', *Phi Delta Kappan*, 90(5), 321+. *Expanded Academic ASAP*. Available at: go.galegroup. com/ps/i.do?p=EAIM&sw=w&u=glasuni&v=2.1&id=GALE%7CA192407565&it=r&asid=76 3501b09933cedf064b4aae76f1e28e, accessed 30 November 2016.

Thompson, N. (2012) *Anti-Discriminatory Practice: Equality, Diversity and Social Justice*. Basingstoke: Palgrave Macmillan.

1.5   A Globalised and Changing World
The Local Impact

A Global Perspective

Our starting point for understanding community development practice is that of global-isation. We live in an increasingly globalised world. No matter who we are or where we live, we consume goods, grown or manufactured from China, Vietnam, the USA, Europe, etc. Skype and FaceTime enable us to see and speak to friends, family, fellow workers and activists almost anywhere on the planet. Refugees from a conflict zone perhaps thousands of miles away from where you live can arrive in your town. Tens of millions of economic migrants are on the move looking for a better life. What happens globally often has a wide-ranging impact on the local. Community development is about making the world a better place. To achieve this, we need to understand the global and local contexts of change.

To fully explore the current state of the world requires a separate book. However, we need a few facts to continue this discussion. At the time of writing this chapter (January 2019) the world population is estimated to be around 7.4 billion people. Of this total:

- 51 per cent live in an urban context
- 78 per cent have electricity
- 87 per cent have access to clean drinking water
- 50 per cent of children live in poverty
- 48 per cent live on less than US$2 a day
- 22 per cent have access to a computer
- 75 per cent have access to a mobile phone
- 30 per cent have access to a computer

If we compare industrialised and developing countries, we can see the human cost of inequality. For example, the average life expectancy is 79 years for industrialised countries and 65 for developing countries. In terms of mortality for children under five years of age, the figures are six for every 1000 births compared to 83 for 1000 births. These figures, though, are not evenly distributed. Iceland has an infant mortality rate of two per thousand births, whereas Afghanistan/Sierra Leone/Liberia/Angola and Niger all exceed 150 deaths per 1000 births.

To counter global inequality the United Nations promoted the Millennium Development Goals that ran between 2000 and 2015. The Goals were:

1. To eradicate extreme poverty and hunger
2. To achieve universal primary education
3. To promote gender equality and empower women

Figure 1.2 UN Sustainable Development Goals © United Nations, 2019

4.   To reduce child mortality
5.   To improve maternal health
6.   To combat HIV/AIDS, malaria, and other diseases
7.   To ensure environmental sustainability
8.   To develop a global partnership for development

Overall, there was progress on all of these goals, but significant global and regional challenges continued. In 2016, the Millennium Development Goals were replaced by 17 Sustainable Development Goals with 169 developmental targets. The Goals are summarised in Figure 1.2 below. It remains to be seen how much progress will be made in taking these goals forward.

The Aftermath Debate

It may be thought that the Sustainable Development Goals only concern developing countries. However, those of us living in Western and developed countries should not be complacent. In 2008, the global financial crash changed the nature of Western economies. Manuel Castells describes the consequences of the crash as the 'Aftermath'. He said:

> Aftermath is being made of attempts to preserve financial capitalism under a new, more exclusionary form. It is also made of the desperate reactions of people left to their own devices. But it is also constructed by people, in different cultures, that seize the moment to reinvent their lives in ways that are both more rewarding and more sustainable.
>
> (Aftermath Project)

The argument of Castells and his colleagues is that the financial crisis in Western countries since 2008 is both structural and multidimensional and marked a tipping point away from the period of economic growth and increasing state expenditure that has been the norm since the resolution of the oil crisis of the 1970s. The authors contend that we are now in a transformatory period similar to the late 1940s where the Western world was reshaped through the Bretton Woods Agreement and the development of welfare states.

Alongside the financial crisis is the loss of national competitiveness of Western countries relative to the growing economies in the developing world. In particular the BRIC countries: Brazil, Russia, India and especially China (although the pace of growth in the BRIC countries has recently slowed, and Brazil in particular is currently facing serious economic difficulties). Perceived economic wisdom is that the loss of competitiveness has been due to state-generated bureaucracy and a loss of innovation and entrepreneurial spirit, partly at least, as an outcome of welfare expenditure. The solution is to promote a freer economy through supply-side changes and creating a more self-reliant culture.

Castells argues that the resolution of these current crises will entail a financial retrenchment of welfare state policies and expenditures. This can be seen in the austerity budgets (with various degrees of severity) in many Western countries. In turn this will lead to new economic and social cultures and movements with a redefinition of the role of the state. Implicit in this argument is a shift of activity from national government to more local structures.

Such social change sits alongside other social trends, such as the decline of social capital as explored by Putnam (2000) and the OECD (2001), and the increasing individualising of society under postmodernity. In an interview, Castells comments that:

> fundamentally this crisis has been about the destruction of the solidarity mechanism in society because that is ultimately what the welfare state is ... And at the same time there has been in the last 20 years an increasing individualisation of society. People see themselves as individuals. So the social institutions were solidarity networks, solidarity among people was dissolved ... When the solidarity networks are dissolved, the institutional solidarity is not able to operate anymore. And when individuals don't have the cultural bound of solidarity and recognising each other as being together in some form, then there is not only an economic crisis but a crisis of society. Of everybody against everybody. Of course we start with immigrants, minorities, but from there we move to someone else ... Therefore from the lack of solidarity in the national societies we go to a lack of solidarity among people in the European context which ultimately also means the possible dissolution of the European Union ... so unless there is a reconstruction of solidarity ties and networks in cultural and social terms, rather than institutional terms, we go towards individualisation of society, increasing aggressiveness and also increasing destructive competition between nation states that ... lead to the disappearance of any common project of living together in Europe at the moment when Europe is becoming marginal in the world.
>
> (VPRO, 2011)

In the view of Castells et al. (2012) there is little possibility of going back to the pre-crisis arrangements and a new mindset is required of politicians and citizens to explore the possible alternative futures that are required. The rise of populist political parties in Western countries, usually (but not exclusively) right wing and anti-migrant, is one of the current outcomes and challenges of this trend.

In summary the authors argue that the financial crisis has exposed the:

- Embedded nature and unsustainability of the long-term debt crisis in Western countries
- That Western countries have unsustainable structural national deficits
- International competitiveness of Western countries is in relative decline

The response to these issues will mean that:

- The consequence of paying down the debt and reducing the structural deficits will be the decline in government expenditure (as %GDP)
- This, in turn, leads to less state involvement in welfare and service provision and a general reduction of the state in economic activity

In time this creates a momentum for:

- Innovation in both the economic and social spheres
- Developing new models of living and collective action

What might these models of living and collective action be, and do we need to completely invent new things, or are there existing ideas and practices that can be adapted? In the UK, for example, we can see these changes taking place. The economy has been growing and unemployment has been falling since 2008. However, many of these jobs are part-time or self-employed. Social programmes are being cut, many welfare benefits have been reduced or frozen, with the consequential increase in food banks.

A further consequence of these social trends is the political unrest of traditional working-class communities, who feel excluded from the apparent benefits of a Western economy and who feel threatened by cuts to social welfare and changes in local demographics through migration. These feelings were clearly expressed in the recent Brexit vote in the UK and the support for Donald Trump in the 2016 US Presidential Election.

Development Issues

As we have noted, an increasing proportion of the world's population live in what the United Nations terms 'Mega Slums' – a slum being usually defined as an urban area, usually having poor housing and limited services. Anna Tibaijuka, who was Under-Secretary General of the United Nations said:

> Make no mistake, we live at a time of unprecedented, rapid, and irreversible urbanisation. The cities growing fastest are those of the developing world, and the fastest growing neighbourhoods are the slums. We therefore have to use every means at our disposal to ensure a new urban era, characterised not only by glittering towers, commercial centres and highways, but also by liveable spaces for the vast majority of our growing urban population. It is a shocking fact that roughly 70 percent of people in African cities live in slums. Urban poverty is now becoming a severe, pervasive – and largely unacknowledged – feature of modern life. Huge numbers of people in towns and cities are suffering levels of deprivation that are often worse than those experienced by the rural poor.

In some countries in sub-Saharan Africa over 90 per cent of the urban population live in slums, in Pakistan the estimate is for over 70 per cent and in India above 30 per cent. Some of these communities are of immense size. For example, the Nez-Chalco-Itza barrio in Mexico City has an estimated population of around 4 million. The Kibera slum in Nairobi is estimated to be anywhere between 200,000 and 1 million. Orangi Town in Karachi is 1 million plus. Khayeltisha near Cape Town has a population of over 400,000 with 40 per cent of its residents under 19 years of age. Given the scale of these communities, they often have their own economy and social systems. Dharavi in Mumbai, with a population estimated to be anything between 600,000 and 1 million, has a vibrant local economy based on recycling as well as traditional industries such as pottery. There are also well-developed community organisations and local support systems. As we see in Section 3 of this volume, there is an international network of Slum/Shack Dwellers that represent the urban poor at a global level.

Nevertheless, there are considerable issues facing the residents of developing world cities. The issues can be summarised as:

- The collapse of existing public services (too many people, not enough money)
- Unemployment and under-employment
- The shortage of affordable housing
- Poor transportation (roads, pavements, buses)
- Unsafe drinking water and lack of sewerage systems
- Crime and violence
- Poor education, welfare and health services
- Environmental collapse
- Corruption
- Continued inward migration increasing ethnic and cultural tension

In developed economies do these problems manifest themselves as well, albeit in different ways and on a lesser scale? If so, have they been made worse by financial restraints after the 2008 crisis? The answer to these questions will depend in part upon local circumstances. It may well be that urban communities in the Western economies can have more in common with developing world issues than might at first be thought. As our discussion of Slum/Shack Dwellers International in Section 3.4 will show, there is much we can learn from development practices and solutions created in the developing world.

Key Learning Points

- We live in a diverse globalised world. Nevertheless, diverse global forces act on local communities
- The UN Sustainable Development Goals set the key global development agenda
- In the developed world the 2008 crash has led to major changes in the role of the state with implications for communities
- We can all learn from each other's experiences no matter where we live
- Issues facing urban communities have commonalities across countries

Learning Tasks

In the community where you live or work, explore the following questions:

- Has the community been significantly affected by a reduction of services since 2008? If so, in what ways has this affected the lives of local people?

- Do any of the issues facing developing world communities (summarised above) affect your local community? If so, in what ways?
- Has there been migration to your community – by people looking for work, by refugees/asylum seekers, etc.? If so, what have been the local consequences of this?
- Do the local effects of all of the above factors change depending upon age, gender, ethnicity, etc.?

Key Reading

Explore the case studies and documentaries at: aftermathproject.com
United Nations Development Project Sustainable Development Goals. Available at: www.undp.org/content/undp/en/home/sustainable-development-goals.html.

References

Aftermath Project. Available at: www.aftermathproject.com/.

Castells, M., Caraca, J., and Cardoso, G. (eds) (2012) *Aftermath: The Cultures of the Economic Crisis*. Oxford: Oxford University Press.

OECD (2001) *The Wellbeing of Nations: The Role of Human and Social Capital*. Paris: OECD.

Putnam, R. (2000) *Bowling Alone: The Collapse and Revival of American Community*. New York: Simon & Schuster.

Tibaijuka, A. (2010) 'Address to World Urban Youth Assembly', 19 March, Rio de Janeiro.

United Nations Development Project. 'Sustainable Development Goals'. Available at: www.undp.org/content/undp/en/home/sustainable-development-goals.html.

VPRO (2011) 'Aftermath of a Crisis', documentary film. Available at: backlight.vpro.nl.

1.6   Living under Neo-Liberalism
Challenges and Opportunities

Introduction

Many of the current debates on the potential for community development practice in both developed and developing economies are often located within a discourse framed by the effects of neo-liberalism. This is because many activists and academics see neo-liberalism as the current dominant economic paradigm. As such, it has a major influence on government policy and expenditure, as well as influencing the broader social and cultural structure of society. Community activity, it is argued, takes place within, and is shaped by, the working of neo-liberalism. Generally, this is argued to be a negative and limiting environment. Such discussion can become heated, often based on people's various ideological positions: you are either for or against neo-liberalism/capitalism/globalisation etc. We suggest that effective practice requires a more thoughtful analysis of how the economy and globalisation affects local communities.

This discussion (adapted from Purcell, 2016) starts to unpack some of the issues around practising community work in a neo-liberal context. Our argument is that community development practice under neo-liberalism has both advantages and disadvantages.

From our previous discussion on values and purpose of community development we have identified a clear commitment to:

- Promoting social justice
- Challenging oppression whether it is based on gender, class, ethnicity, race, religion, sexuality, etc.
- Promoting collective critical educational processes that enable people to reflect on and explore their lives
- Facilitating personal and community empowerment
- The collectivisation of issues
- Building powerful local organisations committed to social change, learning from the examples of Community organising and the developing world examples of Shack/ Slum Dwellers International

With this in mind we need to explore what is neo-liberalism, and whether it hinders (or not) radical practice, and what we might do about it.

What is Neo-liberalism?

According to Saad-Filho and Johnston (2005) 'we live in the age of neo-liberalism', and, as we have noted, this view is shared widely by many social commentators, including writers on community development

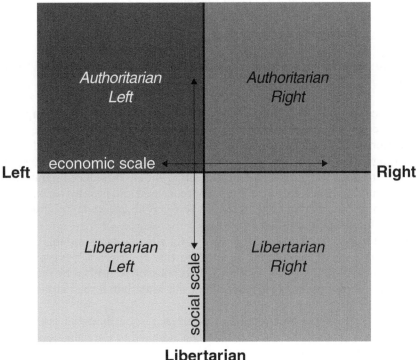

Authoritarian

Authoritarian
Left

Authoritarian
Right

Left economic scale

Right

Libertarian
Left

social scale

Libertarian
Right

Libertarian

Figure 1.3

However, the term 'neo-liberalism' is both contested and applied in a variety of ways. For some it is simply a relabelling of a market economy, for others just an unhelpful term that suggests something new is happening, when what we are experiencing is just the latest manifestation of globalised capitalism. Some people see neo-liberalism as a meta-narrative lens through which all the ills of the world can be portrayed. For others it is simply a slogan or a term of abuse.

In order to understand neo-liberalism, we first have to make the distinction between the moderate political ideology of Liberalism and the economic focused label of Neo-liberalism. The difference is illustrated in Figure 1.3 below (from politicalcompass.org) where Liberal politics sits in the bottom left quadrant and economic neo-liberalism sits in the bottom right quadrant.

This diagram sets neo-liberalism as a free market economic model. However, this is a more recent definition of neo-liberalism. In classical economics neo-liberals sat between laissez-faire free market capitalism on the lower right and state socialist economies on the upper left of the diagram. In doing so, neo-liberalism was seen as representing a strong free market, but one that was, partially at least, regulated by the state to operate in the national interest. (For a full discussion on this debate see Harvey, 2005; Thorsen and Lie, 2006.)

Robbins (1999) has suggested that the neo-liberalism of today is different from that of classical economics, and can be generally characterised as promoting the idea that:

- Sustained economic growth is the way to human progress
- Free markets without government 'interference' would be the most efficient and socially optimal allocation of resources

- Economic globalisation would be beneficial to everyone
- Privatisation removes the inefficiencies of the public sector
- Governments should mainly function to provide the infrastructure to advance the rule of law with respect to property rights and contracts

For these goals to be achieved, a number of social and economic policies need to be put in place, namely:

- The dominance of a free market for all goods, services and movement of capital. The implication here is for deregulation and privatisation of government services.
- The reduction of government expenditure as a percentage of GDP, and the corresponding reduction in taxation. There is some debate about whether government expenditure on education, health and infrastructure should be reduced significantly as these services underpin economic development (educated and healthy workforces and improved transportation of goods). In this respect neo-liberalism is still distinct from classic laissez-faire capitalism.
- The belief that wealth is created by the people at the top of society and this will 'trickle down' to the rest of the population. Inherent in this approach is the growth of the super rich and increasing income inequality. This position is justified by the argument that the poor will eventually become wealthier this way than if the market had been regulated.
- Promotion of the belief in individual and personal responsibility as essential for a fully functioning economy and society. This idea is linked to the reduction in welfare spending that is viewed as both disempowering and a disincentive to work. However, there is not necessarily opposition to minimum or even living wages. There has to be an economic incentive to work and a certain level of wages in society is required to enable consumers to buy the goods being produced. For example, the present Conservative and pro-neo-liberal government in the UK has policies to 'make work pay' and is substantially increasing the minimum wage.

The overall effect of these policies on society is subject to much criticism from a number of perspectives. For example, the neo-liberal economic system tends to concentrate economic power (and by extension political power) in the hands of rich individuals and unaccountable international corporations. Wealth inequality tends to increase both within countries and between countries. It has been estimated for example (globalissues.org), that the richest 85 people in the world have more money than the total income of the poorest 3 billion people. Notwithstanding this, research for the World Bank suggests that the effect of taxation and welfare payments reduces income inequality disparity to a degree. How this works out will vary between countries, their individual tax and welfare policies, and their commitment to progressive and redistributive policies.

The other side of the argument is that both the globalisation of the world economy and the spread of neo-liberal policies have led to sustained economic growth. Over the past 50 years the world economy has grown on average 3.8 per cent per annum. Allowing for the increases in population, growth has still been around 2.1 per cent per annum (Tani, 2015). Consequently, the Millennium Development Goal to halve the 1990 global poverty rate by 2015 was achieved by 2010. That is, according to the World Bank Poverty Review, 896 million people lived on $1.90 a day in 2012 compared to 1.95 billion in 1991. In addition, 2.1 billion lived on less than $3.10 a day (down from 2.9 billion in 1990). Obviously, these figures are still depressingly high, but it should be noted that poverty reduction tends to be greater in countries most connected to the global economy.

It is undeniable that neo-liberalism has also enabled the circumstances where hundreds of millions of people have been able to escape from poverty through the jobs created by capitalist investment. Any consideration of economic growth, a growing middle class and improvements in the annual income of working-class households in China and India, for example, is evidence of this. Advances in technology, whether it be in medicine, communications, transport and, in some cases, for protecting the environment, have been produced because of the profit motive and the reinvestment of profits into research and development by global companies.

Some opponents of neo-liberalism argue that the state should own the key industries of the country and control the major services, and that reducing income inequality should be a prime objective of government. The argument is that state socialist economies will reduce inequality and raise more people out of poverty. However, it is generally the case that non-liberal states and/or state socialist economies have generally not achieved such improvements and often have their own poor record on the environment and poverty alleviation. In China, and to a lesser extent India, it is only when socialist economics was abandoned that spectacular economic growth was achieved. Those countries that remain outside of the globalised economy show little signs of growth and therefore are unable to take people out of poverty and increase state spending on health, education and welfare.

Apart from the economic/inequality discussion, there is a range of other criticisms aimed at neo-liberalism. Writers on the radical side of community development have developed a generalised critique of neo-liberalism. For example, Margaret Ledwith (2011) argues:

- Neo-liberalism = politics of greed
- Individualism lacks a common good
- Market replaces well-being
- Dominant ideology demonises the poor
- and espouses:
- A common sense of privileging the privileged
- Decontextualised practice
- Politics of disposability

This is a strong indictment of the dominant economic system and its impact on society in general, and specifically its impact on the quality of life in poorer communities. We could usefully research the actual impact of the above on communities and our practice. However, we must be careful not to paint ourselves into a corner, where we feel hemmed in by an all-powerful and evil economic, social and political system, with the implication that we are all powerless victims.

In this context it is useful to refer to Gramsci (1971) (we will discuss his ideas in more detail in Section 2). He explored how the dominant economic and social order creates a 'hegemony' that shapes not only how society operates but also how the majority of people think. Paulo Freire (1972) explained this process as magical or naïve consciousness, where people become acculturated by the dominant discourse and fail to critically understand the reasons for their social position and what is in their best interests.

Gramsci (1971) argued that despite the embedded political and cultural power of the dominant order, it is possible to develop a 'counter-hegemony' through people engaging in critical thought and becoming what he termed 'organic intellectuals'. As we discuss in Sections 2 and 3 the process of critical reflection developed by Freire, and the associated range of Popular Education approaches (for example, ActionAid Reflect; Hope and

Timmel, 1984, 1999) provides a way for community workers to help people understand the effect that globalisation and neo-liberalism have on their lives and to explore strategies for change.

Is this Focus on Neo-liberalism Unhelpful?

There is always the other side of the coin. To paraphrase the American radical community organiser Saul Alinsky, nothing is ever 100 per cent one-sided, as the real world is both complex and contradictory. Is it helpful to put neo-liberalism at the centre of our critique of society and label it as the root cause of the problems in our communities? Undeniably, neo-liberalism is a major factor shaping the world, but if we just focus on neo-liberalism then we can easily overlook other critical factors and thereby limit our understanding of the world.

What is being suggested here is that, with neo-liberalism, alongside the negatives discussed above there are positive outcomes that contribute to people's well-being. For many people this has been their route to a better life. It is important we recognise these contradictions and not retreat into a simplified one-dimensional ideological position and forget to make decisions based on facts and critical analysis. Stewart commented:

> Neoliberalism, advanced capitalism, globalisation ... [d]o not in themselves effect-ively describe the complexities of the situation we find ourselves in. The notion of a totalised system, of which everything is always already somehow a part, is not helpful, in the effort to approach a weighted and reeling present.
>
> (Stewart, 2007: 1)

Indeed, as Thorsen and Lie (2006) point out, neo-liberalism itself is not a single integrated body of thought and they question how useful it is to make it the main defining charac-teristic of a society.

Furthermore, is it credible to believe, as some argue, that all governments do is simply implement policies to meet the agenda of neo-liberal driven corporations? To argue this is akin to believing that the world is run by a large secret conspiracy, in which all political leaders are implicated, regardless of their political affiliations. Perhaps it is more credible to suggest that governments have a tendency to promote the interests of multinational corporations because they generate jobs, income, wealth and tax revenues, but that it is not the only consideration driving government policy. Obviously, how this works out will vary country by country, administration by administration.

As noted above some writers choose to analyse community work practice within a neo-liberal context. To some extent this is helpful, as it makes the point that our engagement with the world as practitioners is mediated by economic structures and global processes, which in turn have a symbiotic relationship with government, social policy, social life and the production of cultures within which we operate. However, this only takes us so far. Is community work really helpless to change anything if, as is often implied, neo-liberalism is so monolithic? Is neo-liberalism the only frame of analysis we should adopt? We would suggest the answer is 'no' to both questions.

In Summary

The above analysis suggests that radical practice can operate within the (often consider-able) social and cultural spaces that go with a capitalist liberal democracy. What this looks like will of course vary between countries and cultures.

We are not arguing that neo-liberalism is inherently a good thing. Like most areas of life, it can be both good and bad simultaneously. As we have noted before, the world is complex and contradictory. There are spaces and opportunities for radical practice within neo-liberal environments, and there can be in socialist environments as well, as long as the state allows spaces for community-based creativity to flourish.

As always, we are where we are, and living within a neo-liberal context does offer us opportunities to develop radical practice. As Gramsci commented, 'The point of modernity is to live a life without illusions while not becoming disillusioned.' To do so we need to critically learn from the experience of our own local traditions of practice, as well as incorporate lessons from global practice.

Key Learning Points

- Neo-liberalism is a contested term
- We need to be clear what we mean by neo-liberalism
- For local communities there are both benefits and losses from the effects of neo-liberalism
- Once defined, analysing neo-liberalism can be useful for understanding local communities
- Neo-liberalism cannot be the only framework of analysis for communities – the world is more complex than that

Learning Tasks

In the community where you live or work:

- Research how neo-liberalism makes a positive contribution to the community. This could be through creating employment, creating local assets that could be utilised by the community, opening up opportunities for individuals, creating global links to other communities, etc.
- Research how neo-liberalism makes a negative contribution to the local community. This could be through job losses to other countries, reduction in local services through managerial efficiencies, a reduction in potential community assets, etc.

Such investigations could be developed as a co-learning project with local community-based organisations.

Key Reading

Saad-Filho, A. and Johnston, D. (2005) *Neoliberalism – A Critical Reader*. London: Pluto Press.
Thorsen, D.E. and Lie, A. (2006) *What is Neoliberalism?* Available at: http://folk.uio.no/daget/neo-liberalism.pdf.

References

ActionAid Reflect. 'The Mother Manual'. Available at: www.reflect-action.org/mothermanual.
Gramsci, A. (1971) *Selections from Prison Notebooks*. New York: International Publishers.
Harvey, D. (2005) *A Brief History of Neoliberalism*. Oxford: Oxford University Press.
Hope, A. and Timmel, S. (1984) *Training for Transformation Vols 1–3*. London: ITDG Publishing.
Hope, A. and Timmel, S. (1999) *Training for Transformation Vol. 4*. London: ITDG Publishing.

Ledwith, M. (2011) *Community Development: A Critical Approach* (2nd edn). Bristol: The Policy Press.

Purcell, R. (2016) 'Thoughts on Neoliberalism and Radical Practice', *RCW Journal*, 2(1).

Robbins, R. (1999) *Global Problems and the Culture of Capitalism*. Boston, MA: Allyn and Bacon.

Saad-Filho, A. and Johnston, D. (eds) (2005) *Neoliberalism – A Critical Reader*. London: Pluto Press.

Stewart, K. (2007) *Ordinary Affects*. Durham, NC: Duke University Press.

Tani, D. (2015) 'The World Economy – 50 Years of Near Continuous Growth'. Available at: www.worldeconomics.com/papers/Global%20Growth%20Monitor_7c66ffca-ff86-4e4c-979d-7c5d7a22ef21.paper.

Thorsen, D.E. and Lie, A. (2006) *What is Neoliberalism?* Available at: http://folk.uio.no/daget/neo-liberalism.pdf.

1.7 Community Development in the UK and How We Got Here

Background

Each country will have their own history that shapes the values, policy and practice of community development. Here (drawing on Purcell, 2005), we illustrate a country's example of this process.

Community development in the UK has a long history reaching back to the Victorian philanthropy of the nineteenth century; for example, the Charity Organisation Society, which worked with the urban 'deserving poor'; or the 30 University Settlements based on the Toynbee Hall model of placing 'future leaders' in poor communities to do good works and develop an understanding of poverty. Whilst being more sympathetic to the needs of the poor, and the social conditions within which they lived, the motivation of the Settlements was also about reducing the possibility of civil unrest.

During the inter-war period there was a growth of government-funded interventions. The 1936 Housing Act and the 1937 Physical Training and Recreation Act led to the establishment of community centres in the new suburban housing estates. Partly, the programme was intended to counter the growth and perceived political threat from the National Unemployed Workers Movement.

From 1945, the community centre movement expanded, and a number of reformist legislations were introduced to supplement the development of the new 'Welfare State'. The most important was the 1944 Education Act (1945 in Scotland) that led to the creation of the Youth and Community Service in England. In Scotland, the same process saw the creation of the Community Education Service after the Alexander Report in 1975.

The Ministry of Education (1944) booklet entitled Community Centres, makes clear the social and recreational agenda of the community centres as being:

> [a place where] neighbours come together on an equal footing to enjoy social, recreational and educational activities as members of groups following particular hobbies or on the basis of their common needs or interests in the same locality.
>
> (1944: 6)

During the later phase of the British Empire, the Colonial Office had promoted the use of community development methods to: incorporate the existing local ruling class into the colonial administration; help prepare the administration systems for independence; prevent the spread of communism; and protect the interests of British capital. From the mid-1950s onwards community development workers were returning to the UK and shaping the development of local practice. This development was not without criticism. For example, Batten (1967) commented:

> the community worker does not attempt to decide for people or to lead, guide or persuade them to accept any of his [sic] own conclusions about what is good for them.

He tries to get them to decide for themselves what their needs are, what if anything they are willing to do to meet them, and how they can best organise, plan and act to carry their project through.

The 1960s and the CDPs

By the late 1960s Britain was entering a period of social discontent. Poverty had been 'rediscovered' in a country where the Prime Minister Harold Macmillan had declared that 'we have never had it so good'. Work by Peter Townsend (1954) demonstrated the extent of poor communities. The Fabian Society (1960) outlined the failures of the welfare state, and Titmuss (1962) published an influential book 'Income Distribution and Social Change'.

However, it was the speech in 1969 by Enoch Powell, an ex-Conservative minister, that forced policy change on the government. Powell in his 'Rivers of Blood' speech said 'as I look ahead, I am filled with foreboding. Like the Roman, I seem to see the River Tiber foaming with much blood.' In fact, he was arguing against the Race Relations Bill that sought to prevent racial discrimination, on the grounds that it would enable immigrant communities 'to agitate and campaign against their fellow citizens, and to overawe and dominate the rest'. Sadly, of the 43,000 letters sent to the press commenting on this speech only 800 opposed what Powell had said.

Powell predicted violence on the streets of English cities in response to continuing immigration. In this he was correct as riots broke out in Nottinghill (1976), Southall (1979), St Pauls Bristol (1980), and in 1981 Bristol, Handsworth, and Toxteth. These riots were not caused by immigrant communities dominating their white neighbours, but from continued discrimination against the ethnic minorities and, in some cases, aggressive policing.

In response to the threat of racial violence and the challenge that poverty still existed in the UK, the government introduced a major initiative for community development. This was the Community Development Projects (CDPs). Like much of British social policy, the model comes from the USA – in this case an adaptation of the Community Action Programmes for Juvenile Delinquency and the Model Cities Programme that promoted community action and local participation. The rationale behind these projects was that social and economic problems were not caused by structural problems in the economy, society or political system. Rather, they were products of local circumstances and individual pathology that could be solved through localised small-scale intervention (for the background to this approach see the discussion of Robert Park in Section 2.1 – What is Community, below).

The Home Office described the projects as being:

> A modest attempt at action and research into the better understanding and more comprehensive tackling of social need ... through closer co-ordination of central and local, official and unofficial effort, informed and stimulated by citizen initiative and involvement.

There were 12 CDPs based in Coventry, Liverpool, Southwark, Glyncorrwg, Bately, Birmingham, Canning Town, Cumbria, Newcastle, Oldham, Paisley and North Shields. Each project had a dedicated budget to fund both an action and a research team. The researchers would identify the local social problems, the community work team would organise the local community, and the different methods of intervention would be evaluation to identify 'what works' for replication in other communities.

The CDPs had diverse objectives, with practice and analysis reflecting the different ideological positions of their staff teams. As Green and Chapman (1992) pointed out, the

CDPs exhibited a number of weaknesses in practice and theory. Like many projects at the time they ignored gender and race issues. They tried, and failed, to link community activity to trade unionism, and their analysis of community did not develop into a viable practice theory. Most critical of all was their failure to build political support for community development enabling the government to eventually curtail the projects.

However, the CDPs did produce a number of influential documents that transformed the understanding of community problems and what intervention could and could not achieve. The report, *Costs of Industrial Change* (CDP, 1977a) argued that poverty was caused by unemployment through business decisions taken elsewhere. As such it is an early analysis of the effects of global capitalism on local communities. *Whatever Happened to Council Housing* (CDP, 1976) identified that the poor conditions on many estates were due to government decisions concerning housing policy and the housing market, rather than the fault of tenants. *Gilding the Ghetto* (CDP, 1977b) claimed that urban deprivation is not caused by the deprived themselves but rather that 'the problems of urban poverty ... were the consequence of fundamental inequalities in the economic and political system'. The government's poverty programme, in turn, was not about solving the problem of poverty but about maintaining the status quo and managing the poor.

Broadly, the CDPs developed three approaches to community development, which are still with us in various forms today: Amelioration, Traditional response, Radical response.

Amelioration: The Oldham team was conscious of the impacts of the structural factors on community life. They accepted the view that only major socio-economic change could remedy some of the problems in the Project area, and the corollary that within the local area many problems could not be resolved. The Project team therefore adjusted its practical work programme to the local context and to small-scale self-help ameliorative activities.

Traditional response: Action was designed to effect changes 'in the controllers of resources rather than in those who receive them'. Typical of the ambiguity of this 'middle ground' was the Southwark Project's rejection of conflict-based community action as a means of achieving its goals. Community action was seen as ultimately harmful in that it was sporadic, alienated to the decision makers, and led to group instability. The way to achieve significant change at the local level was to increase access to, and democratic control over, the resources that were already available. Its goal was to radically change the organisation of resources within the local authority, not to act as an outside pressure group.

Radical response: The third grouping of local projects rejected previous definitions of community work and attempted to evolve new forms more fitting with economic realities, that is, to explore the interconnection between the problems encountered in the local project areas and the uneven nature of capitalist development. Rather than just accepting this as a given, or responding eclectically, these projects tried to develop, along with their input at the national level, effective local practices.

Alongside the CDPs, there were more reviews, reports and legislation. The most significant of which was the Gulbenkian Committee review of community work. Their report (1968) commented that community work was essentially:

> concerned with affecting the course of social change through the two processes of analysing social situations and forming relationships with different groups to bring about desirable change ... In short community work is a means of giving life to local democracy.

The report has much in common with the emerging ameliorative approach and identified three main strands of practice: neighbourhood projects, interagency work and research linked to social planning. It is from this document that the characteristic of much of today's practice has developed.

The 1970s Onwards

During the 1970s, 1980s and 1990s community work in Britain was subjected to new social developments: the impact of feminism and race, co-option by the state and reduction in funding.

From the late 1960s feminism had an increasing impact on community development practice. Over the past few decades, feminism has reshaped both the community development agenda and how it is practised, for example, the identification of local issues directly concerning women, as well as the recognition that women bear the brunt of dealing with housing and poverty issues. Feminist analysis and practice also confronted male assumptions and domination of practice. Gender relationships, the use of power within groups, and the understanding that the personal is political, confronted and eventually changed the patriarchal approach of many white male workers.

Alongside the growth of feminist practice, immigration from Africa and the Indian sub-continent, particularly into English cities, pushed a range of ethnic and cultural agendas and perspectives onto the community development agenda. With the entry of the UK into the EU, and free movement of European workers, these agendas have broadened out to include the effects of substantial migration from Eastern Europe. As the Brexit vote in 2016 showed, the anxieties (and hostilities) around immigration and race are still with us and continue to present challenges for practice.

Some community workers actively engaged with these issues, others saw feminism and race as a sub-division of the class system, and something that would be solved with the ending of capitalism. Other workers simply ignored these issues entirely. For other workers, the *process* of the work – how you engage with people, became more important than the *product* of the work – what you actually achieved.

It has been argued that the result of these trends was that community development lost its way. Waddington (1983), in a classic article commenting on the disorientation of many workers, said; '*The plain fact is that many community activities, as we originally conceived them, have simply lost their point. Our current predicament is that we are no longer collectively quite sure of what we are trying to do or how to do it*' (our emphasis). Barr's study in the early 1990s of community workers in Scotland, identified much radical rhetoric amongst generally conservative practice with a confusion of purpose that reinforces Waddington's point. There is no reason to assume that there is currently more clarity about community development practice.

In fact, community work has spent much of the past four decades trying to catch up with how to respond to the social and economic changes that had been driven through as a result of neo-liberalism, globalisation or as policy objectives of the New Right. Another complicating factor for practice has been the incorporation of community development by the state. Currently community development is mostly state sponsored through the central or local financing of projects and jobs. However, community development was traditionally an outlier activity and peripheral to the concerns of government. In the 1970s, many workers agonised over the duality of the job of being a worker of the state, but also working against the state (see London Edinburgh Weekend Return Group, 1980). Such debates are less common these days with workers narrowing the focus of their work to building and sustaining partnerships between relatively powerless community organisations and powerful state institutions.

We can trace the incorporation of community development from the mid-1990s through its intermediary role in the Single Regeneration Budget-funded programmes in England, the partnerships in Scotland, and the Peace and Reconciliation money in Northern Ireland. Social planning is now a major state activity to promote the government's intervention in local communities, and community development has become central to this process. Thomas (1983) defines social planning as 'the assessment of community needs and problems and the systematic planning of strategies for meeting them ... this may involve participative mechanisms like community health councils, planning enquiries and public meetings ... it is intended that such enquiries and consultations will elicit priorities amongst problems and suggest preferred solutions'. Perhaps the majority of community development workers now operate in the social planning context. The amelioration model dominates, with the worker forming and sustaining local groups and linking them to an ever-increasing array of local partnerships. Clearly, local partnerships promote changes for the benefit of the community but as we discuss in Section 3 there are implicit questions around power – that is, individual and community empowerment that does not get addressed within this model of practice.

Running in parallel to the above ameliorative social planning process, but to a far lesser extent, is social enterprise. Research by Demos (a policy think tank) and Paul Brickell (2000) suggests that the traditional structures used by social planners to engage the community have failed and that new radical approaches are required to free local creativity.

Specifically, the usual methods of community involvement are criticised as:

- failing to effectively engage people
- stifling creativity and local initiative
- promoting the idea of dependency upon public bodies
- often dominated by 'professional' community activists who have limited accountability
- deskilling and disabling local people by expecting then to understand and respond to complex issues with inadequate support

Their still relevant argument is that successful regeneration comes not through the bureaucratic structures that community development has become embroiled with, such as partnership management. Instead effective practice comes through mobilising the creativity and resourcefulness of people on the margin. Social enterprises suggest this innovation comes from creative individuals and small social businesses that can cut through red tape and bring their individual skills to play, pulling the local community along behind them. There is some truth to this argument. Although, there are dangers of social enterprises doing things to and for the community, rather than with the community. There is no doubt though, that much of present community development practice lacks creativity and innovation. As we argued in the globalisation discussion above, we are living in times of reduction in social expenditure by the government. The near future probably requires us to develop new ways of doing community development with less reliance upon government funding and systems. These themes are taken up in Section 3, where we explore more effective models of practice.

Key Learning Points

- Community development in the UK has evolved from its nineteenth-century charitable origins
- The evolution of community development has largely been driven by government social policy, created in response to poverty issues

- The mainstream of community development practice focuses on amelioration of social issues within small geographical areas
- Current practice is heavily influenced by government and is largely driven by the consensual partnership model
- Good community development practice will reflect and be sensitive to issues and ideas emanating from local communities, including perspective on gender and ethnicity
- To be more effective, we may need to develop more creative and innovative forms of practice that are less reliant on state funding

Learning Tasks

If you are not in the UK:

- Research the history and development of community development in your country

For everyone:

- How far does feminist ideology influence the nature and practice of community development locally? How far are the different local cultures reflected in community development practice?

Key Reading

Popple, K. (1996/2015) *Analysing Community Work*. Buckingham: Oxford University Press.

References

Batten, T. (1967) *The Non Directive Approach*. Oxford: Oxford University Press.
Brickell, P. (2000) *People before Structures*. London: Demos.
CDP Inter-Project Editorial Team (1976) *Whatever Happened to Council Housing?* London: CDP IIU.
CDP Inter-Project Editorial Team (1977a) *The Costs of Industrial Change*. London: CDP IIU.
CDP Inter-Project Editorial Team (1977b) *Gilding the Ghetto*. London: CDP IIU.
Green, J. and Chapman, A. (1992) 'The British Community Development Project: Lessons for Today', *Community Development Journal*, 27(3), 242–258.
Gulbenkian Committee (1968) *Community Work and Social Change*. London: Longman.
London Edinburgh Weekend Return Group (1980) *In and Against the State*. London: Pluto Press.
Ministry of Education (1944) *Community Centres*. London: HMSO.
Purcell, R. (2005) *Working in the Community: Perspectives for Change*. Morrisville, NC: Lulu Press.
Thomas, D. (1983) *The Making of Community Work*. London: Allen and Unwin.
Titmuss, R.M. (1962) *Income Distribution and Social Change*. London: Allen & Unwin.
Townsend, P. (1954) 'The Meaning of Poverty', *British Journal of Sociology*, 5(2), 130–137.
Waddington, P. (1983) 'Looking Ahead – Community Work in the 1980s', in D. Thomas (ed.), *Community Work in the Eighties*. London: National Institute for Social Work, 66–81.

Section 2
Underpinning Theories

Alongside the contexts within which community development operates (as discussed in Section 1), we also need to consider key theories that underpin practice. Exploring social theory could easily be a task for several books. Therefore, we have identified four critical theories that community development workers need to understand.

First, we discuss what we can usefully understand by the term 'community'. Second, we discuss the nature and application of power from the perspective of Antonio Gramsci and his writings on hegemony. Third, we explore the ideas of Paulo Freire and his insights into critical consciousness. Finally, we explore the nature of everyday life and how this is either liberated or constrained by the social construction of the spaces in which we live.

2.1   What is Community?

Mythology and the Power of Statistics

Community is obviously at the heart of community development, but what do we understand by the term 'community'? If we dig deep back into human history, people lived in small self-supporting groups. They relied on what we now call social capital; a close network of relationships based on trust and reciprocity, that is, the offering of support to others in need in the expectation that they will meet your needs in the future. They were, to adopt a current political phrase, genuinely 'all in it together'.

In the modern world we mostly live in diverse fragmented environments where, paradoxically, due to the numbers of people, we are often isolated. We, of course, have networks and relationships. However, these may not include many of our geographical neighbours, and may be based on family, friends, work colleagues or people with whom we share an interest. Often our networks are dispersed and exclusive; our family does not know our work colleagues, who in turn do not know our friends from school, who also do not know our friends in the sports team.

Social planners have a different view of community from most people's everyday experience. Planners tend to run statistics and plot them on a map, draw lines around the distribution of data and call that a community. In Scotland, for example, the process has led to the creation of data zones based on a number of indicators such as income, employment, crime, education, health, etc. Community development workers are often deployed to work in data zones that are statistically underperforming. There is an assumption that the residents of this area have commonality of interest and they are a functioning community. People may live in close proximity to each other but community is something else. We need to explore what community is and what it is not.

Keith Popple (1996) commented that:

> the dominant view (of community) is an idealised one which always locates a 'golden age' of clearly defined and secure neighbourhoods in the historical period before the present one.

In part this belief can be traced back to Ferdinand Tonnies (2003), the German sociologist who, writing in 1887, developed the concepts of 'gemeinschaft' and 'gessellchaft' – the former referring to a close intimate society with groupings based upon family and neighbourhood relationships that promote feelings of togetherness. This can be idealised as the pre-industrial rural village. In contrast, gessellchaft reflects the more individually focused modern urban environment where people are engaged in multiple relationships driven by function not geography.

Nostalgia and mythology aside, the important development that underpins our current social planning practice comes from Robert Park at the University of Chicago. In particular, we need to explore Park's work on what he called Human Ecology (see Linder et al., 1996). Park also believed that traditional rural communities were based on small, stable and face-to-face relationships. In contrast, community in urban areas only existed in residential neighbourhoods, where interpersonal ties were loose due the diverse nature of the resident's lives. Park was influenced by Social Darwinism and thought that people and neighbourhoods would be in competition with each other, and this led to a range of functional and dysfunctional social behaviours. The pattern of these behaviours could be mapped by the application of statistical methods. If you could identify concentration of behaviours, such as alcoholism, homicides, suicides, and poverty, the city administration could then concentrate its efforts to deal with these behaviours more effectively.

There is of course an attraction to this approach. For example, it defines social problems as being localised rather than systemic, it suggests that it is the fault of people living in the 'hot spot' areas, rather than wider social issues, and implies that concentrated local action can solve these problems. No need therefore, to ask more fundamental questions about the nature of society, distribution of wealth and power.

Social policy in North America, the UK and other countries has often been developed from this perspective. As we discussed in Section 1, the history of community development in the UK has evolved through the deployment of an area approach. The CDPs, for example, focused on 12 hot spot areas. The continuing response to poverty and social exclusion in the UK has been mediated though area strategies operating under a number of titles (Areas of Social Exclusion, Data Zones, etc.).

The area approach can be defended on pragmatic grounds. The state is not going to fundamentally question itself and explore a systemic analysis of poverty. The best we are going to have, as discussed above, is the promotion of an ameliorative approach. There is also going to be resource constraints, so why not concentrate resources to the 'worst' areas? Resources are deployed and social and environmental improvements are made.

However, as we have noted, there is a problem here in relation to defining 'community'. Social planners draw lines on maps based on statistics with some reference to physical geography and long-standing neighbourhoods. But essentially these are artificial constructs that are labelled as communities, with the expectation that the people who live there do (or should) behave as if they were a functioning community. The current trend for gated communities, and the creation of urban villages, is another example of the myth that you can create community through social planning.

This social planning practice leads to local government officials, and sadly many community development workers, referring to 'the community' as if it were a homogeneous entity. Even worse is the selection of individuals as community representatives to sit on partnership bodies. These individuals may represent a community group or organisation, but often they have no means of reporting back to the wider community or ascertaining the views of people they are supposed to represent. It is however, administratively convenient.

Community as Culture

Anthony Cohen (1985) points out that a functioning community is a product of culture, not a reflection of local government structures. He said 'community exists in the minds of its members, and should not be confused with geographical or sociographic assertions of fact'. Or as Geertz (1973) put it, 'Man is an animal suspended in webs of significance he himself has spun' (we should assume that Geertz did mean to include women here, but somehow overlooked saying so).

Community, therefore, can only meaningfully be described by the people within it. Top-down definitions of community that see it in geographical or functional terms are created by people outside the group, often for administrative convenience, and based on definitions that often may make little sense to the 'supposed' community members. These top-down definitions treat communities as *objects* to be defined and organised. The self-definition of communities enables people to become *subjects* with greater potential for power over their lives.

In the modern world we are all part of a number of, often disconnected, micro communities. These micro communities can be based on individuals within our neighbourhood, family who may live great distances apart, friends from school, colleagues from work, parents of our children's friends, those who share a common leisure interest, interest groups around politics, environmental action, LGBT, relationships on social media, and so on.

These communities, whether they are based on geography or shared interests, are built upon a range of ritual activities. These rituals function as symbolic markers and are often reinforced through specific events and activities such as carnivals, fetes, galas, even health days and school events.

Let's take a sports team as an example of a self-defined community. You can be a player, a worker at the club, a season ticket holder, somebody who watches the club on TV, or even someone in another country who has an emotional link to the club. If you feel that this team is part of your identity you have self-defined into that community.

The specific example we are using here is Celtic F.C. in Scotland. The club has a distinct history, being formed in 1888 with the aim of helping relieve poverty amongst the immigrant Irish population in the East End of Glasgow. Flowing from this is a range of symbolism, ritual and myths, and buying into this helps to build feelings of belonging and community. For example:

- Symbolic home – the ground at Parkhead is also significantly known as 'Paradise'. There are other symbolic places where ritual activities take place including dedicated pubs and clubs.
- Underpinning mythology – being linked to Ireland, Irish Republicanism, Catholicism, working class, even though you may never have visited Ireland or have Irish relatives.
- Shared History – Lisbon Lions, Jinky, Jock, Henrik, etc. If you know who these people are then you are part of the community.
- Ritual events – 'Old Firm' matches where Celtic play their greatest rival, Rangers F.C.
- Ritual dress – wearing the team colours.
- Ritual songs – singing 'You'll Never Walk Alone'
- Shared 'rhythmic muscular bonding' (dance) – crowd performance as in 'stand up if you hate Rangers'.
- Shared visual icons, flags, colours
- Levels of participation – season ticket, occasional attendee, TV watcher, vague emotional attachment
- Defines itself by a boundary – *what it is not*: Rangers F.C.

All functioning communities have some of these characteristics. By identifying micro communities, understanding what makes them function, and what people feel they gain from being community members, the community development worker begins to understand the lives of people they are working with. Bringing together these micro communities provides a basis for organising, developing social capital and creating a wider functioning network of people.

With community being a cultural phenomenon, it is influenced by a range of social and economic forces and utilised in various ways. The next discussion looks at how hegemony shapes culture. This is followed by an introduction to Freirean theory that explores how culture can create limitations to the way we see and experience the world. We then discuss the tactics people use to navigate their ways through the experience of everyday life.

Key Learning Points

- There is a continuing myth that communities functioned better in the past
- Many so-called communities today are defined by planners on the basis of administrative convenience
- Community is a product of self-identification with a group, based on culture, not by administrative structures
- Communities function through deploying a range of cultural rituals and reinforcing activities
- There is no such thing as a meaningful overarching community – we all live and function through our own set of micro communities
- Community development workers need to identify the various micro communities to which people belong. They are the basis for building social capital and creating more integrated networks of people.

Learning Tasks

- Identify both the geographical area and communities of interest of which you are a part: do these micro communities have anything in common, do they have overlapping members?
- Think about two significant communities of your choice. Explore the following questions:
  - What rituals and symbols are used to build community identity? Do they work? How could they be improved?
  - In what ways does the community define its boundary? Give examples. Does it work? Is this boundary helpful?
  - What is the 'official' story of their community, and how far do individuals identify with it? How far is this story myth or fact?
  - Where does power reside in defining and using concepts of community?

Key Reading

Although an anthropological text, Cohen's classic book provides a short and fascinating introduction to seeing community as a product of culture:

Cohen, A. (1985) *The Symbolic Construction of Community*. London: Routledge.

References

Cohen, A. (1985) *The Symbolic Construction of Community*. London: Routledge.
Geertz, C. (1973) *The Interpretation of Cultures*. New York: Basic Books.
Linder, R., Gaines, J., and Chalmers, M. (1996) *The Reportage of Urban Culture: Robert Park and the Chicago School*. Cambridge: Cambridge University Press.
Popple, K. (1996/2015) *Analysing Community Work*. Buckingham: Oxford University Press.
Tonnies, F. (2003) *Community and Society*. New York: Dover Publications.

2.2 Gramsci/Hegemony and the Nature of Power

Introduction

In order to develop Community Development practice that is both effective and which aims to deal with root causes of social problems, rather than just the surface manifestations, we must have some sort of explanatory framework that helps us understand the way our world functions. From our perspective, the work of Antonio Gramsci is of great help in this respect.

Gramsci was born in Sardinia, Italy, in 1891. He was active in the Italian Communist Party and was for a time its leader. In 1926, fascist police arrested Gramsci for his work against Mussolini and, despite his parliamentary immunity, he was brought to Regina Coeli, the famous Roman prison. At his trial the prosecutor, who clearly understood the power of ideas, said 'for twenty years we must stop this brain from functioning'. Whilst in prison Gramsci spent much of his time rethinking and writing about many aspects of Marxism, developing 'a revolutionary strategy for social transformation in Western Europe' (Mayo, 1999: 35). His main concern was to challenge the teleology embedded with Marx's analysis and explain why the Marxist prediction of a proletarian revolution had not happened. The core of Gramsci's ideas can be found in the book: Selections from Prison Notebooks (1971) However, for the purposes of this book, we will concentrate on five central strands of Gramsci's thinking – the role of Civil Society, Hegemony and Counter-Hegemony, Tactics of Change and the role of the Organic Intellectual.

Civil Society

Gramsci was perplexed by the fact that the Marxist prediction that there would be a proletarian revolution had not come to pass and was driven to seek an explanation for this. Whereas it may be thought that social domination is something which emanates from the state or elites exercising their personal power, Gramsci points to the influence of Civil Society in creating relations of social power and maintaining them through structures and cultural practices that not only shape behaviour but also shape our sense of ourselves, our aspirations and our moral standards. It is in this that he begins to see why the people did not spontaneously rebel against the contradictions between the powerful and the powerless within society: these aspirations and moral standards produced by civil society, create a common-sense view of the world that supports the status quo. We will explore this in more detail under Hegemony.

And so, the term Civil Society is used to denote the civil spaces and institutions that lie outside the state and its direct political control. Whereas the state's influence is seen through the enacting of laws supported by the judiciary, the police and the army, Civil

Society exercises influence through a network of spaces, organisations and agencies which include the economy, churches and other faith groups, the family, education, the arts, the media etc. in a more diffuse and pervasive way.

The interconnected nature of civil society can be seen by considering the case of education. In its relationship to the economy, particular forms of learning and knowledge are valued by business and these then become the forms of knowledge that are validated by education. Whilst it is possible to step outside that system of learning, the economy punishes you by restricting your access to certain jobs and the money that goes with them. It is therefore in people's interests to go with the existing system. This may be strengthened by faith groups whose moral discourse supports obedience, compliance and hard work. The media will produce material that reinforces, in a multiplicity of ways, a version of the 'good life' underpinned by education and consumption. Finally, families, whose support is actively sought by schools, will reinforce the message that working hard at school is the (only) way to ensure a good life. Not that good connections with the economy and support from family and religion is essentially bad but it does tend to valorise uncritically the system which exists, and which supports much of the inequality in our world.

The interconnected nature of social phenomena as outlined above leads us to the recognition that in Community Development, our political action – by which we mean any participative action for reflection and change – cannot only have the state as its focus, since the state is not the only agent of social influence and control, but must reflect and act on the network of influences which are found within Civil Society since 'In Gramsci's formulation, power is both centralised in the coercive apparatuses of the state and diffused across other institutional sites' (Caroll and Ratner, 2001: 6).

Hegemony

Gramsci develops the concept of Hegemony, building on the earlier concept of Ideology and so we will start our examination of this issue there. In this context Ideology does not simply mean a set of ideas held by an individual or group, but rather it is the process of presenting a partial truth which masks an underlying reality and which advantages certain sections within society. According to Marx (Marx et al. 1974) ideology naturalises, it historicises, and it eternalises. That is:

- 'ideological structures appear to be natural, 'according to the order of things' (naturalization);
- ideological structures appear to be the logical conclusion to an historical development (historicization);
- there is an assumption that now that this (natural) state of affairs has been reached, things will be that way, barring regression (eternalization)'.

(Lye, 2008)

Allman discusses it in these terms:

> Ideology or ideological refers to any thought, behaviour or even symbols that serve to distort our dialectical understanding of reality. (Ideological statements) refer to aspects of our reality that are real, and in that sense true, but only a partial truth or fragments of something we cannot fully understand unless we grasp it in its entirety. In this way they distort the truth and thus prevent us from fully comprehending a situation – in other words they tend to frame our thinking within certain horizons or parameters.

(Allman, 2001: 7)

Brookfield offers us the simple definition that: 'When a belief seems natural and obvious and when it serves to reproduce existing systems, structures and behaviours, it is ideological' (Brookfield, 2005: 67).

A useful tool for exploring practically the existence of ideological statements within our media is provided by John Lye (2008). In the form of questions, these can be run against any television programme, film, newspaper or magazine, or indeed the text of this book.

- 'What are the assumptions about what is natural, just and right?
- What (and who) do these assumptions distort or obscure?
- What are the power relations? How are they made to appear as if they are normal or good? What negative aspects are excluded?
- Look for binaries, oppositions (good/evil, natural/unnatural, tame/wild, young/old). Which term of the binary is privileged, what is repressed or devalued by this privileging of one term over the other?
- What people, classes, areas of life, experiences, are 'left out', silenced?
- What cultural assumptions and what 'myths' shape experience and evaluation? To demystify, pay attention to the particulars, the specifics, the concrete reality, with all its blemishes and contradictions.
- What enthymemes can you see in the 'logic' of the text? In a general sense, enthymemes are statements which exclude the expression of key assumptions which ground conclusions – e.g. 'Karen studies really hard. She'll ace this exam for sure'. Unspoken assumption: What it takes (all it takes?) to 'ace' an examination is hard study.
- How does the style of presentation contribute to the meaning of the text? Style always contains meaning.
- What 'utopic kernel', that is, vision of human possibility, appears to lie at the heart of the understanding of the ideology? The assumption is that there will be some vision of the good that drives that ideological perspective's imagination of the world.'

(Lye, 2008)

Ideology therefore frames our discourses about the issues in our life. It embeds within us a 'common-sense' understanding of our world. An example of this might be the way some marginalised communities limit the range of opportunities that they consider to be appropriate for them. For instance, the uptake of higher education within many working-class communities in the UK has remained stubbornly low, despite a range of initiatives from government to widen access. There are many factors why this is the case – unsupportive school environments, labelling of themselves and their community as deprived or failing, peer groups and families that resist, lack of community role models etc. – all of which lead to the people themselves believing and feeling that higher education is not an appropriate opportunity for them. This is a deeply regrettable situation. Not because higher education is necessarily the only credible option for people, but, if people frame themselves or are framed as 'non-participants in higher education' without their having thought about the issue and come up with their own conclusion, then they are being limited by something other than their own ability. Gramsci understands that limiting factor to be the outworking of hegemony. Hegemony has been defined as the situation where '... Dominant groups in society, including fundamentally but not exclusively the ruling class, maintain their dominance by securing the "spontaneous consent" of subordinate groups, including the working class, through the negotiated construction of a political and ideological consensus which incorporates both dominant and dominated groups' (Strinati, 1995: 165).

The complicated network of institutions and organisations found in civil society and the state work together in a way that maintains the status quo; it keeps the powerful, powerful. As discussed above, the education system teaches people their place within society, stratifying people for particular roles and rewarding particular forms of knowledge and behaviour. The media portrays our world in a way that defines a broad range of issues including what we should aspire to, what it means to be a man or woman, who is valuable within society and who is not and how we view insiders and outsiders. The economy privileges certain types of knowledge and behaviours and rewards them financially and with cultural prestige. The list could go on, but we see that, by constant repetition from a multiplicity of sources, strong cultural messages are embedded within people's consciousness. The effect of this is that they think and feel this common sense, internalising cultural standards and values even if it shows them in a negative light. People then become self-policing, generally recognising that it is in their own interests to go along with the way things are.

Hegemony is constantly shifting and renegotiating in order to maintain consent whilst protecting the status quo. An example of this is seen in the tradition of protests at the global G20 summits. It is expected that there will be major protests wherever the G20 summit occurs and provision is made for that. However, this happens within very controlled boundaries. In examining the protests at the Brisbane G20 summit in 2014, where new legislation and policing tactics were seen as Draconian, Legrand and Bronitt (2015) note that ensuring that individuals have an 'equality of protest opportunity' is a new policing responsibility in the twenty-first century (2015: 5). Seen through the lens of hegemony, this can be seen as strategies deployed to maintain consent. So long as people feel they have the opportunity to protest and have their voices heard they are prepared to consent with the way the world is. They may not be happy with it, but they have the impression that they are able to influence through their action. Whereas these protests are powerful performances, which can at best give a sense of cohesion to social movement or at least give people a temporary sense of being part of something, it is clear that its impact on global capitalism is very limited. And so, hegemony gains consent without relinquishing power or challenging the status quo.

However, when this general consent within society breaks down, more oppressive state apparatus can be deployed; the law, the police and the army can all be deployed quickly to restore order. However, this is a difficult and resource intensive position to be in and so the state always seeks to return to the hegemonic position of consent. This has been seen in the various riots that have happened within the UK over the years. The pattern is as follows: civil unrest flares up and the police and army are deployed in the short term. In the longer term, youth work and community work resources are introduced to the communities where the unrest was apparent, giving the community the impression that the concerns are being listened to but also providing diversionary activity which may be very useful but may also deflect from the central concerns which remain untouched.

Counter-Hegemony

Counter-hegemony addresses the need to break that ideological bond that exists between those in power and the rest of society and build up a 'counter-hegemony' to that of the ruling class; the hegemony of the many rather than the hegemony of the few. We can note here that hegemony in itself is not necessarily an oppressive force rather it is the form of hegemony that we see in operation at this point in history since it is a hegemony that benefits the few at the expense of the many. In essence, the development of counter-hegemony has two fundamental aims, to weaken the hegemony of the dominant group and to build its own political culture within the spaces of the old society.

> The revolutionary forces have to take civil society before they take the state, and therefore have to build a coalition of oppositional groups united under a hegemonic banner which usurps the dominant or prevailing hegemony.
>
> (Strinati, 1995: 169)

To have an impact we must see structural change and ideological change as part of the same struggle; changed thinking and changed action as part of the same process. This is important because hegemony is experienced as an internalised reality, which is both understood and felt, it is not just an abstract structure. Therefore, any attempt at developing an alternative society must locate itself in the cognitive and affective experiences of the people as well as within the sphere of organising and political activities.

The challenge then faced by organisations seeking to promote this form of social change is to build structures and approaches that enable people to develop alternative ways of thinking and acting in an unequal world. Carroll and Ratner (2001) suggest that social action organisations must provide an ongoing basis for alternative formations of identity and community through a process of politicising their constituents and transforming their received identity scripts. They must also provide an ongoing basis for alternative modes of satisfying needs and nurturing the capacity of their community to take action. Finally, they must develop a repertoire of collective action that dynamically and visibly contests hegemonic relations and practices. However, they warn that as groups begin to exercise power they face two challenges to maintaining counter-hegemonic activity. These come in the form of marginalising and colonising moves by both capital and state. In the first move, access to funding and places at the negotiating table are denied. If this fails and the organisation continues to grow in power and influence, the state will try to mainstream the organisation, paradoxically trying to give funding while at the same time neutralising their effect through bureaucracy, policies and constricting guidelines.

Counter-hegemony is change that reshapes the balance of social power away from ruling elites into the hands of people who are marginalised in the current social order. It comes about through a process of critical thinking and collective action which produces people with a new vision of themselves and their society and new organisations which provide an abbreviated experience of transformed relationships and a power base for political change; it leads to increased levels of social justice, solidarity, participation and security.

> The revolutionary forces have to take civil society before they take the state, and therefore have to build a coalition of oppositional groups united under a hegemonic banner which usurps the dominant or prevailing hegemony.
>
> (Strinati, 1995: 169)

Tactics of Change

Gramsci describes two forms of counter-hegemonic tactics, the War of Manoeuvre and the War of Position.

War of Manoeuvre is only possible when the state is off balance and rules by force and when its hegemony is weak or fractured. It is understood as a frontal attack whose main goal is winning quickly. As such it is unlikely to be appropriate or effective within well-established democracies. Examples of these approaches were seen during the Arab spring where high levels of civil unrest were matched by states whose hegemony was fractured or weakened. The difficulty with this approach is that it fails to take seriously the challenge that the counter-hegemonic project is an ideological one, an intellectual and emotional one, and finally a structural one. The speed of action normally means that the ideological, intellectual and emotional work has not been done widely enough across society. The upshot of this is that the only model that people have of power is the one existed before, since that has not been subject to critical scrutiny leading to alternative models. As Freire (2000) warns us,

> almost always, during the initial stage of the struggle, the oppressed, instead of striving for liberation, tend themselves to become oppressors, or 'sub-oppressors'. The very structure of their thought has been conditioned by the contradictions of the concrete, existential situation by which they were shaped. Their ideal is to be men; but for them, to be men is to be oppressors. This is their model of humanity.
>
> (2000: 45)

It is no surprise, therefore, when the structures that rise up to replace the old order turn out to be no better that those they replaced. This is echoed by Gramsci, 'How is it possible to consider the present, and quite specific present, with a mode of thought elaborated in the past which is often remote and superseded?' (1971: 324).

And so, we turn to the War of Position, which is envisaged as a long struggle which happens across a broad range of institutions in civil society. The aim of this approach is the development of a different 'common sense' through cultural and ideological struggle which takes place within an intricate system of political 'trenches', for example, newspapers, trade unions, cultural organisations, women's groups and community organisations. 'The revolutionary forces have to take civil society before they take the state, and therefore have to build a coalition of oppositional groups united under a hegemonic banner which usurps the dominant or prevailing hegemony' (Strinati, 1995: 169).

Community development potentially has a central role to play in this process given its ability to work with marginalised groups of people in an informal educative process. However, since great emphasis is placed on localised forms of practice the possibility of developing this social movement for change is minimised. However, the possibility to support the development of counter-hegemony remains but will only be realised if we stick to the fundamentals of good practice. First, we hold to a particular analysis. This is based on the understanding that the current system is oppressive, working for the few at the expense of the many. We recognise that people are subjects not objects, able to be active in their own lives and that people are, at least in part, solutions to community issues, not just problems to be fixed. We reject the individualising narrative that blames individuals for their situation whilst leaving structural issues unanalysed and unchanged. Second, we have a unique approach to practice. We are committed to doing work with people and not doing work to them. We recognise that process and product are both important – this is a vital distinction in our target-driven age. Finally, we must hold our values, discussed above, which are predicated on a commitment to Social Justice. Based on those fundamentals of good practice we have four interlinking processes.

Working with Individuals

This is the bedrock of youth and community work. The ability to develop relationships with people, to win their trust and to be a positive influence in their lives is essential to all forms of practice. But there are some essential dynamics that set the Community Development approach apart from other professional caring relationships. First, we always start with the lived experience of the people we are working with; not the agency agenda, not the funders' ideas and not government policy. This both honours the capacity of the participants to think and act, and maximises the possibility of true ownership and co-production of any subsequent work. Second, we engage in a process of re-seeing the world, in other words, making problematic the assumptions, the history, the narratives and the barriers that limit the opportunities of the people we are working with. We have more to say on this in the chapter on Freirean learning. Finally, we have as a central focus, the discovery of personal power. This is more important than goals around engagement, participation or other externally set targets. If, after working with us, people do not realise and are capable of exercising, more of their personal power, then we have failed. All of this is set in an attitude of optimism about people; everyone has the potential to become more and so we work actively with people to develop a vision of a different world for them, their community and the wider world.

Working with Groups

The next, or indeed, parallel step is collectivising those individual issues and personal power, which is achieved by forming and working with groups. Groups, in Community Development terms, are more than communal get togethers; at their best, they are experiments in a new way of being. This could be understood with reference to group theory (Hyman, 1942). This identifies a normative reference group, which provides an individual with values, attitudes and behaviour patterns, and a comparative reference group, which provides an individual with alternative standards and points of reference. Where people find themselves part of unhelpful and limiting situations, community groups can act as a comparative group, where alternative ways of being, thinking and acting together can be explored. It is possible that we provide a space where people can be heard and valued for their ideas for the first time, enabling them to create new knowledge and new possibilities, recognising that they are strong on their own but even stronger together.

Building Power Organisations

In the UK, practice often stops at the point of developing and working with groups but that is not enough if we are to foster social change and lay the foundations of a counter-hegemonic movement. We need to develop power organisations. We discuss this more fully elsewhere but essentially the overarching intention of both our individual and group work is the building of people power where people collectively get active, make demands and develop tactics to address the issues of social injustice that impact on their lives.

Developing Networks Locally, Nationally and Internationally

Finally, once we have individuals who have discovered and are exercising their individual power, have groups that are exploring new ways of thinking, being and acting together, and organisations that are exercising political power in their lives, we must continue the process of collectivising. If we can agree that our world has become globalised and that many of the structural issues act at a global as well as a local level, any movement that seeks to develop alternatives must also act at those levels. One of the opportunities presented by the twenty-first century is the ability to communicate and link across the world in ways that have hitherto been unimaginable. We have the possibility to develop local/global networks, based on shared values and commitment to global social justice and to develop a different common sense of what it means to be human, what the economy is, how we do politics and how we ultimately humanise our world.

The Role of the Organic Intellectual

Gramsci saw the role of the intellectual as a crucial one in this process of creating counter-hegemony. He contrasts this new way of being an intellectual with Traditional intellectuals whom he saw as those who do regard themselves as autonomous and independent of the dominant social group and are regarded as such by the population at large. They seem autonomous and independent and possibly as irrelevant in the context of fundamental social change.

He envisaged a new type of intellectual that would be intimately involved in these change processes. 'The mode of being of the new intellectual can no longer consist in eloquence ... but in active participation in practical life, as constructor, organiser, permanent persuader and not just a simple orator ...' (Gramsci, 1971: 10).

This role ties in with Freire's notion of conscientisation where 'The starting point of critical elaboration is the consciousness of what one really is ...' (Gramsci, 1971: 323). He envisages the criticality and historical perspective of the intellectual marrying up with the understanding and feeling of the people in order to develop a praxis for change.

Finally, it rejects the prevalent individualist focus which education has taken on. So, rather than being concerned with the development of individual skills, knowledge and understanding, the aspiration is for change on a societal level. As Smith (1994) describes 'Their purpose is not necessarily individual advancement, but human well-being as a whole' (1994: 127). I believe that community workers, youth workers and adult education workers are well placed to take on the role of the organic intellectual, navigating, with the people, that space between theory and practice, critical reflection and action.

Key Learning Points

- The current social order, which disadvantages many, is produced by the action of the state and civil society working in mutually reinforcing ways
- The process of hegemony creates a 'common sense' whereby people consent to that given social order
- Community Development could be part of a social movement for change, supporting people to develop new ways of thinking, acting and associating
- Because of the global nature of hegemony, fundamental social change must embody thinking, acting and working together at local, national and global levels
- Community Development workers are well placed to support this thinking and acting at all levels

Learning Tasks

Consider:
- Are community workers organic intellectuals? If so, what might your role be at local, national and global levels?

Key Reading

McNally, M. (2015) *Antonio Gramsci*. Basingstoke: Palgrave Macmillan.

References

Allman, P. (2001) *Critical Education Against Global Capitalism*. Santa Barbara, CA: Greenwood Press.

Brookfield, S. (2005) *The Power of Critical Theory for Adult Learning and Teaching*. Milton Keynes: Open University Press.

Carroll, W. and Ratner, R. (2001) 'Sustaining Oppositional Cultures in 'Post-socialist Times': A Comparative Study of Three Social Movement Organisations', *Sociology*, 35(3), 605–629.

Freire, P. (2000) *Pedagogy of the Oppressed*, 30th anniversary edn. London and New York: Continuum.

Gramsci, A. (1971) *Selections from Prison Notebooks*. New York: International Publishers.

Hyman, H.H. (1942) *The Psychology of Status. Archives of Psychology*. New York: Columbia University.

Legrand, T. and Bronitt, S. (2015) 'Policing the G20 Protests: "Too Much Order with Too Little Law" Revisited', *Queensland Review*, 22, 3–14. doi:10.1017/qre.2015.2.

Lye, J. (2008) 'Ideology: A Brief Guide'. Available at: www.brocku.ca/english/jlye/ideology.ph, accessed 10 November 2016.

Marx, K., Engels, F., Arthur, C.J., and Marx, K. (1974) *The German Ideology*. London: Lawrence & Wishart.

Mayo, P. (1999) *Gramsci, Freire, and Adult Education: Possibilities for Transformative Action*. London: Zed Books.

Smith, M.K. (1994) *Local Education: Community, Conversation, Praxis*. Buckingham: Open University Press.

Strinati, D. (1995) *An Introduction to Theories of Popular Culture*. London: Routledge.

2.3   Freire and Critical Consciousness

Introduction

If we accept the fundamental premise that community development is not about service delivery but is a process of individual and collective learning for social change, then we must ask ourselves some fundamental questions about those educative processes. What is the purpose of learning? Under what circumstances and in what conditions do people learn best? What is the role of the educator, in what ways is that problematic and what challenges do we face as educators? It is into this context that Paulo Freire speaks most clearly and is therefore of greatest use to the community development practitioner. However, it is imperative that we understand Freire's work as an approach, not just a method. An approach has a history, a set of values, a vision of a transformed world and a set of ontological and epistemological commitments. It is to these underlying ideas and assumptions that we turn our attention.

At its heart, the Freirean approach has two basic assumptions, the possibility of humanisation and the historical reality of dehumanisation. Freire's pedagogy is not merely concerned with the acquisition of skills and knowledge; rather, it is going for something much deeper, to enable people to become more fully human. He goes on to describe his understanding of what this true humanity looks like.

For, apart from inquiry, apart from the praxis, individuals cannot be truly human. 'Knowledge emerges only through invention and re-invention, through the restless, impatient, continuing, hopeful inquiry human beings pursue in the world, with the world, and with each other' (Freire, 2000 : 72).

He foregrounds this creativity and invention as being the ontological vocation of human beings and it is this vision of humanity that drives the educative process. The obverse of this is the current, dehumanised, condition that humanity finds itself in. This is seen in every situation where creativity and invention are replaced by prescription, stifling and oppressing the human impulse to think and create. Again, the Freirean educative process is driven by a desire to strip out these negative forces both within the thinking of participants and in the social relationships within the educative process itself. More on this later.

> I consider the fundamental theme of our epoch to be that of domination – which implies its opposite, the theme of liberation, as the objective to be achieved ... In order to achieve humanization, which presupposes the elimination of dehumanizing oppression, it is absolutely necessary to surmount the limit-situations in which men are reduced to things.
>
> (Freire, 2000: 93)

And so, his vision of authentic humanity is made clear, as is his understanding of the world as it is. This gives rise to his analysis and for the purposes of this book we will focus on three elements of that analysis: the constructed nature of the world, the constructed nature of our subjectivities and the political nature of education.

He offers a very clear analysis of the world, suggesting that all social phenomena are produced by the complex interplay of opposing structural forces: Labour/capital, rich/poor and oppressor/oppressed. These binary oppositions are seen by some as an oversimplification of the way the world works. That is undoubtedly true, however this typology opens up a way of thinking about the world which is very helpful for us as community development practitioners. It gives us a way of thinking dialectically about our world and therefore gives us an opportunity to understand not just symptoms that we deal with in our day-to-day practice but the root causes of those phenomena.

That the world is typified by inequality is very easy to see. The shocking truth is ably illuminated by Oxfam's (2017) report on wealth inequality: 'the wealth of the poorest half of the world's population – that's 3.6 billion people – has fallen by a trillion dollars since 2010. This 38 per cent drop has occurred despite the global population increasing by around 400 million people during that period. Meanwhile the wealth of the richest 62 has increased by more than half a trillion dollars to $1.76tr. Just nine of the "62" are women.' Where Freire is helpful to us is in making the connection between that global level and our lived experience; the unequal power relations we see at the global level and replicated in every social encounter we have.

To explore that idea in more detail, let us consider Freire's second area of analysis. That is, the understanding that people's subjectivities are constructed by the complex interrelationships between themselves and their material conditions – their environment, social conditions and social relations. This can be more simply explained by the idea that people learn what they live. In community development, we may work with people who have experienced poverty, educational failure and an environment where experts tell them how to think and what decisions to make. Their subjectivity, the sense of who they are and how they understand the world, is shaped by those experiences. People learn passivity and silence in the face of these forces. Freire's pedagogy recognises that, in order to change people's subjectivities, we must change their social reality. Of course, community development cannot transform people's social experience wholesale. It can, however, provide contexts where people experience being heard, being valued and feeling part of a group where change is possible (Beck and Purcell, 2010). Paula Allman (2001) talks of this as being an abbreviate experience of transformed social relationships which are the foundation for genuine participation in change processes. It is within these contexts that people's confidence grows, their sense of personal power develops and a desire for further, more comprehensive change can be fostered. Community development's emphasis on group-work processes recognises this dynamic but we must reflect carefully on the processes within that group work and the impact that they have.

As a worker in this process we must recognise that we exist within these pre-set, unequal power relationships. Because of our status as workers, gained from organisations, education and experience, we automatically hold a position of power – whether we like it or not. And so, part of our practice must be to struggle to transform those power relationships. Within many marginalised communities, people have grown to expect someone else to make decisions for them; to tell them how to feel and what to think. We, as community workers, enter into a relationship with the group that's already shaped by those pre-existing assumptions. Again, whether we like it or not, groups will defer to our perceived power and if you want to change that situation we have to be prepared to struggle.

This leads us to Freire's final area of analysis which is an understanding that no education is neutral, it either domesticates and shapes people to function within the given social order or it liberates people to be critical agents for change in their thinking, their practice and their wider world. From this analysis, he posits two basic forms of education: Banking Education and Problem Posing Education.

Banking Education is described by Margaret Ledwith (2011: 100) as an act of cultural invasion – involving the imposition of one's values, assumptions and perceptions of the world on others, silencing and disempowering them. The roles within Banking Education are clearly delineated along the lines of power with the teacher being powerful and the taught being powerless. The teacher has the power to define questions, to validate answers and to prescribe processes. The role of the learner is to listen, remember and repeat. The process of learning is, again, one that is decided in advance by the teacher. The knowledge that is to be transferred is researched by the teacher, whose role then becomes the efficient transfer of that existing knowledge so that learners can remember and accurately repeat that knowledge.

Of course, as we have already seen, people learn what they live and so the learners learn a number of important life lessons. They learn that knowledge is fixed and external to them and therefore in order to learn they must be taught by experts. This is generally a pacified position, which is reflected in many other areas of life, creating what Freire terms, 'the culture of silence'.

By contrast, Freire's **Problem Posing** approach to education has a specific aim, that of helping learners to develop critical consciousness. This is a state where people see themselves and the issues they are dealing with in the context of their wider social reality and, through that deeper understanding, become capable of making change in their lives. As Jesson and Newman (2004) put it, 'they cease to be objects and become writers of their own story'. Before going on to consider the theoretical underpinnings of the problem-posing approach, let us explore Freire's understanding of consciousness.

Within Freire's typology there are three levels of consciousness. First, Magical Consciousness: In this state people are passive and accepting of their lot in life; their belief is that the situation is inevitable and unchangeable. This level of consciousness is typified by statements like, 'that's just the way is!'. People feel powerless to change their situations; they feel like the locus for control for their life is external to themselves. Where people have no belief in the possibility of change, change becomes very difficult. Having lost connection with their sense of human agency, they are forced to rely on the influence and energies of others and, in doing so, become passive.

The second level of consciousness to which he refers is Naïve Consciousness. In this state people recognise their personal problems but do not make the connection to wider social or structural issues. This level of consciousness is often typified by feelings of anger and frustration. People recognise injustice, feel that there is something wrong but also feel unable to do anything about it. This is potentially fertile ground for the community worker. In the UK, we are socialised to be suspicious and uncomfortable with too much emotion, especially negative emotion. And yet, emotion is often the engine that drives change. If people are angry, frustrated or afraid they are more likely to seek an answer for the situation than if they are feeling perfectly calm. A skilled community worker can harness these so-called negative feelings as a springboard into critical analysis and action. The process of how this is achieved will be explored later.

The final level of consciousness that Freire outlines is Critical Consciousness. In this state, people recognise that the situations they find themselves in are neither entirely of their own making nor the product of some invisible and unknowable forces, but they come to recognise that structures of society are unjust and the discrimination they produce affects them, the way they think and feel about their lives, and the opportunities that are open or closed to them. The intention of this approach is that this awareness leads to collective action for change but there is a danger that the process gets stuck at the stage of analysis and is not translated into action. Both the skill of the worker and the energy of the group are required to ensure that this process has an impact on the real-life situations within which people live.

The process which is at the heart of Problem Posing Education is that of Dialogue, which Freire says lies at the heart of this process of humanisation. Ledwith describes Dialogue as horizontal communication between equals involved in critical enquiry (Ledwith, 2011). This horizontal communication is predicated on the transformation of two key relationships; first, transformed social relationships (teacher/learners and learner/teachers); and second, a transformed relationship to knowledge itself whereby all participants (both teachers and learners) become creators, rather than consumers, of knowledge.

The relationship between teachers and learners transforms from a one-way process of information transfer, to a model of co-investigation. This is not to say that teachers do not teach. There is a powerful role for teachers to research existing knowledge and to present that to the learning group, but this is presented not as a finished article but as a starting point – a question to be explored, a problem to be solved. In this process, the thinking of group members and also the thinking as expressed in the 'knowledge object' (existing knowledge), is collectively focused on 'what do we think?' and 'where has that thinking come from?' And so, embedded within this process is the possibility of the creation of new knowledge and recognition and the exploration of metacognitive processes – we think about our thinking and in that process our thinking transforms. In this process the teacher knows the starting point and the process but not the end point of the learning, since that is produced by the co-investigation of the learning group. This is an exciting process but also a risky one as it entails the teacher giving away that power to define and to control and opens up the agency of the whole learning group to explore, nurturing the critical curiosity of the group and deliberately making spaces within which to create new knowledge. This process of education has the potential for, not just individual change but transformation on a societal level since, rather than passively consuming the received wisdom on any subject, it deliberately questions and challenges what is known and, as seen above, seeks to link transformed thinking to transformative action. Paula Allman suggests that until society itself is transformed, dialogic communication and learning will remain counter-hegemonic (Allman, 2001: 176).

We can see then that the Freirean approach is not educational in the traditional narrow sense of the word but as a cultural process for change. And so, let us finally consider Freire's view on the role of culture within his pedagogy.

First, he warns of the danger of an uncritical practice where no consideration is given to the relationship between learners and teachers and learners and knowledge as discussed above. He talks about such practice as being a form of Cultural Invasion. The impact of such practice is that people begin to see reality through the eyes of the invaders, accept imposed norms and values, see themselves as inferiors and finally become powerless.

Cultural invasion is undertaken by well-meaning workers who do not have critically reflective practice. They assume that they understand the problems that are being experienced by the community and that they have a well thought out solution to those problems. They therefore see their role as persuading the community to see things their way and implement their solutions. This overlooks the fact that there are many ways to understand the issues and many ways to deal with problems. More importantly, it assumes that the values, views, analysis and solutions of the worker are pre-eminent, dismissing people's expertise in their own life. Even if this happens to be true in a particular situation, people learn what they live. This top-down, prescriptive approach teaches them that someone else knows and they do not know. That external knowledge is valuable, and their knowledge is not. In short, they have learned to be more reliant and more disempowered – even if that particular intervention sorts out their short-term problem.

These top-down forms of practice which are repeated through politics, health, education, housing and the rest, produce what Freire describes as the Culture of Silence. Within this culture, the world is named by others on their behalf. One example, which I currently find disturbing, is that of young people being described as NEETS – Not in Education, Employment or Training (Miraz-Davies, 2016). I find this particularly pernicious since the entirety of the young person's identity is summed up by what they are not. This pathological model of deficit typifies the Cultural Invasion transforming creative critical multidimensional people into objects, into problems to be solved. It is little wonder that within this Culture of Silence people feel ignorant, become dependent and realise very clearly that their knowledge and insights are less valuable than that of experts.

The cultural process which Freire suggests is more emancipatory and transformational is Cultural Action for Freedom. Within this form of practice Culture is created through Praxis – the integration of action and reflection. As Clifford Geertz (1973) says 'Man is an animal suspended in webs of significance he himself has spun. I take culture to be those webs, and the analysis of it to be therefore not an experimental science in search of law but an interpretive one in search of meaning' and so this process of making culture is a collective exploration of our world and the many relationships we have to it, what that means and what we wanted it to mean.

Let us conclude this chapter by considering five key qualities of the worker in these educative processes.

1. Personal decision to engage in a process of self-transformation

Since the educative process is no longer a one-way street, we must be open to our thinking and practice being challenged; this calls for humility and trust. It acknowledges the fact that we are people in process and that we require other subjects of knowing to aid us in that process.

2. Exercising authority but not being authoritarian

There is a delicate balance to be struck on this issue. Leadership which allows people to think and to function effectively in a group is essential, but leadership which dominates, and stifles creativity is oppressive. This balance can be found through maintaining and openness and reflexivity within the group since an examination of the relationships and the power within the group are always part of the learning.

3. Being directive but not manipulative

The Freirean process is, in a sense, a directive one since it constantly invites people to reflect and challenge existing knowledge, their attitudes and assumptions and the status quo. Similarly, it deliberately makes connections between individual experience and wider societal forces. However, it is not manipulative in the sense that it is transparent about its assumptions and intentions. Also, although the process is directive in that sense, the outcomes are within the gift of the group to shape; the worker does not know the end point at the start of the process and so the power to choose and to shape remains with the group.

4. Balance the need for structure with the need for openness

Following on from the previous point, people are more able to think and to be creative within some sort of structure. The Freirean use of codifications and dialogue give clear structure but allow for the analysis of the group to shape the process.

5. Know that you do not know – or do not fully know

This is a fundamental characteristic of the skilled worker. It acknowledges the reality that all knowledge is provisional and dynamic and fosters the critical curiosity that is essential for energetic educational practice. It opens up the possibility of genuine dialogue since the questions posed are genuine ones; in traditional forms of education, teachers ask questions to which they already know the answers. Finally, it undermines the cultural norm that the expert knows all and being wrong or uncertain is a weakness; not knowing is an essential precursor to searching for a deeper understanding.

Key Learning Points

- Community development is not about service delivery but about collective learning and change
- Our current social order dehumanises people
- Community development enables people to connect with their agency and creativity
- Through dialogue and critical reflection, people are prepared to act for change

Learning Tasks

The Freirean approach supports people to move from magical to critical consciousness.

- Can you think of a time in your life when you felt powerless and that the situation was unchangeable?
- How did that change for you?
- How can that understanding help you when you are working with community groups?

Key Reading

Beck, D. and Purcell, R. (2010) *Popular Education for Youth and Community Work*. Exeter: Learning Matters.
Freire, P. (1972) *Pedagogy of the Oppressed*. London: Penguin.

References

Allman, P. (2001) *Critical Education Against Global Capitalism*. Santa Barbara, CA: Greenwood Press.
Beck, D. and Purcell, R. (2010) *Popular Education for Youth and Community Work*. Exeter: Learning Matters.
Freire, P. (2000) *Pedagogy of the Oppressed*, 30th anniversary edn. London and New York: Continuum.
Geertz, C. (1973) *The Interpretation of Cultures*. New York: Basic Books.

Jesson, J. and Newman, M. (2004) 'Radical Adult Education and Learning', in G. Foley (ed.), *Understanding Adult Education and Training*. New South Wales: Allen & Unwin.

Ledwith, M. (2011) *Community Development: A Critical Approach*, 2nd edn. Bristol: The Policy Press.

Miraz-Davies, J. (2016) *NEET: Young People Not in Education, Employment or Training*. London: House of Commons Library.

Oxfam (2017) 'An Economy for the 99%'. Available at: www-cdn.oxfam.org/s3fs-public/file_attachments/bp-economy-for-99-percent-160117-en.pdf.

2.4 Space and Everyday Life in Communities

Introduction

As we discussed in the introduction to this book effective community development is not simply organising people into delivering community-focused tasks. Instead, it is a social change process underpinned by an educational interaction, which facilitates people reflecting on their lives and identifying changes they wish to make through collective action.

In the previous two discussions we have identified the way culture, operating through hegemonic processes, shapes an understanding of how we see the broader society and our place within it. Freire shows us the importance of critically inspecting this received understanding and developing a more critical perspective. An essential part of this understanding comes from reflecting on the nature of what has become known as 'everyday life', and our personal response to this by deploying a set of 'tactics' to get us through the day. Kathleen Stewart (2007) describes it thus:

> Everyday life is a life lived on the level of surging effects, impacts suffered or barely avoided. It takes everything we have. But it also spawns a series of little somethings dreamed up in the course of things.

Analysis of Space

Purcell (2012) suggests that the world has been divided into functional spaces, within which everyday life takes place. Lefebvre commented, 'space is a social product controlled by dominant classes and interests' (Lefebvre, 1991). This includes everything from workplaces, schools, shopping malls, to community centres and domestic living spaces.

The effect of this is that those who control space in an urban area also control what can and cannot happen. Lefebvre uses religion as an example: without churches or spaces in which to hold religious ceremonies and promote its ideology, a religion cannot function. Purcell suggests the same principle holds true to private shopping malls as sites of consumption with restricted codes of public behaviours, gang territories in neighbourhoods and even what happens/does not happen within a community centre. What happens and where it happens is an outcome of ideological conflict and, as Gramsci suggested, potentially a site of hegemonic/counter-hegemonic struggle. Increasingly this struggle manifests itself in virtual space through the Internet, but the meaning of this for community development is a separate story.

Everyday Life

Since the 1960s, ideas loosely called 'theories of everyday life' have been developed. These theories take Lefebvre's argument of the primacy of space as given, and explore how ideology, social control and potential resistance may be played out through the lived experience in the everyday lives of ordinary people. The key ideas come from Michel de Certeau, *The Practice of Everyday Life* (1984), but also include key texts by Guy Debord, *Society of the Spectacle* (1982); Henri Lefebvre, *The Critique of Everyday Life* (2008); and Raoul Vaneigen, *The Revolution of Everyday Life* (2006).

Overall, these writings explore the postmodernist belief that in advanced capitalist societies social relationships are in decline, with face-to-face interactions being replaced by virtual friends, and our involvement with the world increasingly mediated by images from TV, computers and publications that suggest that human satisfaction is a product of consumption. As such, our lives are becoming 'inauthentic'. From a different ideological position, the work of Putnam (2000) on the decline of social capital in modern society reinforces this argument. Or as Debord wrote in *Society of the Spectacle* 'all that was once directly lived has become mere representation' (1992: thesis 1).

Raoul Vaneigem (2006) who, along with Debord, was a key member of the French Situationist International, also explored the nature of everyday life. He argued that the way capitalism functions distorts the nature of social relationships. People's relationships and lives in general are overwhelmingly defined by the need to produce and consume, rather than interact with others in more socially useful ways. Vaneigem asked, what can be done to change this? – a question that should also be relevant for community development workers.

This is also a question explored by de Certeau. His argument was that institutions and government organisations in society always act in their own sectional interest (for a wider discussion of this, see Illich, 1995, 2005). These self-interests are promoted through the control of space, which promotes certain activities that favour the institution and restrict alternative actions. This process was termed by de Certeau as 'strategies'.

A strategy may enjoy status as a product of the dominant order, or be sanctioned by the powers that be. Michael Shapiro suggests that strategies belong to those who have legitimate positions within the social order and consequently are part of 'a centralized surveillance network for controlling the population' (1992: 103). This may be overstating the degree of co-ordination of strategies, although it can be argued that increasing control of the population is a clear outcome.

Purcell notes that strategies can manifest themselves physically through the sites (space) of operations. Institutional strategies are also promoted through social and cultural products (for example, laws, language, rituals, commercial goods, literature, art, inventions and discourse). In an urban area the physical space and the activities of people within it will be controlled through a variety of direct/indirect and formal/informal strategies. Our lives and the way we perceive the world, through the way work, leisure, and our movement around the city is both organised and restricted, is shaped by the deployment of strategies.

Tactics of Everyday Life

However, people are not simply passive. Within everyday activity there is an abundance of opportunities for ordinary people to subvert the rituals, representations and processes that institutions seek to impose upon them; in effect, to make their lives more livable. De Certeau called these responses 'tactics'. Given the individualised nature of modern life, tactics are often just fragmented and isolated. Tactics can be both functional or dysfunctional in terms of self-interest, and either positive or negative in terms of social change. Nevertheless, according to de Certeau, in any everyday activity lies an abundance of opportunities for ordinary people to subvert the rituals and representations that institutions seek to impose upon them; in effect to try, often in an unconscious way, to remake part of the world in their personal interest.

Conquergood (1992: 82) described tactics as a 'performance repertoire of displaced, disenfranchised and dominated people deploying improvisational savvy'. Similarly, de Certeau saw tactics as often spontaneous and the seizing of a moment of opportunity. Individualised tactics therefore can take many forms and are often quite small, for example, taking a long coffee break or using the work computer to book a holiday.

Tactics may also include emotional responses: the middle-age crisis, buying a motorbike, having a younger boy/girlfriend or maybe sexual deviancy. Sometimes they are politically focused and can include street protests or boycotting goods. The 2016 Brexit vote has been described as an act of protest by people who feel themselves to be otherwise powerless in society. A similar argument has been used to explain much of the support for Donald Trump in the 2016 US Presidential election. Tactics may also include random acts such as parking illegally, flash mobbing or simply spontaneously helping others (random acts of kindness).

It could be suggested that collectivised critical consciousness will produce more positive tactical outcomes. If community development workers better understood how strategies operated, then they could work with people to devise tactics for developmental ends. Such an approach would have its challenges, as Conquergood makes clear, tactics 'resist systematizing and totalizing discourses because they are dispersed and nomadic; they are difficult to administer because they cannot be pinned down' (1992: 83).

So, what can community development workers do to assist people with understanding how their lives are shaped by the modern world, and to develop a more functional repertoire of personal and social change-orientated tactics? A useful starting point could be to consider the manifestation of the global economy and culture in local everyday life and its effect on how we construct our identities (see, for example, Giddens, 1991). Another would be to explore the effects of the modern phenomena of the merging of work with the commodification of leisure activities (Slater, 1997). A third approach could explore the decline of the traditions of public life and its replacement by privatised activities in public space (Sennet, 2002).

Transgression

Related to the nature of existing and potential tactics are acts of transgression; that is, the breaking of social norms and engagement in activities unacceptable to dominant social groups and organisations, and in conflict to the formal/informal rules of a particular space. De Certeau thought that everyday life works by a process of poaching (his word for transgressing) on the territory of others, recombining the rules and products that already exist in culture in a way that is influenced, but never wholly determined, by those rules and products.

Transgression can take many forms from the individual to the collective, from the socially dysfunctional to the functional. Transgression can also be a tactical expression of need and/or defiance by powerless individuals and groups. For example, individual transgressions could be graffiti on the side of walls. Is this vandalism or cultural expression? In some areas of the USA this is criminalised, in other areas graffiti artists are paid to paint positive messages about HIV prevention, safe sex, etc. Is young people wandering around a housing estate or hanging out in bus stops a social threat, or simply a tactical social act by people with nowhere else to go? On a political level, are acts of civil disobedience, such as blocking roads as part of an environmental protest, legitimate or not? We discuss this particular question further in Section 3.

This raises the question of what forms of transgressions should community development workers actively support (positive transgression)? Which ones should they confront (negative transgression)? Are there situations where workers should collude with, or deliberately ignore, transgressive behaviour? Should these decisions be made by the worker based on their own values, by the employing agency as hegemonic control, or by members of the community themselves with the risk that this is one section of the community simply exerting power over another social/cultural/ethnic group?

Key Learning Points

- The world is divided into elements of space that are controlled by institutions and government organisations in their own interest
- This process of controlling spaces is termed by de Certeau as 'strategies'
- How we interact (or are prevented from interacting) with these spaces shapes our understanding of the world and how we see ourselves
- In responding to the way spaces are organised, we developed a set (repertoire) of personal 'tactics'
- Tactics are usually individualised and can be personally functional or dysfunctional, socially progressive or repressive
- Tactics can often be transgressive, and again these can be personally functional or dysfunctional, socially progressive or repressive
- Community development can help people understand the effect of space, and facilitate the development of more function and socially progressive tactics

Learning Tasks

- Identify a community space, for example a community centre. How is this space organised, by whom, for what explicit/implicit purposes, whose interests does this organisation of space really serve? How could this space be better organised for inclusive community development purposes?
- What is your repertoire of tactics? List them according to whether they are functional or dysfunctional, both for you and for the wider community? Are there tactics you would wish to change?

Key Reading

Highmore, B. (2002) *Everyday Life and Cultural Theory*. London: Routledge.

References

Conquergood, D. (1992) 'Ethnography, Rhetoric, and Performance', *Quarterly Journal of Speech*, 78, 80–123.
Debord, G. (1992) *Society of the Spectacle*. London: Rebel Press.
de Certeau, M. (1984) *The Practice of Everyday Life*, trans. Steven Rendall. Berkeley, CA: University of California Press.
Giddens, A. (1991) *Modernity and Self Identity*. Cambridge: Polity Press.

Illich, I. (1995) *Deschooling Society*. London: Marion Boyars,.

Illich, I. (2005) *Disabling Professions*. London: Marion Boyars,.

Lefebvre, H. (1991) *The Production of Space*. Oxford: Wiley Blackwell.

Lefebvre, H. (2008) *The Critique of Everyday Life, Vols 1–3*. London: Verso.

Purcell, R. (2012) 'Community Development and Everyday Life', *Community Development Journal*, 47(2), 266–281.

Putnam R. (2000) *Bowling Alone: The Collapse and Revival of American Community*. New York: Simon & Schuster.

Sennet, R. (2002) *The Fall of Public Man*. London: Penguin.

Shapiro, M. (1992) *Reading the Postmodern Polity: Political Theory as Textual Practice*. Minneapolis, MN: University of Minnesota.

Slater, D. (1997) *Consumer Culture and Modernity*. Cambridge: Polity Press.

Stewart, K. (2007) *Ordinary Affects*. Durham, NC: Duke University Press.

Vaneigen, R. (2006) *The Revolution of Everyday Life*. London: Rebel Press.

Section 3
Models of Practice

In this section we discuss a range of practice models. We start with an overview of practice as it is experienced in the UK. Next, we look at Direct Action, which provides a counterpoint to the dominant practice model. We then move on to explore four successful international models of practice: Community Organising from the USA; the Slum Dwellers International (SDI) approach that is used in cities across the developing world; how to apply the ideas of Freire in practice; and the Asset Based Community Development approach from the USA, widely used across the world. Finally, we attempt to pull many of these themes together and suggest a possible Integrated Model of Practice.

3.1   Overview of Current Practice

Where We Are Now in the UK

As we discussed in Section 1 the majority of community development practice in the UK has evolved in the Ameliorist tradition. That is, recognising that many community problems are due to wider social and economic structural issues, and with increasing globalisation this is ever more so. However, it is not the role (so Ameliorists would argue) to challenge these wider issues; they are too large, too complicated and anyway community development should be about bringing social stability not promoting political unrest. Consequently, community development practice has tended to be focused in small community settings, or small groups within communities, and be concerned with making some aspects of everyday life just a little bit better.

There are some classic texts of how to practise community work in this way, for example, Henderson and Thomas (2001), Henderson (2012) and Twelvetrees (2008). These books defined the nature of community development practice for a generation of UK workers. In Skills in Neighbourhood Work, Henderson and Thomas idealised practice within closely defined geographical areas that were real or imagined functioning neighbourhoods. The goal of the worker was to establish and support small groups within these localities to provide mutual support, deliver a service, represent particular interests, liaise with the local state, or act as agents of the local state.

These groups were usually dependent upon external funding, and often competed amongst themselves for whatever grants were available. This system of a multiplicity of small groups who are all broadly seeking the same end of improving community life, but at the same time in competition with each other for resources, has been defined as pluralism. The result of this is that the potential for community power is dissipated and community groups can at best expect to be in a client relationship with the local state. As we shall see later the ideas of Community Organising sit as a direct rejection of this model.

The Skills in Neighbourhood Work model identifies nine steps for practice. This is a process model where the worker systematically works through the following steps:

1. Entering the neighbourhood
2. Getting to Know the neighbourhood
3. What Next: needs, goals and rules
4. Making contacts and bringing people together
5. Forming and Building organisations
6. Helping to clarify goals and priorities
7. Keeping the organisation going
8. Dealing with friends and enemies
9. Leaving and endings

In one sense this is a very practical approach to undertaking community development work. The book, which is still a widely recommended text, is a great resource for an inexperienced worker asking themselves the basic questions such as: How do I get to know local people? How do I identify local issues? How can I create and sustain a community group? and so on.

There some strong arguments in favour of taking this neighbourhood approach. It does reflect the reality that most community projects have a local focus, and that, as we have seen in Sections 1 and 2, social policies are based on identifying small local areas of need. For some residents the neighbourhood is where they spend most of their time and is the location of their family and friendship networks.

On the other hand, there are serious critiques of this approach. As we have said, the classic neighbourhood model chooses to ignore wider social and economic issues such as globalisation, structural inequality, climate change, and the distribution of power. It often has little to say in the debates about wider social changes driven by feminism, minority communities, personal and sexual identity, cultural change, etc. Being a process model of practice, it tends to ignore what many workers believe to be key theoretical ideas deriving from Gramsci and Freire, and, being too influenced by communitarianism, defaults to an implicit acceptance of the status quo. The neighbourhood approach also ignores the divisive effects of having groups competing with each other, and promotes the idea that all geographical neighbourhoods are, by default, a functioning community (or could be).

Community Planning

Over the past 20 years or so this multiplicity of small neighbourhood groups has been increasingly linked to the local state through the development of social/community planning and the creation of partnerships.

Firmly in the model developed by Robert Park (Park and Burgess, 2019), this model seeks to better manage local communities through an organised area approach. In particular, the community planning approach identifies small areas of need through the analysis of data sets; can bring together a wider range of key service providers (e.g. Health, Police, Local Government, Housing); and gives local community representatives a seat at the table. In many areas, Community Planning is the system and if a community group wants grants and support it has to fit into the priorities and process of the local partnership structure. Like it or not, if you want to succeed as a small and relatively powerless community group you need to be assimilated into the system.

In some ways the partnership model is a welcome development as it shares information and co-ordinates action. Local people's views are heard and may sometimes influence decision-making. There can be questions over who the community representatives are: representatives of the local tenant or residents association: long-standing community activists; friends of the local councillor; members of a particular political party; or simply individuals who have no constituency in the community. There are also questions of how the community representative knows what the various sub-groupings of the community think about any issue, and how they report back and build in accountability. These questions can, of course, be overcome, but they are usually ignored. There is also the wider issue that not all players are equal. The Police and Health Service, for example, have huge power and control over resources. They are not going to accede to anything that they fundamentally disagree with. Consequently, how much real power in decision-making do the community representatives really have? The answer, of course, given the nature of small community groups, is not very much.

Community Work and Social Systems

Of course, the ameliorist/pluralist/neighbourhood work approach is just one of many ways of conceptualising and developing practice. Let us consider other forms of practice, taking a snapshot of different global examples. One way to do this is to construct a frame of analysis within which we can analyse the different models. Purcell (2016) views community development practice (in its widest sense) in terms of authoritarian/libertarian–open system/closed system dimensions. He defines these terms as:

- Authoritarian = regulation, defined limits of action, government control
- Libertarian = individual rights, autonomy of action, self-determination
- Closed System = stable, controlled, predictable, reproducible
- Open System = complex and diverse, allows new and creative approaches

In Figure 3.1 below a selection of different types of community development are mapped against the authoritarian/libertarian–open system/ – closed system dimensions. The chart is intended to be illustrative and is not based on any detailed mapping of collected data analysed through complex metrics. It is simply diagrammatic and used to illustrate the diversity of approaches. For convenience, the traditional UK model of community development, based on small and localised groups that we have been discussing, is placed in the

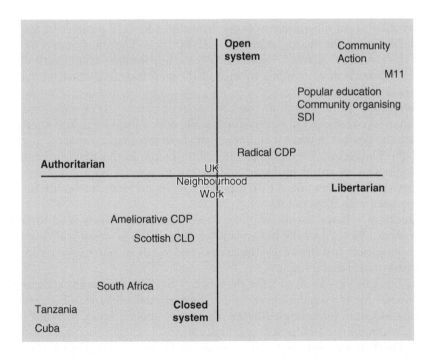

Figure 3.1

centre of the diagram. This is not to suggest that UK practice is the centre of the community development world. Readers in other countries can populate the diagram as appropriate with their own examples.

Purcell notes that generalising about models of practice is always open to debate as it can be criticised as oversimplifying. However, we need to start the discussion somewhere. Based on his research, Purcell offers the following explanation of why different models were placed where they are.

- **Cuba** – Community development within Cuba is mostly the top-down delivery of activities to communities. It operates under the auspices of the state in quite prescribed forms.
- **Tanzania** – This example relates to rural activities that are formulated by the government as part of an overall development strategy. At the local level, community development activity is focused on mobilising local village communities to meet specific targets set by government, for example, assisting in the construction of local school buildings. Communities are charged with deciding how to complete the task and have little effective input into what these tasks might be.
- **South Africa** – There is an extensive community development programme in the townships. Much of this work involves the community development worker acting as an intermediary between local people and government policy and funding opportunities.
- **Scottish CLD** – Community Learning and Development in Scotland is well developed in policy terms, and much activity is routed into partnership arrangements with major resource-holders. Often this is time-limited engagement with specific small-scale objectives. There is some freedom to operate within the overall policy framework.
- **Ameliorative CDP** – An illustrative example from the UK CDP projects of the late 1960s and becoming the major model of UK practice. The ameliorative strand recognised the structural nature of social problems but thought community development was incapable of responding to such challenges. Instead it concentrated on largely self-help initiatives.
- **UK Neighbourhood Work** – a traditional UK model of practice. It operates within a pluralistic analysis of society. Often very small scale, with a local focus and limited in scope, but can be flexible in what is attempted and how it is done.
- **Radical CDP** – The alternative model to the CDP projects. In this case it recognised the structural nature of social problems and looked to operate on a large scale for social change. It failed to achieve this, especially in its ambition to build effective campaigning links with trade unions.
- **Popular Education** – Based on the work of Paulo Freire and widely used in South America, southern Africa and the Indian sub-continent. Can be small scale but very flexible in application and driven by the desires and needs of participants with the goal of transformative social change.
- **Community Organising** – Evolved from the work of Saul Alinsky and is represented by the Industrial Areas Foundation and their international affiliates. This category also includes ACORN International as an alternative model. Seeks to build large autonomous community-based power organisations.
- **Slum/Shack Dwellers International** – An international network based in mega slums. Seeks to build mainly women-focused autonomous powerful organisations dedicated to making the slum more livable and integrated into the wider society.

- **Direct Action/M11** – This example refers to the long British tradition of taking direct action for emotive causes, for example, on the environment. The M11 motorway protest in London was a noticeable example of large-scale opposition to urban road building.

Purcell argues that this diagram illustrates the diverse nature of practice that is possible from top-down and closed systems to open and bottom-up alternatives. He suggests that, within the UK, the models of practice vary from quite limited in scope where community work is located tightly into a local authority programme and policy framework, to potentially the more radical where there is some independence from the local state.

Internationally, the countries where open/libertarian societies are prevalent (for example the USA, Western Europe) are more likely to have community work organisations developing a critical analysis of society and challenging accepted norms and structures. Many of these countries will be operating a neo-liberal economy. We know from Gramsci that despite the force of hegemony that a modern capitalist state generates, it is still possible to engage in reformist and maybe revolutionary activity and build a counter-hegemonic opposition. Given the less than revolutionary aims of community work, Purcell argues that a neo-liberal environment can be conducive to open, creative and power-challenging models of practice.

Conversely, the closed/authoritarian approaches (in both capitalist and socialist countries) are most likely to constrain community work practice to being conformist and uncritical of the status quo, allowing little challenge to authority. In these contexts, the main community work focus is to implement government programmes and policies. Purcell notes that some may argue that socialist countries through their opposition to neo-liberalism are inherently radical, and therefore community work in these settings must therefore also be radical. This, of course, depends upon what your definition of 'radical' might be, and the actual policies of the government. Despite the rhetoric of most governments, especially authoritarian ones, the outcomes can turn out to be weak on actually promoting the key objectives of community development such as social justice, challenging oppression and promoting empowered citizens with independent powerful civic organisations.

Purcell concludes that the more power the state has over civic life the more closed the model of practice will be. In contrast, the less power the state deploys the greater the potential for open models of practice. In the next discussions we look at more radical forms of work including Direct Action, Community Organising, Paulo Freire and Slum Dwellers International.

Key Learning Points

In this discussion we have explored:

- The current dominant model of community development practice in the UK, and found
- That the dominant model is based on producing ameliorative outcomes for small-scale community groups operating within a local neighbourhood focus
- That community development has been largely incorporated into a local state-led social planning framework, based on a local partnership model
- That a snapshot of global practice models is built around an authoritarian/libertarian – closed system/open system analytical framework
- That the more creative and people-driven models of community development are most likely to be found in open system–liberal societies
- That more closed system–authoritarian societies are more likely to use community development-like activities as means of delivering top-down government policies

Learning Tasks

Select a neighbourhood where you live or work and map the community groups operating in the area:

- What do they do?
- How many members do they have?
- What do they achieve?
- What do they wish to achieve?
- What is their relationship to the local state?
- Are they dependent on third party funding?
- What do you conclude from this?

Key Reading

For an insight into the practice of the dominant UK ameliorative model read:
Henderson, P. (2012) *Skills in Neighbourhood Work*. London: Routledge.

References

Henderson, P. (2012) *Skills in Neighbourhood Work*. London: Routledge.
Henderson, P. and Thomas, D. (2001) *Skills in Neighbourhood Work*. London: Routledge.
Park, R. and Burgess, E. (2019) *The City*. Chicago, IL: University of Chicago Press.
Purcell, R. (2016) 'Thoughts on Neoliberalism and Radical Practice', *RCW Journal*, 2(1).
Twelvetrees, A. (2008) *Community Work*. Basingstoke: Palgrave Macmillan.

3.2   Direct Action

Introduction

This book concentrates on the role and activity of community development in its various forms. Running alongside community development activity is, of course, a wide range of other forms of social and civic engagement, and political action. The range of activity is extensive from volunteering, care activities, befriending to, at the other end of the spectrum, political activity, which sometimes moves into direct action approaches. Community development workers need to understand why people resort to direct action, the values and principles of such activity, how it is organised and what it does and does not achieve. There will be times when community development workers and/or the people they are working with feel they have to resort to direct action methods. If you are promoting consensual ameliorative work then this is less likely. If you are a community organiser then direct action will be part of your toolkit.

Direct action is an integral feature of contemporary societies. For example, the American Civil Rights Movement gained much of its success through engaging in direct action. Dr Martin Luther King Jr pointed out that he came to direct action through relating the work of Ghandi to Christian doctrine and the morality of confronting evil. He said that he was fascinated by the idea of 'refusing to co-operate with an evil system' that promoted segregation and racial discrimination (King, 2011).

Dr King's idea of non-violent direct action was based upon six key principles, which he outlined in his book Stride Towards Freedom. These principles can be summarised as:

> **First,** one can resist evil without resorting to violence
> **Second,** non-violence seeks to win the 'friendship and understanding' of the opponent, not to humiliate him
> **Third,** evil itself, not the people committing evil acts, should be opposed
> **Fourth,** those committed to non-violence must be willing to suffer without retaliation, as suffering itself can be redemptive
> **Fifth,** non-violent resistance avoids 'external physical violence' and 'internal violence of spirit' as well: 'The nonviolent resister not only refuses to shoot his opponent but he also refuses to hate him'. The resister should be motivated by love in the sense of the Greek word agape, which means 'understanding', or 'redeeming good will for all men'
> The **sixth** principle is that the non-violent resister must have a 'deep faith in the future', stemming from the conviction that 'the universe is on the side of justice'
> (King, 1958, 2011)

One of the current motivating forces for direct action is that mainstream political parties appear to have lost the ability (if they ever had it) to aggregate issues into coherent ideological packages linked to the aspirations of the diverse social groups that comprise contemporary society. The way governments operate tends to ignore minority views. Sometimes these minority groups can be extensive, and on occasion can become a majority. For example, the 2016 Brexit vote in the UK was driven significantly by white working-class voters in areas subject to post-industrial decline. People felt the mainstream parties had forgotten them. The vote to leave the European Union was a protest about remote bureaucracies, and the perceived threat to culture and way of life from immigration. This is not direct action in itself but a sign that it might not be far away if large numbers of people continue to feel ignored. The 2016 presidential election in the USA could be analysed in a similar fashion.

Alongside the above points, there is the continuing trend for single-issue campaigns that are self-defined as the most important thing, compared to which all other social and economic issues become insignificant. Often, such campaigns are climate change/environmentally focused. If you believe that you are saving the planet then most forms of protest become acceptable. Other examples of long-running, single-issue campaigns are prolife protests, anti-hunting and animal welfare. Such actions include blocking motorways and airport runways, to smaller 'actions' that are designed to attract the maximum media attention. Due to the strength of feeling there can be an 'all or nothing approach' where compromise is seen as selling out. Sometimes the issues are closely focused (e.g. stop fracking in this area) where a success can be identified, or vague and therefore impossible to resolve. The Occupy Movement would be an example of this. In 2011, protesters in London set up camp demanding a better world. The camp issued a statement (*The Guardian*, 17 October 2011) explaining their action and demands:

1   The current system is unsustainable. It is undemocratic and unjust. We need alternatives; this is where we work towards them.
2   We are of all ethnicities, backgrounds, genders, generations, sexualities dis/abilities and faiths. We stand together with occupations all over the world.
3   We refuse to pay for the banks' crisis.
4   We do not accept the cuts as either necessary or inevitable. We demand an end to global tax injustice and our democracy representing corporations instead of the people.
5   We want regulators to be genuinely independent of the industries they regulate.
6   We support the strike on 30 November and the student action on 9 November, and actions to defend our health services, welfare, education and employment, and to stop wars and arms dealing.
7   We want structural change towards authentic global equality. The world's resources must go towards caring for people and the planet, not the military, corporate profits or the rich.
8   The present economic system pollutes land, sea and air, is causing massive loss of natural species and environments, and is accelerating humanity towards irreversible climate change. We call for a positive, sustainable economic system that benefits present and future generations.
9   We stand in solidarity with the global oppressed and we call for an end to the actions of our government and others in causing this oppression.

Over the next few months the protest began to fall away as participants became disillusioned with the protest. This was inevitable, as organisations are kept alive through building on success. In this case the demands were either vague (how do you know when you have succeeded) or impossible to achieve as they are asking for global change.

In February 2012, the camp was evicted. It is estimated (*Bloomberg L.P.*, 23 April 2012) that the camp cost London authorities over £1million from monitoring, policing and legal fees. Although a wide range of issues was raised across the media there was no discernible win from the occupation. It does illustrate that feeling strongly about an issue, and getting exposure in the media is not enough. To make real gains you need to have a tight organisation and specific realisable demands (see the discussion on community organising below).

There is also the danger that direct action can move public opinion against your cause. The 2016 blocking of the runway at London City Airport by nine protestors is a case in point. White climate change protestors, who had decided to support the London Black Lives Matter campaign, took the action. The protestors argued that climate change was racist in that it disproportionately affected Black people specifically in London and generally in Africa. It was suggested that the airport was mainly used by business people engaged in capitalist activity. As capitalism is destroying the planet, the closing of the airport was therefore justified. The majority of public opinion appeared to be in disagreement, and it is likely the action damaged the prospects of the Black Lives Matter campaign in London.

Direct action has a wide range of possible tactics. Gene Sharp (1980) has identified 198 different tactics for non-violent action (The Albert Einstein Institution has a summary of all 198 tactics online at aeinstein.org/nonviolentaction/198-methods-of-nonviolent-action). These tactics can be organised into six categories of possible action:

1. **Persuasion:** speeches, letters, leaflets, lobbying, exhibitions, vigils, processions, public gatherings, walk-outs, etc.
2. **Non Co-operation:** ostracism, boycott, strikes, stay-at-home, etc.
3. **Economic Boycott:** consumer boycott, rent strikes, lockouts, embargos, blacklisting traders, etc.
4. **Strikes:** symbolic strikes, group actions, industrial strikes, slowdowns, work-to-rule, sit-ins, selective strikes of key personnel, etc.
5. **Political Non Co-operation:** withholding support, refusal to comply, sit-downs, breaking 'unjust' laws, legal delaying tactics, etc.
6. **Non-Violent Interventions:** fasting, harassment, sit-ins, pray-ins, land seizures, work-ons, blockades, etc.

These tactics have all proved effective at various times. However, as a main strategy of direct action is to involve the media there is a constant pressure to innovate and undertake new forms of action. Repeating the same tactic can lead to boredom amongst participants and disinterest by media organisations.

Running through direct action is a belief and a willingness to undertake civil disobedience. Such activity was famously defended by John Rawls (1971) who defined civil disobedience as a public, non-violent and conscious breach of the law undertaken with the aim of bringing about a change in laws or government policy. Do community development workers simply watch as their community members take such actions? Or do they personally join in, or absent themselves on moral/legal/pragmatic grounds? What criteria should workers use to help make such decisions? Referring back to the values and principles of community development is helpful here. However, such decisions are usually made as a reflection of the personality and ideological views of the individual practitioner.

As the history of community organising shows us, there are times when workers need to decide their position on such actions. If you are engaged in community organising then direct action will happen sooner or later. It is this form of activity that we explore in the next discussion.

Key Learning Points

- Direct action is a continuing feature of civic and political life
- A belief in the legitimacy of direct action can be based upon moral or religious doctrine
- Direct action usually operates outside of community development activity, but there will be times when community development workers are potentially draw into direct action
- Direct action is usually based on single issues that participants believe to be of overriding importance
- These issues can be local and focused, but can also range to the global and diverse
- The tactics of direct action are often designed to attract high levels of media attention
- Direct action can mobilise public opinion either for or against your issue
- Direct action is often viewed as a moral act

Learning Tasks

Identify a local example of direct action and consider:

- What was the objective of the activists?
- Why did they choose to use direct action tactics?
- Did these tactics work?
- Could the result have been achieved (or exceeded) in other ways?
- Do you consider these actions to be legitimate? If so, why?

Key Reading

A Toolbox for Revolution. Available at: beautifultrouble.org/tactic/direct-action/.

References

Bloomberg L.P., 23 April 2012.
King, M.L., Jr (1958) *Stride Toward Freedom: The Montgomery Story*. New York: Harper & Row.
King, M.L. (2011) *Stride Towards Freedom: The Montgomery Story*. London: Souvenir Press.
Rawls, J. (1971) *A Theory of Justice*. Cambridge, MA: Harvard University Press.
Sharp, G. (1980) *The Politics of Non Violent Action: Method of Von Violent Action Part 2*. New York: Sargent.
The Guardian (2011) 'Occupy London Stock Exchange – the Initial Statement'. Available at: www.theguardian.com/commentisfree/2011/oct/17/occupy-london-stock-exchange-occupylsx.

3.3 Community Organising

Introduction

Davis Merritt Jr sums up the community organising perspective: '*the only way for our community to be a better place to live is for the people of the community to understand and accept their personal responsibility for what happens*'. For practitioners in the UK the above quote can be contentious. The mythologised view of the welfare state and benevolent local government, has led to the idea that social problems should (and will) be solved by external organisations. As we have discussed above, our learned experience of community development in the UK is that communities are relatively powerless to tackle major issues. Often the failure to solve local housing problems, environmental issues and unemployment lead to local anger, but seldom to the idea that if it is our problem then we have to take the lead in fixing it. The benefit from taking responsibility for our own problems is that the issue is more likely to be fixed, and in a way that works best for us. Community organising is about this – to fix our problems we need to come together, organise, get the job done ourselves and in our own way. In doing so there will be significant gains in terms of personal, collective and organisational empowerment.

Saul Alinsky, the grandfather of community organising, often quoted the slavery abolitionist Fredrick Douglass who said, 'power concedes nothing without a demand, it never has and it never will'. Alinsky's point is that poor communities remain poor because they are discriminated against in a broad range of economic and social ways: jobs, housing, local services, political representation, etc. Just asking the powerful to do the right thing is not going to change the situation. The only way the poor and the oppressed are going to have a better life is through building their own collective organisations that will accumulate power so that marginalised people can claim their fair share of society. As Alinsky said: 'Change comes from power, and power comes from organisation. In order to Act, people must get together.' For Alinsky this was about making democracy work for everyone. These ideas are set out in his classic book *Rules for Radicals* (Alinsky, 1971).

Community organising in the way we use the term today starts with Alinsky in the Back of the Yards area of Chicago in the 1930s. The 'Yards' was the meat-packing district and the processing plants were the main employers in the area. The local community was poor with desperate housing and social conditions, with many immigrants from Eastern Europe. In association with local leaders, Alinsky built a coalition of local groups, trade unions and the Catholic Church to form the Back of the Yards Neighbourhood Council (BYNC). Over the years the BYNC has provided a range of services for local people, renovated local housing, supported trade unions action for better wages and working conditions, and made demands on the Chicago City Administration to improve its support to the area.

Since the creation of BYNC, community organising has evolved. There are now diverse models of how to practise community organising both within the USA and across the world (for a fuller discussion see Beck and Purcell, 2013). A main form of community organising practice, and the direct descendant of the Alinsky model is the Industrial Areas Foundation (industrialareasfoundation.org). Currently, the IAF organises in 23 states and 24 cities in the USA, and has affiliate organisations in the UK, Canada, Germany and Australia. The IAF has an organisational model, the key features of which focus on:

- Campaigning on winnable issues
- Using the winning of issues to further build the membership and power of the organisation
- Identifying and building local leadership
- Developing a network of communication throughout the community based upon personal contacts
- Promoting participation through people making decisions and taking responsibility for themselves and their community
- Using research to understand issues, planning effective actions to promote the issues, and evaluating and learning from campaigns

Central to the deployment of the IAF model are Community Organisers. These key workers build the organisation locally by linking with existing local leaders and organisations as well as creating new forms of organisation. Alinsky saw the community organisers as requiring a special set of characteristics that include curiosity about the world; an irreverence for existing structures and power systems; imagination for new ways of thinking; a blurred vision of what a better community might be like; a strong ego along with bucket loads of self-confidence; a sense of humour to get through the hard times; and what he called the need to be a 'well integrated political schizoid'. By this Alinsky meant that although campaigns are built on a 100 per cent vs. 0 per cent approach, in reality most issues cut 52 per cent vs. 48 per cent and the goal is to be able to move into constructive negotiation and compromise when the time is right. As Alinsky commented, 'compromise always puts you ahead'.

Underpinning campaigning is a set of rules defined by Alinsky (1971):

1. Power is not only what you have but what the enemy thinks you have
2. Never go outside the experience of your people
3. Whenever possible, go outside of the experience of the enemy
4. Make the enemy live up to their own book of rules
5. Ridicule is man's most potent weapon
6. A good tactic is one that your people enjoy
7. A tactic that drags on too long becomes a drag
8. Keep the pressure on with different tactics and actions, and utilise all events of the period for your purpose
9. The threat is usually more terrifying than the thing itself
10. The major premise for tactics is the development of operations that will maintain a constant pressure upon the opposition
11. If you push a negative hard and deep enough, it will break through into its counterside
12. The price of a successful attack is a constructive alternative
13. Pick the target, freeze it, personalise it, and polarise it

One of the criticisms of community organising is that it is culturally specific to the USA and therefore the model does not translate well to other cultures. For example, some commentators (for example, Henderson and Salmon, 1995) suggest the focus on conflict does not work in the UK where, as we discussed above, the tradition is for very small-scale self-help organisations operating formally or informally under the hegemony of the local state.

However, this is not the case as is evidenced by the success of the IAF affiliate Citizens UK (citizensuk.org), with alliances comprised of local organisations, faith groups, schools, universities, and trade unions operating across the country, for example, in London, Birmingham, Nottingham and Leeds.

In Wales, the Cardiff Citizens and Vale of Glamorgan Citizens was formed in October 2014, via a Founding Assembly of 700 people representing more than a hundred organisations. Now known as Citizens Cymru Wales their current goals include:

- Tackling poverty and inequality through the promotion of the living wage
- Making local services accountable and responsive to the needs and views of local people
- Building a welcoming community that is supportive of people and open to immigrants and refugees
- Overcoming powerlessness through developing local leader, supporting young people to become socially active and promoting voter registration schemes

In London, community organisations negotiated an agreement with the 2012 Olympic organisation to respond to local demands to make the games community friendly. This resulted in an agreement for six People Promises:

1. Affordable homes to be provided for local people through a Community Land Trust and mutual home ownership
2. Funding to be set aside to improve local schools and health services
3. The University of East London to be the main Higher Education beneficiary of the sports legacy
4. £2 million to be committed for a Construction Academy to train local people for the coming construction jobs
5. That at least 30 per cent of the jobs created by the Olympics would be set aside for local people
6. That the Lower Lea Valley Area would be designated a 'Living Wage Zone'

There are, of course, other models of community organising as well as the IAF. The most important of these alternatives is ACORN (Association of Community Organisations for Reform Now) established by Wade Rathke in 1970. At its height ACORN had in excess of 500,000 members operating in more than 1,200 local chapters in over 100 US cities. The main areas of work included voter registration, health care, affordable housing and local social issues. In 2010, ACORN closed its US operation after a fabricated sting operation by conservative activists led to the loss of core funding. ACORN International (acorninternational.org) continues to work in 16 countries including Argentina, Canada, India, Italy, Kenya, Mexico, Peru, and the UK, with a particular focus on mega slums (for example, Dharavi in Mumbai and Korogocho in Nairobi).

John Atlas (2010) has written a definitive history of ACORN, within which he has described the organising model. When moving into a new area, Atlas suggests the following actions:

1. The community organiser analyses the local demographics, politics, issues, and the current local leadership.
2. The organiser drives around the local area (the windshield tour) to get a feel of the area.

3. The organiser meets with local leaders and starts to build working relationships.
4. ACORN is primarily interested in building a new local organisation of individuals coming together. (In contrast, IAF is more concerned with creating a broad organisation through creating a coalition of existing organisations.)
5. The organiser and local leaders identify potential allies and enemies.
6. The organiser and local people undertake a programme of 'door-knocking' to identify local issues that are important to residents and to sign up members. The objective would be to knock on every door over an eight-week period and sign up 10 per cent of households. Membership dues are often a notional payment each month. The money would pay for the local organisation, but also creates a sense of ownership and involvement amongst the members.
7. Within two months local people should be standing up at local meetings and be prepared to take action on issues they have defined.
8. In areas that had multiple chapters an executive committee should be established to co-ordinate campaigns.
9. The objective is to empower local people to take action on issues fundamental to their lives, not solve their problems for them.
10. Once a local organisation is established, local people and the new emerging leadership would make the decisions and run the organisation.

The key feature of this approach is the speed in which the organisation develops. All community organising is based on the principle of identifying a local issue that can be successfully addressed quickly and easily. This positive result builds confidence and belief in local people that change is possible, and that the new organisation is a route to this change. Success therefore builds the organisation, which in turn increases the membership, enabling bigger and more complex issues to be tackled, so further increasing membership.

Also central to community organising is the development of local leadership. Alinsky usefully described a leader as somebody 'who has a following'. This might be someone who holds an official position such as the chair of a local organisation; a local person you go to for help with welfare benefits; or somebody with an extensive network of friends and contacts. These local leaders and those with leadership potential are trained, supported and nurtured to take on ever more demanding roles and are the future of the organisation. In North America, this emphasis on leadership is nothing new. In the UK, leadership training is comparatively rare. As we will see in Section 4, the UK places emphasis on capacity building, but this is mainly about training people to function as a committee member within a local partnership setting. Training people to become independent leaders of a powerful autonomous organisation is not often on the agenda.

As we have said at the start of this chapter, community organising has taken many forms since the early days of Alinsky. One of the most interesting and effective organisations today is Slum Dwellers International. Much of their operating model can be linked to the principles and practices of community organising. However, there is a distinctiveness about their organisation, and this is explored in the next discussion.

Key Learning Points

- Community organising is about individuals and local communities taking responsibility for, and solving, local issues
- Success is achieved through building powerful autonomous local organisations
- Success leads to more members, a stronger organisation, which in turn leads to more success and more members ...

- Community organisations need to be prepared to fight vigorous campaigns to achieve their goals. However, most campaigns lead to negotiation and compromise
- One of the main community organising models is the IAF, which builds coalitions of organisations to maximise local power
- Another model is ACORN where individuals are recruited to build a new local organisation
- Identifying local leaders and building leadership capacity is central to successful community organising

Learning Tasks

Consider and discuss the following questions:

- How far are local problems the responsibility of local people to solve?
- Could you see yourself as a community organiser?
- What do you think of the 13 Rules?
- If there was a local community organisation where you live would you want to join it?

Key Reading

Beck, D. and Purcell, R. (2013) *International Community Organising: Taking Power, Making Change*. Bristol: The Policy Press.

References

Alinsky, S. (1971) *Rules for Radicals*. New York: Random House.

Atlas, J. (2010) *Seeds of Change: The Story of ACORN*. Nashville, TN: Vanderbilt University Press.

Beck, D. and Purcell, R. (2013) *International Community Organising: Taking Power, Making Change*. Bristol: The Policy Press.

Henderson, P. and Salmon, H. (1995) *Community Organising: The UK Context*. London: Community Development Foundation/Churches Community Work Alliance.

3.4   Slum Dwellers International

Introduction

Slum Dwellers International (knowyourcity.info) was officially launched in 1996. SDI, as it is generally known, is an international network representing the urban poor. The network brought together large-scale federations in six Asian countries, four African countries and one in Latin America.

Currently the SDI Network operates in Asia: Cambodia, India, Nepal, Philippines, Sri Lanka, Thailand; Africa: Ghana, Kenya, Malawi, Namibia, South Africa, Tanzania, Zambia, Zimbabwe, Uganda; and Latin America: Brazil. There are also emerging initiatives in Indonesia, East Timor, Mongolia; Africa: Lesotho, Swaziland, Madagascar, Angola; and Latin America. Overall, SDI works in 478 cities across 32 countries and represents millions of people. SDI is active with the United Nations and the World Urban Forum.

In some ways, SDI reflects the basic principles of community organising. For example, emphasis is placed on recruiting broadly across the community; large-scale direct action will be undertaken when required with the ultimate goal of forcing state and city authorities to the negotiating table. However, SDI has its own set of guiding principles and modes of action, which makes it a unique and powerful organisation. The lessons learned from successfully organising large-scale and very poor urban communities in the developing world can be transferred to the developed world.

SDI describes its guiding principles thus:

1. A '*voice* of the urban poor' and not a voice *for* the urban poor.
2. Daily *saving* by members is a mobilising and developmental tool, creating accountability, self-reliance and financial and human resource management skills.
3. The participation of *women* and of the most marginalised members of slum communities is central.
4. Community *learning* and solidarity through horizontal exchange programmes.
5. *Incremental* human settlement development.
6. Grass-roots-driven gathering of *information* through surveys, enumerations and settlement profiles.
7. Solution-finding through *negotiations* and dialogue.
8. Community-based *shelter* training, including house modelling, community action planning and community design.
9. Small core groups of *professionals* to provide technical and financial support to federations.
10. Consistent *engagement* with local authorities through urban poor funds, enumeration data and citywide development strategies.
11. International *advocacy* in order to strengthen local city level initiatives.

These principles are worth exploring in some detail, but first let us set the context within which this model has been developed and tested. Dharavi is a mega slum in Mumbai, India. It is a place both the authors know well, and is a good example of SDI practice.

Dharavi has a population that is estimated to be anywhere between 600,000 and 1 million people. Local government services are almost non-existent. As there is only a minimal welfare system, everyone needs some kind of income to buy food, medicine, etc. There is, of course, a local economy running to meet the basic needs of the population. In terms of asset-based development, the few financial and environmental assets are balanced by the large pool of people and human capital.

In the UK, for example, many community groups are small and operate within a generally well-serviced housing estate, city neighbourhood or rural community. To an outsider, Dharavi can seem chaotic, and UK community workers arriving in Dharavi are usually overwhelmed by the scale of the place. They are, however, impressed by the energy of the local people and the commitment and achievements of local community projects. If you can successfully organise in Dharavi you can certainly organise in the developed cities of the West.

The first SDI principle is being the *Voice* of the poor. That is, local people and communities can and will speak for themselves. They do not need outsiders or 'experts' to speak on their behalf. This point is also about owning your own problems and seeing your community as the major part of the solution. This is a very empowering position to adopt, and sits in contrast to the alternative of being a victim and/or dependent upon outside agencies or government to solve your problems for you. In the USA, for example, such a position is not unusual. However, in countries with more interventionist governments, the idea that the state/local state will/should solve these problems for you is an obstacle to effective organising at a local level.

Second, the SDI model engages directly with the poverty of the people and actively encourages *women to save money*. There are many benefits to this – there is money in the family to deal with emergencies, but equally important is the direct experience of making decisions and starting to take control of your life. It also recognises that people will not become active in their community if they are weighed down by debt or worrying about how to feed the children. In the UK and Ireland there are similar experiences through, for example, locally based Credit Unions that help people to save and provide cheap loans. Promoting local savings schemes could be more widely adopted in the West.

The third principle is that *community organisations need to be built around women*. This approach directly challenges embedded structural discrimination against women. It also recognises that it is women who care for the children and who have to deal with many of the day-to-day issues that community organisations can tackle. It is claimed that in many communities men are often self-focused and disengaged from these struggles. Of course, men are involved in SDI organisation, but the lead role of women is prioritised.

Importance is also given to *community learning*. Knowledge and skill development, learning through action and reflection is embedded into practice. Learning from each other and sharing experiences across groups, communities and in the case of SDI, across the network, underpins developing and extending effective practice. Community organising has a similar practice of learning for action and structured reflections. Unfortunately, not all examples of practice take learning as important. In the UK there can be a thread of amateurism running through community work practice with small neighbourhood groups.

SDI recognises that the majority of their member communities have a population of tens of thousands, if not hundreds of thousands. It is simply not possible to systematically rebuild these communities. The only practical way forward is through *incremental development*. For example, by improving local sanitation, extending electricity and potable water supply, improving health case, extending education (and making education equally accessible to girls). By moving forward incrementally as part of a long-term community-owned development plan, change becomes possible.

Another underpinning practice is the *collection of information* and statistics about the local community. There are several reasons for this approach. When local people themselves investigate local issues, they become equipped and confident to make the argument for change. Organisations are then in a position to challenge state/city governments with facts from the ground. Local research uncovers wider social and economic problems that otherwise stay hidden. Myths about the community (such as the scale of immigration) can be effectively challenged. We could ask ourselves how well we, and our local community groups, really know the community. Simply living in a community is not the same as truly knowing that community.

Like community organising, SDI recognises that change comes through *negotiations and dialogue* with powerholders. It may take campaigning and direct action to get the other side to negotiate, but ultimately compromises can be found and, as Saul Alinsky said, 'compromise always puts you ahead'.

SDI represents slum dwellers so *shelter and housing* are key issues. Like all community action local people need to be in the lead in looking for solutions.

It is clear that for SDI local people take the lead and make the decisions in local organisations. However, technical expertise is required to support community initiatives. For larger organisations this expertise can be directly employed by the organisation. In other cases, it is a partnership relationship with NGOs. However, decision-making and the power relationship need to be clear.

Social change is a long-haul activity. Consequently, SDI is clear on the importance of constant engagement with state/city governments. As we said above, compromise puts you ahead, but that is just a staging post in a long campaign for continued improvements to make the slums more habitable.

Finally, SDI recognises the multiple levels within which they operate. Many improvements are the result of local action and negotiation. In other cases, ***external pressure and advocacy*** from the wider SDI network, NGOs and other actors may need to be deployed. International campaigning and work through the United Nations, high-level policy papers and publicity campaigns can all have a local benefit. There is a history, in the UK at least, of local groups fighting the city government without the help of the wider organisation, and often without the support of other local community groups. Working out who else can support you and building a coalition of mutual support should be basic to everyone's practice.

These SDI guiding principles need to be seen as the components of an integrated model. The model can be configured as shown in Figure 3.2 below.

Key Learning Points

The SDI model is an integrated approach that has been developed in poor communities across the world. It offers us many lessons for effective practice. This is especially important in terms of:

- The key role of women in development
- The importance of stabilising family finances

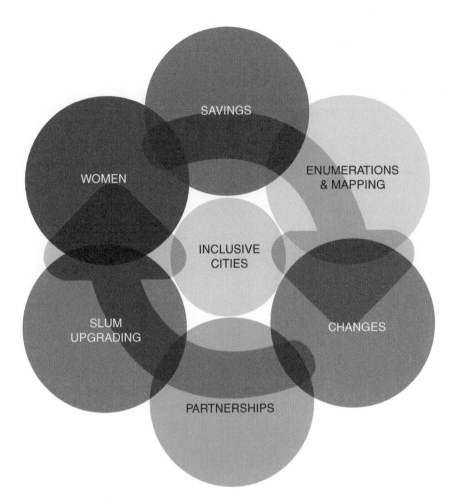

Figure 3.2 SDI Model

- The role of community research
- Recognising the importance of shared learning, skill and knowledge development
- Building a power base to make negotiations work
- The role of experts and external agencies as support for community organisations

Learning Tasks

For your country, and your local community in particular, think about the relevance of:

- Development work being led by women
- Families prioritising savings
- Development work being underpinned by community research and knowledge/skill development
- External agencies working for local communities, rather than leading local communities
- Can you envisage which apply to the whole SDI model in your community?

Key Reading

Look at the following websites and explore the material they contain. There are links to various SDI campaigns, publications and resource material:

http://sdinet.org/
http://knowyourcity.info/

3.5 Freire and Popular Education

Introduction

Following on from the Chapter 2.3 in which we explored the theoretical underpinnings of the Freirean approach, this chapter looks at how this approach is operationalised in practice. Beginning with considering some basic ideas around participation, we will then examine the building blocks of transformational education. These are:

- identifying the generative theme
- developing codes
- engaging in dialogue
- taking and reflecting on action

Freirean approaches to education, which are variously described as problem posing, transformational education, democratic learning and animation, fall under the broader term of 'participative methods'. The main rationale for participative methods is the belief that people themselves are best placed to know what their problems are and, with the right support, can develop the most appropriate solutions to those problems. It is, therefore, incumbent on workers to develop approaches that tap into that local knowledge and capacity for change. To do anything else is to impose external culture and values and, even for the best of reasons, further disempower the communities with which we work. As Paulo Freire puts it:

> One cannot expect positive results from an educational or political action program which fails to respect the particular view of the world held by the people. Such a program constitutes cultural invasion, good intentions notwithstanding.
>
> (Freire, 1972: 93)

As previously discussed, there is no such thing as a neutral position in formal or informal education, and therefore it has to be recognised that youth and community work is all about taking sides. Social Justice is a core value-underpinning practice, with the implication that we work with, and on behalf of, those experiencing injustice. As the great American community organiser Saul Alinsky commented, this means taking the side of the have-nots, those who are left out and overlooked (Alinsky, 1971). Workers, therefore, have to find ways to maximise the genuine participation of people in their practice.

Social policy in the UK has developed approaches to community planning and regeneration which have purportedly had community participation at their heart. In the 1980s the advent of enterprises like City Challenge and the Single Regeneration Budget were major policy initiatives that set the tone for all of the subsequent community planning initiatives. However, some evaluations suggest that the level of community participation was largely tokenistic (DETR, 1998; Rhodes et al., 2005). Rhodes et al. (2007) indicate that community representation tended to be tokenistic; few projects were led by community groups and those that were had lesser funding and a shorter duration than projects led by the local authority or private sector. This is no new phenomenon, as the classic analysis by Shelly Arnstein (1969) reveals: not everything which claims to be participative gives local people a genuine say in the issues that affect their lives. Often what is described by professionals as participation is simply information-giving, or a consultation exercise where the community is presented with a limited range of pre-determined options. Even where partnership structures are established there are usually significant power and resource imbalances between the community and agencies. Genuine examples of participation where the community has equality are ones that attend to those imbalances.

As a result, youth and community workers often find themselves in the situation where they are tasked with encouraging local people to participate in issues, services and events that have been decided and designed outside the community. These range from trying to get people to use the new one-stop shop, getting participants for pre-decided training courses, to persuading people to engage in local authority-led community planning processes. There are several implications which flow from this model of practice. First, the fundamental power relationships within the community have not changed; external bodies are still making decisions on behalf of local people, albeit with some marginal choices being left to them. Second, the worker has to supply large amounts of time and emotional energy trying to persuade people that these are issues and services that are important to them. This can lead to workers burning out and communities feeling as if they are being battered by regular waves on new policies and initiatives and becoming even more 'apathetic' and 'hard to reach'. This calls into question the sustainability of this model, both for workers and communities. Finally, if all of this energy and effort is going into working with issues that are not necessarily the community's main concern, it means that our practice masks these real concerns and further silences and disempowers the community. If we truly aspire to empowering practice, alternative ways of working must be found. In the rest of this chapter we suggest that the Freirean approach offers a way of working with communities in genuinely participative ways. Let us then consider the role of the worker in this alternative model of practice.

As Peter McLaren puts it: 'We require of revolutionary movement of educators informed by a principled ethics of compassion and social justice, a social ethos based on solidarity and social interdependence' (2000: 451). Unlike the work of Batten (1967), whose response to the challenge of enabling people to take control of their own lives is that of non-direction, theorists such as Freire, McLaren and Ledwith suggest an approach to practice which is underpinned by particular concerns and commitments. Ledwith (2011) identifies five vital areas: a commitment to collective action for social and environmental justice; a process of empowerment through critical consciousness and participation; an analysis of power and discrimination; an understanding of the dominant ideas; and the wider political context and collective action based on this analysis which deals with root causes and not just symptoms. It is clear from this that the worker is not a blank canvas who, with no previous experience or values, seeks only to work with the community's agenda. Rather they are intentionally agents of change seeking to encourage sustainable social change through critical reflection and collective action.

This focus on collective action is particularly important at the early part of the twenty-first century because of the dominant ideology of the individual (O'Flynn, 2009) that shapes social policy and practice. Explanations of social problems centre increasingly around individual pathology or family inadequacies. Putnam's work (2000) also alerts us to the erosion of social capital in our postmodern world. The networks of formal relationships – trade unions, churches, clubs and organisations – and the nuclearisation of the family have meant that people increasingly face social problems on their own. In addition to this, we understand from the work of Gramsci et al. (1971) that the process of hegemony embeds the values and identity of the ruling class in the minds of those who are ruled. This renders the experience of people in marginalised communities normal, inevitable and unchangeable. It also casts the response to social issues in the terms of the current dominant discourse. It becomes clear then that approaches to empowerment of communities must engage people in processes of critical reflection, otherwise they will inevitably respond to symptoms rather than root causes and even the symptoms will be understood and responded to in the light of the dominant discourse of individual pathology.

And so, the role of the worker in a model of practice, which leads to genuine empowerment, is this. First, to have a thorough understanding of the issues that are important to the local community. Second, to understand the wider social and political context that gives rise to those local conditions. Third, to develop processes whereby local people can critically reflect on their experiences in the context of the wider world. And finally, to support a process of collective action that aims to achieve personal and social transformation.

To galvanise community action, the worker must first identify issues about which people have a passion and a willingness to take some action. Freire calls these issues 'generative themes'. He identifies domination and liberation as the overarching or global generative themes that are expressed at every level within society; people experience them as boundary situations. An example of a boundary situation from community-based education is the very common experience of working with a group of community activists who, although intelligent and able, feel stupid and non-educatable. This understanding of themselves could have been produced by things teachers have said to them, failing in formal education, and believing when they are told by other members of the community that education is not for them. However it is produced, it feels like a real and insurmountable barrier that will effectively keep them from risking education; which further strengthens the barrier. Only when they begin to see an alternative future for themselves and are able to see the injustice of the education system that failed them and a society that is prepared to put them on the scrapheap – and get angry about it – do they have the ability to challenge that barrier.

Freire describes this participative process between workers and the people as one in which they seek to investigate the generative theme:

> For precisely this reason, the methodology proposed requires that the investigators and the people (who would normally be considered objects of that investigation) should act as *co-investigators*. The more active an attitude men and women take in regard to the exploration of their thematics, the more they deepen their critical awareness of reality and, in spelling out those thematics, take possession of that reality.
>
> (Freire, 1972: 78)

Traditional forms of practice do not start with the generative themes of the community; rather, they rely on qualitative and quantitative research methods to provide an evidence base for practice. The inherent danger in these approaches is that inevitably the workers' experience and value base will shape the issues focused on, and the questions asked will in turn shape the answers obtained and the action that results. For example, an organisation which has been set up to deliver skills training to get people back into work may well carry out some initial research to identify what the community wants. It will, of course, ask training-related questions and get training-related answers. This will then justify the action they take within the community as being 'community-led'. It is obvious that if you asked the same group of people different questions, you would get a very different picture of what the community needed.

Often these studies treat local communities and the people within them as data sets to be analysed. Needs are usually ascribed according to agency priorities rather than the openly expressed views of local people. The overall effect is to treat people as objects for analysis and organisation, rather than subjects who have the right to self-determination. The Freirean approach seeks to reverse these power relationships and support local people to both define the needs of the area in which they live and the solution to their problems. Key to this process is the identification of generative themes.

One practical way of identifying a generative theme within a community is by carrying out a listening survey. Listening in this context denotes a permanent attitude on the part of the subject who is listening, of being open to the word of the other, to the gesture of the other, to the differences of the other (Freire, 1998: 107). The key skill in a listening survey is having an open mind. As Purcell commented:

> For this [listening survey] to work it is important to adopt the Zen approach of *expecting nothing*. That is to be open to any thing and any interpretation and not to approach with a mind fixed on particular sets of issues or an attachment to a specific course of action.
>
> (Purcell, 2005: 239)

A listening survey can be a challenging task as people's feelings may be contradictory and are seldom clearly expressed. Often a 'presenting issue', such as young people on the streets, may be a symptom that hides the underlying issues (for example, the lack of youth provision and difficult home environments).

Hope and Timmel (1999) outline the nature of a listening survey. Teams of workers, often made up of a mixture of development workers and local people, seek to identify the issues within the community about which people have the strongest feelings. The process is to find situations where people are involved in informal conversations – shops, bars, outside schools, waiting rooms, etc. – and listen for the issues about which people are worried, happy, sad, angry or fearful. In particular the team is listening for issues that relate to six themes that are common to groups of people living together:

1. Basic physical needs
2. Relationships between people
3. Community decision-making processes and structures
4. Education and socialisation
5. Recreation and beliefs
6. Values

The themes identified form the basis for the critical co-investigation that follows. As a first step, the grid below can be used to take initial issues and set them in the context of wider society.

Grid on Generative Themes

Theme	Economic causes of the problem	Who controls the decision-making on the problem	What are the culture, values and beliefs held about the problem	What is the present national, provincial, local policy on the problem
Young people drinking on street corners	Limited disposable income Access to cheap drink Lack of job prospects Few youth venues	Parents Shop owners Police Local authority	Drinking is a sign of being grown up Need to drink to be accepted by peer group	WHO Declaration on Young People and Alcohol, 2001 Crime & Disorder Act 1998 Parenting Orders Confiscation of Alcohol (Young Persons) Act 1997

Developing Codes

The next step in the process of a transformational practice is developing processes that enable people to question the social reality in which they live, with all its injustices and contradictions, but which they experience as normality. In Freirean education, this process begins by developing codes.

A code is a concrete representation of people's lived experience, which is used in the context of dialogue to engage people in critical reflection and action in order to effect social change. They are not just the use of visual aids to generate discussion. They are the product of identifying a generative theme and carefully devising an image, a song, a play, a piece of text, or other experiences that will allow the group to fully explore and act on that theme. They pose questions, rather than give answers; as Ira Shor (1993: 26) says, 'a process of questioning answers rather than merely answering questions'. Through this process people cease to be objects and become writers of their own story (Jesson and Newman, 2004).

The use of codes and what can be used as codes is limited only by the imagination of the worker. The strength of the code is that it accesses people's visual and creative resources and utilises them to think deeply and solve problems. They are risky, of course, because the worker has no control over the end point – groups actually do take control over their own destinies, even if it is only for a short time. It is, however, this experience of taking power that provides the motivation to continue the process of asking questions, making demands and not settling for the way things are at present. Codes provide an emotional, enjoyable way of becoming active in your own life and the life of your community.

For example, a group could be presented with photographs of housing conditions on their estate. This has the effect of enabling them to see again images that have become invisible to them. It is at this stage that the problem-posing method starts.

A typical range of questions that the group might explore is:

- What do you see happening?
- Why is it happening this way?
- How do people feel in this situation?
- Whose interest does it serve?
- Who holds power in this situation?

- Is your experience the same or different to this?
- Are there any things happening economically or politically which are having an impact on this situation?
- Is there anything being done to improve this situation?
- Is there anything we could do to improve it?
- How might we do this?
- Who else could be involved?

(Hope and Timmel, 1999)

The result of these discussions will be a critical understanding of the issue; personal awareness of the individual's relationship to the issue; understanding that the issue is experienced collectively; and an outline for a programme of action. The role of the worker is to facilitate this process, to learn from it, but not to direct it. This suggests a democratisation of learning since the knowledge that is created, and the conclusions that are drawn, are not within the gift of the worker but are created by the group. It also indicates a shifting of power from the individual expert to the group. Not that this is an easy or automatic process – far from it. Because of the unequal social relations we all live in, we automatically default to our socially conditioned roles. It is therefore very common for workers to feel that they must have all the answers and for the groups they are working with to defer to their expertise and look for direction and answers. These ingrained social roles must be struggled against if real empowerment is to be achieved.

Engaging in Dialogue

At the heart of this process is dialogue. Freire describes dialogue as a form of revolutionary communication (Freire, 1972) He is not describing a mere conversation, but an intentional process of communication set in a context of two transformed relationships; first, the relationship between teachers and learners and second, the relationship between learners and knowledge.

> Educator and learners all become learners assuming the same attitude as cognitive subjects discovering knowledge through one another and through the objects they try to know. It is not a situation where one knows and the others do not; it is rather a search, by all, at the same time to discover something by the act of knowing which cannot exhaust all the possibilities in the relation between object and subject.
>
> (Freire, 1976: 115)

In order to achieve this transformation, the worker must understand the culture and community which is the social location of the learner and then to cross the border in that way to act in solidarity with the learners; no longer seen as the other (Mayo, 1999). The starting point for this learning process is that no one fully knows; neither the teacher nor the learner, but that together we can discover new knowledge. This does not mean that the worker has the same role as the learner but that they have complementary roles in the group as the whole group both teaches and learns.

As an example, a youth worker might want to discuss sexual health with a group of young people. In a traditional form of practice what was to be learned would be decided by the worker; this could be the use of condoms, the nature of sexual diseases and available health resources. The worker might then set up group discussions, videos, distribute leaflets and arrange visits to other projects in order to enable the group to learn what the worker had decided were the important lessons for the group. We can see that in this model, the worker does not learn, only teaches and the group learns. No matter how well meaning, this is external knowledge imposed on the group from outside. For people to act on knowledge they must believe in it, and this is unlikely to happen when it is simply the case of adults once again telling them what is right and wrong. Perhaps this is one of the reasons why sexual health amongst young people in the UK is so bad.

By contrast a transformational approach to the subject of sexual health would be qualitatively different. The worker, realising she does not know all there is to know about the sexual health issues that are important to the group, would seek to know what young people understand, experience and feel about sexual health issues, as well as understanding the received wisdom about safe sex practices. These elements would then be explored by the group through dialogue. Within this, understandings and assumptions would be challenged in order to develop an authentic understanding of how people are positioned within the issue. The outcome of the dialogue would not be known since it is developed by the group and not the worker. They might think that issues of identity and power are more central to them in making positive decisions about their sexual behaviour. This might also include much of the information contained in the traditional approach but the young people themselves would decide what was useful and how it fitted into their own understanding of the world. In this way an internal impetus for change is developed rather than the external imposition of the traditional approach.

In the above example we see the second transformed relationship; the relationship between learners and knowledge. Within transformative education, existing knowledge is the starting point and is to be critically examined through the co-investigation of the learning group. Through this process of co-investigation new understandings are developed and new knowledge is created. Because this knowledge is created and owned by the group, it has power.

Part of the effectiveness of this social approach to learning is its ability to enable us to analyse our assumptions – why we think the things we think. This can reveal the boundaries that block us from developing new ideas and new action.

Taking and Reflecting on Action

The final phase of the Freirean process is taking and reflecting on action. Freire said, 'Functionally, oppression is domesticating. To no longer be prey to its force, one must emerge from it and turn upon it. This can be done only by means of the praxis: reflection and action upon the world in order to transform it.' Understanding that the world is an oppressive place, or even making connections between personal circumstances and the structural forces that produce them, is fine as far as it goes, but as Marx said, 'The philosophers have only interpreted the world, in various ways; the point, however, is to change it' (Marx et al., 2001: 170). Freire strongly warns against Action without Reflection = mindless activism (acting without thinking) Reflection without Action = verbalism = 'blah' (Freire et al., 1998: 68).

Key Learning Points

- Authentic practice is based on the genuine participation of the community
- Workers must seek out the Generative Themes within communities in order to harness the energy and passion needed to achieve social change
- Genuine participation will come about through engaging people in the critical examination of their lives and providing structures to support action on the themes that emerge

- Community Development is understood as a Praxis, thinking and acting combined to achieve personal and social change
- This approach to working with people acts as an antidote and stands as a critique of top-down approaches, which seek to ameliorate symptoms and pacify people, rather than empowerment, which leads to change

Learning Tasks

With another person, visit somewhere where people congregate – café, pub, bus stop, school gates. Then, *working separately*

- Listen out for issues that people are concerned, happy or angry about
- Summarise the issues
- Make one suggestion for action
- Compare your findings with those of the other person
- Discuss
- Imagine you have been asked to work on the issues of sexual health with a group of young people. Devise a code that would allow the group to explore the issue and come up with their own responses, rather than having answers imposed on them
- What are the ethical issues involved in this activity and how would you deal with them?

Key Reading

Beck, D. and Purcell, R. (2010) *Popular Education Practice for Youth and Community Development Work*. Exeter: Learning Matters.

Hope, A. and Timmel, S. (1999) *Training for Transformation, 1–4*. London: ITDG Publishing.

This is, in many ways, classic text of Popular Education Practice, providing a wide range of ways to both think about and practice Popular Education in ways that are accessible to youth and community groups. There is a variety of exercises that are spelled out in detail; as with all material, the worker should adapt to suit the needs of their particular group.

Sheehy, M. and Warner, C. (2001) *Partners Companion Manual to Training for Transformation*. Dublin: Partners.

This is a compilation of the exercises, processes and methods designed and used by facilitators over several years and drawing on experience of workshops in the north and south of Ireland, the UK and across the world.

References

Alinsky, S. (1971) *Rules for Radicals*. New York: Random House.

Arnstein, S. (1969) 'A Ladder of Citizen Participation', in *JAIP*, 35(4).

Batten, T. (1967) *The Non Directive Approach*. Oxford: Oxford University Press.

DETR (Department of Environment, Transport and the Regions) (1998) *Evaluation of the Single Regeneration Budget Challenge Fund – A Partnership for Regeneration: An Interim Evaluation*. London: HMSO.

Freire, P. (1972) *Pedagogy of the Oppressed*. London: Penguin.

Freire, P. (1976) *Education: The Practice of Freedom*. London: Writers and Readers Publishing Cooperative.

Freire, P., Clarke, P., Macedo, D.P., Aronowitz, S., and Dawson Books (1998) *Pedagogy of Freedom: Ethics, Democracy, and Civic Courage*. Lanham, MD: Rowman & Littlefield Publishers.

Gramsci, A. 1971 *Selections from Prison Notebooks*. London: International Publishers.

Gramsci, A., Hoare, Q., and Nowell-Smith, G. (1971) *Selections from the Prison Notebooks of Antonio Gramsci*. London: Lawrence & Wishart.

Hope, A. and Timmel, S. (1999) *Training for Transformation, 4.* London: ITDG Publishing.

Jesson, J. and Newman, M. (2004) 'Radical Adult Education and Learning', in G. Foley (ed.), *Understanding Adult Education and Training.* New South Wales: Allen & Unwin.

Ledwith, M. (2011) *Community Development: A Critical Approach*, 2nd edn. Bristol: The Policy Press.

Marx, K., Engels, F., Arthur, C.J., and Ebooks Corporation Limited (2001) *The German Ideology.* London: The Electric Book Company.

Mayo, P. (1999) *Gramsci, Freire, and Adult Education: Possibilities for Transformative Action.* London: Zed Books.

McLaren, P. (2000) *Che Guevara, Paulo Freire, and the Pedagogy of Revolution* . Lanham, MD and Oxford: Rowman & Littlefield.

O'Flynn, M. (2009) *Profitable Ideas: The Ideology of the Individual in Capitalist Development.* Leiden: Brill.

Purcell, R. (2005) *Working in the Community: Perspectives for Change.* Morrisville, NC: Lulu Press.

Putnam R. (2000) *Bowling Alone: The Collapse and Revival of American Community.* New York: Simon & Schuster.

Rhodes, J., Tyler, P., and Brennan, A. (2005) 'Assessing the Effect of Area-Based Initiatives on Local Area Outcomes: Some Thoughts Based on the National Evaluation of the Single Regeneration Budget in England', *Urban Studies*, 42(11), 1919–1946.

Rhodes, J., Tyler, P., and Brennan, A. (2007) *The Single Regeneration Budget: Final Evaluation.* Cambridge: Department of Land Economy.

Shor, I. (1993) *Education is Politics: Paulo Freire's Critical Pedagogy.* New York: Routledge.

3.6 Asset-Based Community Development and Social Capital

Introduction

This chapter explores the nature of the resources available to communities. There is an assumption that well-heeled middle-class areas have lots of resources available, but poorer deprived communities do not. Indeed, in the UK this assumption has shaped practice to the point where many workers and community groups believe that unless they can acquire a grant (from the local state, Lottery, etc.) then little is possible. This is not to say that the right grant funding is unwelcome, as it can be of major significance. But there are dangers of 'chasing grants' where the local organisation simply does what funders want, rather than what the community needs. Or the community just does nothing because there is no grant.

If we look, for example, at what is achieved in the USA by autonomous community organisations using a variety of resources, then a world of possibilities opens up. For example, the authors on a recent trip to Detroit visited a number of self-funded projects. One was a community laundry/coffee shop/English classroom based in an old industrial unit. Outside, an arts venue space was being developed. At the other end of the scale was an old car factory now being used as an income-generating storage facility, housing units for homeless people, and starter units for new community enterprises. Some of the case studies below also explore community-funded initiatives.

In every community there is a range of resources that can be used for community purposes. Some of these are *hard* resources such as buildings and land, others are *soft* resources based around people, such as those who are in the existing local organisations; what knowledge, experience and skills do they have and what time do they have to commit to local projects? But more important than this is the nature of relationships between people, and the degree of trust and supportive networks that exist. These resources are generally known in the developing professions as Assets, and for our purposes the approach is Asset Based Community Development (ABCD).

ABCD was pulled together as a working approach in the 1960s (see, for example, Kretzmann and McKnight, 1993), although, you can trace the roots back to Alinsky and his approach of building 'an organisation of organisations' in Chicago during the 1930s.

The Asset Model

There are seven types of Assets (sometimes called Capitals) that are either currently used, or could be used by the community. Assets can be labelled in different ways, for example:

- **Physical** – usually buildings, but can be other structures such as bike tracks
- **Economic** – local businesses and what they can offer in terms of sponsorship, funding, investment either to enhance the community (new businesses/jobs), or specifically to support community projects

- **Environmental** – parks, gardens, surrounding landscape that are used or could be used for community purposes.
- **Institutional** – the formal and informal ways in which the local community can influence external decision makers. This includes voting, lobbying politicians as well as organising direct action.
- **Human** – the totality of what local people know, the skills they have and experiences they can share (including those who may work in the area but do not live there), local leaders and potential leaders. *The most important human asset is time* – to give to community activity either as a regular commitment or for specific events over the year. Regardless of income, education, skills etc., everyone can contribute something, and be able to commit time to building the community.
- **Social** – the relationships between people and how they interrelate to each other (see the section on Social Capital below).
- **Cultural** – how local people see themselves and their community. The belief in the possibility of change.

As can be seen this is a broad list. Often categories overlap. For example, a local business can offer physical space, expertise and financial support if it is involved in community activity. An example could be a Garden Centre supporting a local community-run environmental improvement project which may also have an impact on social relationships.

If a community is exploring its needs and moving to a stage of planning action (using the Reflection–Vision–Planning–Action model), then it would be essential to map the actual and potential assets before undertaking detailed planning. In doing so, resources can be uncovered that had not previously been thought about, and the community avoids the trap of trying to achieve the impossible, or just sitting back hoping grants will be offered. The asset approach enables communities to develop realistic plans based upon what resources are available to them. This is important because it shows that local change is in their hands, and not dependent upon external bodies offering money.

Asset Mapping

Community asset mapping can be undertaken in a number of ways. What is essential is that it is undertaken by community members, and not by external 'experts'. By involving community members it becomes a group-building, skills-development and knowledge-creating experience for the community.

One way of approaching this task is for the worker to facilitate the following processes:

1. Organise and brief teams, each exploring one of the asset headings.
2. Pool what people already know and what comes out of discussion. This phase usually identifies the obvious resources.
3. Walking the neighbourhood to see what has been missed in the discussion.
4. Tabulating assets. It is important here to identify between existing community assets and potential community assets – with the latter annotated with what might be required to realise it as an asset. This can be done through lists or writing on a large map of the area
5. Arrange a further collective discussion, which will uncover other assets and identify where specific assets headings overlap.

Social Capital

Of all the assets under discussion, social capital is perhaps the most important in terms of enabling community development to take place. Robert Putnam in his ground-breaking work *Bowling Alone* (Putnam, 2000) showed how the decline in collective community activity (bowling and other group activities), due to TV and people spending more time at home, had undermined social relationships and the quality of life in middle America. In the age of social media where we increasingly live physically isolated lives, the importance of social capital is central to our quality of life experience. As Putnam said 'social capital can be thought of as the glue that binds a community together'.

Arising from Putnam's work, social capital is normally described as: *the networks, norms, relationships, values and informal sanctions that shape the quantity and co-operative quality of a society's social interactions.* The degree of social capital in a community is usually determined by the interrelationship of a range of factors. The key factors are thought to be the impact from:

1. history and culture
2. whether social structures are flat or hierarchical
3. the family
4. education
5. the built environment
6. residential mobility
7. economic inequalities and social class
8. the strength and characteristics of civil society
9. and patterns of individual consumption and personal values

The mix of the above factors works to build or reduce social capital in community-based networking relationships in three main ways: through *bonding* social capital (e.g. amongst family members or ethnic groups); *bridging* social capital (e.g. across different ethnic groups); and *linking* social capital (e.g. between different social classes). Overall, if the operation of these processes leads to trust between individuals and groups, then people will work with and support each other (through reciprocal actions), and the level of social capital will be high. If these factors undermine trust then the possibility of mutual inter-action and support declines and social capital will be lower.

Where there are high levels of social capital people will:

1. feel they are part of the community
2. feel useful and be able to make a real contribution to the community
3. participate in local community networks and organisations
4. pull together for the common good in floods and bush fires they
5. welcome strangers
6. all help out with something but no one will do everything

However, if there is low or no social capital in the group, neighbourhood or community, it will be less likely for those people to work together for the common good. If there is no social capital present the causes may be that:

- the human capital required for social capital's core building blocks is absent e.g. self-esteem, trust, communication skills
- there are inadequate levels of material well-being – people are struggling for survival

- there is inadequate physical infrastructure – such as places to meet, public spaces, telephones, newspapers
- the human, economic and physical infrastructure pre-requisites are present but there have been no opportunities to develop the networks and interconnections between people.

Community development workers need, therefore, to understand the level of social capital in the community. If social capital is high and there are many functioning networks in the community, organising will be easier. If there is low social capital, then work will need to be done to start building trust between individuals and groups before mutually supportive community activity can be achieved.

Key Learning Points

- It is important for community development to recognise that in any community there will be a range of assets that are either community resources, or have the potential to be so. Identifying these assets is a skill-sharing/bonding community activity
- The most important asset is social capital, as it is the building block upon which community trust, cohesion, development and quality of life is built
- The success of community development is built on identifying and effectively using community assets

Learning Tasks

- Undertake an **asset-mapping exercise** where you live or work. The scale of the exercise depends upon how many people are involved. Be mindful to follow the procedure below:
  - Identify the obvious resources under the seven asset headings
  - Walk the community to identify new assets
  - List the assets and identify if they are an existing or potential community asset
  - Think through a range of uses to which these assets could be deployed
- Undertake a **social capital assessment** within a community. A simple way to do this is to conduct a survey (door to door, or interview people in the street). Sample questions to ask are:
  - In an emergency could you rely on a neighbour for help?
  - Do people in the local community support each other or do they keep to themselves?
  - Does your family live locally?
  - Do your friends live locally?
  - Are you a member of any local groups (formal/informal)?

The purpose of the questions is to produce a snapshot view of: the degree of trust between people, if a neighbour's help in the time of need can be expected, and the degree of interconnectedness in the community.

Key Reading

Field, J. (2008) *Social Capital (Key Ideas)*. Abingdon: Routledge. Available at: https://sustaining community.wordpress.com/resources-for-students/strengths-based-approaches/.

References

Field, J. (2008) *Social Capital (Key Ideas)*. Abingdon: Routledge.

Kretzmann, J. and McKnight, J. (1993) *Building Communities from the Inside Out: A Path Towards Finding and Mobilizing Community Assets*. Evanston, IL: ACTA.

Putnam, R. (2000) *Bowling Alone: The Collapse and Revival of American Community*. New York: Simon & Schuster.

3.7 Integrated Models of Practice

Introduction

In this chapter we take stock of where we have got to and pull together the, sometimes diverse, models of practice. As we have said, our aim with the book is to equip practitioners, whether they are paid (or unpaid) workers, local activists, or concerned citizens to develop their own toolkit of theories and practice from which they can build appropriate and effective community groups and organisations.

Our Integrated Practice Models is a suggested way to implement an effective community development strategy. It is based on nine steps, built around eight key questions the workers need to ask themselves. The steps are:

1 Knowing your Values and Core Purposes

The first questions are why are you doing this work, who are you doing it for and are there ulterior motives at play?

If you are a paid community development worker, then your employer is likely to be sending you there for a pre-determined purpose. What is this purpose and how does it fit with the values we set out earlier? If you are an activist you may have a freer hand in what you do. Basically, are you working for the community and reflecting their expressed needs, or for somebody else's agenda? Can you combine the two agendas in a meaningful way?

The purpose of community development is clear. It is about social change, social and collective empowerment, and helping people to have a better quality of life. These goals link to wider issues around anti-discriminatory practice, human rights, etc.

2 What is the Community?

Before we can effectively work in a community we need to understand it. But we have to recognise that a community is a fluid and diffuse thing. Let us consider a housing estate where people of different ages, occupations, education and possibly religion and ethnicity live together. It would be very rare for everyone there to hold the same opinion about anything. If we look carefully enough, we can see diverse networks, family and informal groupings where interests, experience and opinions (on certain areas) are shared. In reality, the world is composed of numerous micro communities, and the job of the community development worker is to understand this diversity and see where commonalities exist and can be created. Not everyone can or will be involved in community activity.

What should the aim be for community involvement? This of course depends upon the nature of the community and what you want people to be involved in. For a neighbourhood housing area, an achievable goal would be for 30 per cent of the population to be involved in some kind of community activity in a year. This is an ambitious but achievable target over time.

3 How Everyday Power is Deployed

Communities exist in socially constructed space. That is, everything concerning the community: the buildings that have been built, how they are used, who owns them, what people live/work there, who is not there (age/gender/ethnicity/etc.), what people do and do not do – all happen in a socio-economic and cultural context. Underpinning all this is the distribution of power; some people are able to make decisions on how this space operates, most people do not. It is necessary to think through 'hegemony', how it plays out locally and the potential for counter-hegemonic development.

4 Everyday Life Strategies and Tactics

As we have discussed, power is not monolithic. De Certeau (1984) describes how people with power develop strategies to control things in their own interests, what he called 'strategies'. In contrast, people develop daily 'tactics' to make life more liveable. As a local worker you need to understand the main tactics being deployed: are they functional (in that they make people's lives better), dysfunctional, individualised, or do they have the possibility of being utilised for social change?

5 Knowing the Community's Needs

You now know the diverse networks in the community, the distribution of power and the key players, and how people respond to living there through their daily tactics. How do you build on this knowledge to work with local people to identify what they wish to do?

Sometimes this is easy. For example, a child on their way to school may be injured by a car. As a result, there are local protests about speeding traffic. Sometimes, though, the presenting issue is not the actual problem. A classic example is the often complaint about teenagers roaming the streets causing trouble, and the expressed possible solution of extra policing. However, the actual problem is more likely to be the absence of youth facilities leaving young people nowhere to go in the evenings and weekends. The positive response in this situation is focusing on the needs of young people, not forcing them off the streets.

Identifying the needs of local people involves various processes of interactive enquiry. There are many techniques that can be used, and some are more effective than others. The most effective involve time and effort.

First, it cannot be stressed too much that just relying on professionals talking to each other about local needs, asking questions on Facebook, questionnaires, or simply guessing, are failed strategies.

Effective techniques always involve personal engagement with local people. We discuss these techniques elsewhere in the book, but to summarise these involve:

- Listening surveys where you hear local conversations and/or engage individuals in discussion over a cup of tea
- Knocking on doors and talking to residents
- Working with local groups to map the local area, identifying things they like and things they want to change
- Local people taking photographs as a PhotoVoice exercise
- Accompanying local people on a psychogeographic walk

Once you have collected this data you need to engage in a facilitated process with local people to explore what this means to them. If you have properly engaged with local people in the data collection process, you will have a lot of people wanting to be part of this discussion.

This facilitated process could usefully follow the Freirean model and explore the RVPA model. In this model 'generative themes' are developed from the data, and linked 'codes' using images/text from the data are created. The first phase of discussion is one of *Reflection* where people think about what they like/dislike about living in the area. The second phase is about a *Vision* of how the area could be, and the specific things (object-ives) you want to achieve. The third phase is one of *Planning* what to do to implement the vision. The fourth phase is taking *Action* on the plan. Because local people have been fully engaged throughout this process and have generated the vision and plan themselves, they will be fully motivated to take action. Once *Action* is completed the RVPA cycle starts again building on what has been achieved and learned from the completed process.

6 Assets, Local Resources and Leadership

This section is linked to mapping the community and planning for action, but is worthy of a separate comment. As the communities in which we work are often poor and under-resourced, it is important to make an accurate map of local assets that can (or might) be deployed for community development purposes. It is common for community organisations to rely only on their own resources and ignore the wider assets and resources that exist locally. Engaging with local assets should be part of the planning/action phases. It is worth remembering that the biggest asset in poor communities is local people. The question to be explored here is one of mobilisation, knowledge and skill development. This can take some time and effort to work through, but is worth it in terms of individual and collective benefits.

A key question is one of leadership (this is discussed more fully in Chapter 4.5). As we know, the community development worker is an adviser to community groups, they are not leaders of those groups. This is true informally as well as formally. Avoid being the community development worker who pulls the strings of a community organisation.

Saul Alinsky helpfully described a leader as somebody who has a following. Often this following is informal, and based on the person's knowledge, experience and personality. Community development workers should identify actual and potential leaders and work supportively with them to develop skills and confidence.

7 Organising Models

In the planning process there needs to be thoughtful consideration of how the existing or emerging community organisation wants to organise itself. This decision should be based on what is appropriate to most effectively meet the planned objectives.

The default position is usually what local people are used to. In the UK, this is usually a committee/office bearers' model. There is nothing wrong with this when used appropri-ately. However, a collective model or less formal models can sometimes be useful in the right circumstance. Below we identify the key options for organising in the community:

1. **For Large-scale Campaigning** the traditional Community organising model of the IAF is proven to work. As we have noted, its democratic structure enables the involve-ment of diverse groups and individuals. Alternatively, the SDI model offers a distinct women-led approach to large-scale development.

2. **For Building Large Neghbourhood Organisations** working on diverse issues. The distinct model developed by ACORN provides a readymade way of quickly building a democratic organisation, and moving swiftly to the action phase.
3. **Working with Smaller Groups** involves its own challenges, and the Forming–Storming–Norming–Performing process discussed in Chapter 4.6 is helpful. Additionally, the Freirean process provides a more intensive approach to working with groups. Both of these models can be applied within the larger operation of the IAF, SDI and ACORN models.
4. **Combining the Above.** Sometimes it is appropriate to create hybrid models, for example, Freirean groups exploring the experience of mental health, which feed into a larger campaigning structure. What is important is to see all of the above models as templates that can be adapted according to local circumstances.

8 RVPA Approach to Planning

Although this was originally developed for working with the Freirean model, it is important to systematically work through a version of the RVPA process as appropriate to the organisational approach that has been adopted. The stages of the model are:

1. Facilitating people to **REFLECT** upon their lives, the nature of the community, what they like and dislike.
2. To develop a **VISION** of what they want their lives to be and desired improvements in the community.
3. To **PLAN** how these desired changes can be implemented (in the context of the available resources for change as identified through Asset Mapping.
4. To take **ACTION** to deliver the plan as appropriate for the organisational model being used.

RVPA is a circular and repeating process. The identified plan is used to build the monitoring and evaluation framework. The Evaluation process becomes part of the Reflection stage for the next cycle of visioning, planning and action.

9 Monitoring and Evaluation

In any development activity, monitoring and evaluation is essential, otherwise it is impossible to know if the objectives are being met, and what is to be learned from the work. Many community development organisations fail to properly identify what they are trying to achieve. They simply talk about 'working with young people', 'supporting the elderly', or 'fighting poverty' without defining clear and realisable objectives. This can be through poor advice from the community worker. Although, if you don't define objectives and don't measure achievement then you can never fail.

Defining objectives is part of the Vision phase of development. In the Planning phase you set out the monitoring and evaluation plan, and monitoring is implemented as part of the Action Phase. The final part of the Action phase is the evaluation. The data from evaluation becomes part of the new RVPA cycle.

In the case studies discussed in Section 5 we can see various ways where some of these steps have been utilised. In the commentary to the case studies, we discuss how the Integrated Model could be of assistance to the work in hand.

Key Learning Points

- The art of community development practice is to work with many dimensions at one time
- The worker needs to remain constant to the values of CD, and be able to analyse the community through applying social theories. From this analysis a range of practice models can be selected and applied
- What is essential is that the worker is flexible and creative in making these choices

Learning Tasks

- Select a piece of community development work
- Work through the nine steps outlined above
- Compare your findings with the current practice

Key Reading

Revisit the relevant section of the book, exploring theory and practice around Freire and Community Organising, as appropriate for the action required.

Reference

De Certeau, M. (1984) *The Practice of Everyday Life*, Trans. Steven Rendall, Berkeley, CA: University of California Press.

Section 4

Practice Issues for Community Development Work

In this section we consider some of the broader issues that impact upon practice. Firstly, we return to the question of community, and with the help of Psychogeography and Photovoice techniques, explore how we can better understand the reality of peoples' experience. We then move on to some core issues around creating a better community – how to promote empowerment, and thus build capacity, capability and resilience. Underpinning all these activities is the requirement for effective local leadership and community groups. We discuss how leaders and groups can be facilitated and sustained. Finally, we discuss the importance of having a monitoring and evaluation framework. Without such a framework it is impossible to truly know if what we are doing in the community is effective, what works and how to improve practice.

4.1 Understanding the Community
Psychogeography and PhotoVoice

Introduction

Fundamental to working successfully in the community is developing a detailed understanding of the community itself. As we explored in our previous discussions on the nature of community, it is important to recognise that there is no such thing as an overarching community where everyone has the same experience, sees the locality in the same way and expresses the same views. The reality is that we work with multiple small micro communities that reflect diversity in life experiences, needs and desires. The question we discuss here is how to begin to understand this diversity and complexity.

Traditionally, community development workers tended to rely on area profiles, often compiled by local agencies, as their source of local information about the community. Usually, these profiles are statistical documents and often provide detailed information collected against a number of social and economic indicators. These area profiles seldom undertake broader asset mapping, and are more concerned about statistically identifying deficits in the community than exploring potential resources for change. (An exception to this is the SDI approach where community members are directly involved in developing local statistics that reflect the needs and experience of local people.)

For example, we might know from an area profile that there is a high number of lone parents and elderly. But was does this tell us? Being a lone parent or being elderly is not in itself a social problem. The day-to-day experience of elderly people might be OK, or it might not be. What are the needs of local elderly people, and how do we find this out? What we need to do is to explore people's experiences, needs and wants through dialogue with them. This is not the same as completing a questionnaire or asking people 'off the cuff' questions about the community. To facilitate people thinking through what they experience, and what they want, is a process. As we explore elsewhere, popular education approaches built around listening surveys, codification, and discussing generative themes provide a robust approach to this end. The Community Organising/ACORN approach of knocking on doors and engaging people directly is another effective way of both understanding community needs and starting to directly involve local people in the process of change. In this section, we focus on two further methods, psychogeography and PhotoVoice, which can be used to explore the nature of the community. They can be used separately, together, and in conjunction with popular education of community organising work.

Underpinning the above methods is an understanding that the spaces within which we live and work are not neutral. The street, shopping malls, workplaces, schools, community centres etc., are controlled by somebody with a clear purpose, and therefore is also a reflection of power and ideology. We explored this more in the above section on Space and Everyday Life. PhotoVoice and psychogeographic exploration are helpful in understanding the nature of spaces that dominate and, to a varying extent, control our lives.

Psychogeography

One of the ways of getting to know the community is to walk around it at various times of day and on different days of the week, to see who is around, who is not there, what is happening, and to feel the 'vibe on the street'. This has to be done on foot. ACORN uses the 'windshield tour' but walking is more effective. You have to tune your senses to hear the sounds of the street, and see the detail of what is there. This takes effort and you have to forget about anything else and concentrate on what is.

This author has written extensively on this approach (Purcell, 2012). There is a long social history to the seemingly simple task of walking around and looking at what is going on. The classic description of this activity is known as being a 'flaneur', that is a stroller and observer of modern life. The term was first used in the late nineteenth century and is attributed to Baudelaire (1995) in reference to the new bourgeois class who spent much of the day watching life from the comforts of a Parisian café. In the 1930s Walter Benjamin, in his classic *Arcades Project* (Benjamin, 1999) gave the flaneur a Marxist makeover, and the Surrealist Andre Breton practised strolling along the streets of Paris as a way to 'reframe the mundane aspects of everyday life with something marvellous' – that is, to learn to see and experience in a different way.

In the late 1950s, again in Paris, the Situationists further refined walking around. Guy Debord (1955) created what he termed Psychogeography, which he defined as 'the study of the precise laws and specific effects of the geographical environment, consciously organized or not, on the emotions and behaviour of individuals'. For Debord, life in the city was always exciting and challenging if you were alert enough to see it, to feel it. It is PSYCHO geography because walking down the street impacts on your physical and mental state. He said city life was characterised by a 'sudden change of ambience in a street within the space of a few metres; the evident division of a city into zones of distinct psychic atmospheres and the appealing or repellent character of certain places' (Debord, 1955). This may initially sound a dubious statement, but if you have ever walked down a dark and empty street late at night and felt rising panic, or sat in a city park on a sunny day watching your children play and felt really happy and content, then you know what this means. Our modern and increasing practice of walking around with headphones blocking out the local environment shuts us of from the immediacy of experiencing the city.

These focused walks are generally known as 'Derives' and they are a tested technique to engage with an urban area, and interrogate the nature of space. Community development workers can usefully get to know an area more deeply through undertaking a derive. It is also very useful to undertake a derive with local people. By facilitating the walk with open questions, local people can re-see where they live and this opens up discussions of what people like, what they do not like, and begin discussions of what they might want.

For a successful derive, several pre-conditions are necessary. Sensitising questions (as listed below) need to be set out before the walk. It is important that people focus on the questions as well as being open to seeing, hearing and feeling experiences as they walk. Avoid chit-chat, using mobile phones, headphones and distractions.

Suggested sensitising questions:

1. Who owns/controls this space?
2. Is it public or private space, or mixed?
3. How is the space used, e.g. to include people (who is included and why, what are they doing)?
4. How is the space used to exclude people (who is not there, why)?

5. How is this space experienced according to different class/gender/sexuality/ethnicity/culture/age (as appropriate)?
6. Are there signs of transgression?
7. What is the ideological nature of this space, does it promote hegemony and if so how, what is normal/acceptable behaviour?
8. Can you see institutional strategies of control?
9. Can you see individuals or groups using tactics as defensive/ offensive responses?
10. What psychogeographic issues arise from the above, for individuals for various groups/sub-cultures?
11. Is there a community development response to these issues?

PhotoVoice

Photography is used extensively in community development work to document a place, situation or activity, as a campaign tool, to produce promotional activity, as part of a community arts programme, and in this case as a method of exploring a community or social question.

There are three main ways of using photography for such developmental activities: photo-elicitation, photo-novella and PhotoVoice. To fully explore these three methods is beyond the scope of this section, but a short summary is useful as there can be confusion over the various methods (for more detailed discussion see Purcell, 2009).

Photo-elicitation was originally developed by anthropologists to record social and ritual events. The resulting photographs are then explored with participants to trigger discussion about the activity under question. The method has become widespread in development work, for example, in memory retrieval with elders, ethnic identification, with children and as part of programme evaluations. In photo-elicitation, the photographs are usually taken by the worker on subjects of their choice, and relate to an issue that has often been decided by an external agency. Local people are often the object of someone else's study, rather than being in control of the process.

In contrast, the photo-novella approach moves the power balance back to the participant. People photograph an aspect of their lives that is important to them. Hurworth (2003) explains that 'A key component of the photo novella process is dialogue where participants show their photographs and talk about their significance and meaning. This grounding of the real images in real experience ... makes the photographs infinitely more valuable than a set of images created by outsiders.'

PhotoVoice was developed in the USA by Wang and Burris (for a broader discussion see Wang and Burris, 1997). The first project was with homeless men who were given cameras to document their lives on the street from their own perspective. The resulting photographs were used as publicity and campaigning material. The key point was that the photographs made the situation of the men visible and very public. In addition, it gave a mechanism for the men to speak about their experiences and needs, and provided a mechanism to engage politicians. The role of the workers was to support and facilitate, not lead and direct. In contrast to photo-elicitation, PhotoVoice enables people to be in control of a development process directly related to their expressed needs.

In their article, Wang and Burris identify the various stages of a PhotoVoice project as:

- Conceptualising the problem and devising the initial theme
- Conducting PhotoVoice training
- Considering ethical issues in photographing people and communities

- Defining broader goals and objectives
- Taking pictures
- Codifying issues, themes, and theories
- Facilitating group discussion
- Critical reflection and dialogue
- Reaching policymakers, donors, media, researchers, and others who may be mobilised to create change

Like much of community development practice, how the project is set up can determine the success or otherwise of the endeavour. Most people's experience of photography is about snaps of family, selfies and holidays. To suggest photographing where you live, or more challengingly, aspects of your life can feel difficult. Choices need to be made between handing out cameras, or using mobile phones as both have their own advantages and disadvantages. Talking through what is being asked and showing examples of where a community has used PhotoVoice before is an important part of establishing the project properly. Training workers in how to run a PhotoVoice project is useful. It is not just handing out cameras to people and hoping for the best.

PhotoVoice is a powerful method if applied correctly. It can stand alone and provide an effective way for people to reflect critically on aspects of their lives, and the community. It can be used to supplement a psychogeographic derive. It is also a useful tool as part of a popular education programme.

Key Learning Points

For effective community development work it is important that the worker understands the complex and diverse nature of the community within which they practice. As we have stressed throughout this book, it is also important to facilitate local people to critically reflect on their lives and where they live.

Psychogeography – going for a planned structured walk, and facilitating discussion around sensitising questions – can lead to a greater understanding and re-seeing of the community.

PhotoVoice is another approach and complementary to re-seeing the community, and creates a body of material that can be codified and discussed as part of a popular education programme.

Learning Tasks

- Using the guidelines for a derive, go to a place you have never visited before and undertake a derive of around two hours, using the above guidelines. Do not read about the place or look at it on Google streetview before you go, as this will undermine the impact of the first encounter with the space

Key Reading

As an example of the modern derive, set in New York, see:

Jacks, B. (2006) 'Walking the City: Manhattan Projects', *Places*, 18(1). Available at: http://repositories.cdlib.org/cgi/viewcontent.cgi?article=1965&context=ced/places.

Derives can be recorded and explored through factual, visual, literary approaches or a combination of these. For a literary factual, historical and sometimes mystical account, see:

Sinclair, I. (2002) *London Orbital*. London: Granta.

PhotoVoice is a UK-based agency that uses photography for development purposes. Explore their website at: https://photovoice.org.

For a general discussion of photography and community development see:

Purcell, R. (2009) 'Images for Change: Community Development, Community Arts and Photography', *Community Development Journal*, 44(1), January.

References

Baudelaire, C. (1995) *The Painter of Modern Life*. London: Phaidon Press.

Benjamin, W. (1999) *The Arcades Project*. Cambridge, MA: Belknap Press.

Debord, G. (1955) 'Introduction', to a *Critique of Urban Geography*, Les Le'vres Nues #6. Available at: www.cddc.vt.edu/sionline/presitu/geography.html.

Hurworth, R. (2003) 'Photo Interviewing for Research: Social Research Update, 40', University of Surrey, Guildford. Available at: http://sru.soc.surrey.ac.uk/SRU40.html.

Purcell, R. (2009) 'Images for Change: Community Development, Community Arts and Photography', *Community Development Journal*, 44(1, January), 111–122.

Purcell, R. (2012) 'Community Development and Everyday Life', *Community Development Journal*, 47(2), 266–281.

Wang, C. and Burris, M.A. (1997) 'Photovoice: Concept, Methodology, and Use for Participatory Needs Assessment', *Health Education and Behaviour*, 24(3), 369–387.

4.2   Promoting Empowerment

Introduction

There is no doubt that empowerment is a contested term. In the past few years we have seen empowerment promised through yoga – 'Empowerment is about having the ability and confidence to turn towards and really feel the moment deeply' (Tomlinson, 2018); taking on debt, with one credit company claiming they had empowered 880,000 customers by lending them money with an interest rate of nearly 50 per cent APR; and through using makeup, 'Empowerment takes shape in many forms, and makeup is one of those forms' (Zubair, 2016).

A recent conversation we had with a community worker reveals the confusion that exists even in community development practice. He stated that he had recently being doing 'empowering work' with a carers group. It transpired that this group had been set up by the local authority to provide a place where carers of children with disabilities could have some respite and engage in social and educational activities. The funding for the childcare workers, hire of the premises and putting on the programme for the carers came from the local authority. However, due to pressure on local budgets, this funding was being withdrawn and the community worker was sent in to support the group. His plan was to 'empower' them by helping them to form a committee, draw up a constitution and make them responsible for raising all the required funding. His view was that this was empowering practice because the group would now be fully in charge of their group. What he did not seem to see was that the decisions had all been imposed on the group, they were losing the very elements of the group that made it useful for them and they had gained additional pressure and responsibilities in their already difficult lives. This type of approach is not uncommon; many movements which start with radical intentions end up being drawn into 'the system' by being given buildings to run, staff to manage and service-level agreements to meet – thereby diverting them from their original mission and robbing them of their power to challenge the status quo (Beck and Purcell, 2010).

So, as community development practitioners, whose main focus is developing empowered individuals, groups and communities, we need a clear framework with which to understand what it is, and a sense of what elements need to be in place to support community empowerment.

Empowerment

Put simply, empowerment is a process through which people and/or communities increase their control or mastery over their own lives and the decisions that affect their lives (Macharia, 2005). It produces a community that is 'confident, resilient, energetic and independent. It is well networked. It has a high degree of social capital. It is confident enough to imagine a better future for itself and is in a position to take control of that future. It has the breadth of vision to be able to enlist others and other agencies in helping it to deliver its ambitions' (Elliot, 2014).

In 2018, the International Association for Community Development reaffirmed community development as a process where:

> people concerned with human rights, economic, social and environmental justice act collectively to change societal circumstances. With good processes determining good outcomes, community development will continue to address power imbalances and strengthen the capacities of rights holders to define, claim and realise their rights by holding stakeholders to account. Supporting and valuing the diversity of communities, community workers will continue to address the causes and consequences of marginalisation and oppression on the basis of key factors including but not exclusive to, gender, 'race' and class.
>
> (IACD, 2018)

We understand that an empowered community will demonstrate:

- Individuals who are creative, confident, questioning and critical
- Groups that are autonomous, supportive experiments in transformed social relationships
- A strong community infrastructure
- Policies, agenda and spending shaped by (or at least with) the community
- Processes which recognise and challenge the structural nature of inequality
- A demonstrable shift of power from the haves to the have-nots

Moving on to consider the elements which must be in place to support empowerment, Ledwith and Springett (2010: 20), drawing on the work of Fay (1987), suggest four interconnected theories which must be in place if workers are to effectively practice in an empowering way. These are theories of false consciousness, crisis, educational action and transformative action. Using these as a template, we now explore the elements of empowering practice.

False Consciousness

This begins to respond to questions around why people accept the situations they are in or the explanations that they are given for those situations in an uncritical way, often thinking that their circumstances are natural, inevitable and unchangeable. In general terms, if people believe that change is impossible, they are right. Only when there is a belief in the possibility of change, can change happen.

The role of the worker, then, is to make problematic this situation and to open up new ways of thinking. We talk in Chapters 2.3 and 3.5 about the use of critical pedagogy to support people in this process but there are many other ways of supporting this process. On an individual basis, peer mentoring can be effective. People from similar situations who have become more empowered, act as an image of what is possible, but they can outline possible strategies for change, identify potential barriers and offer personal support through the change process. On a collective level there are two ways this can be tackled: (1) drawing on the thinking of Alinsky (1971) achieving small victories supports personal and group empowerment – this is discussed in more detail in Chapter 3; (2) seeing examples of excellent practice can challenge existing thinking and offer new ways of operating. This can be achieved in several ways. First, by visiting successful projects and discussing their origins and development with participants. Second, new technologies have opened up the potential for groups to collaborate and share practice throughout the world. Finally, there is an important role for workers to locate and share research, case studies and evaluations of models and approaches that are successful. Making these types of resources available to people helps to share the collective learning of our field.

Dealing with entrenched bias and prejudice is also an element of this aspect of practice, since this acts as a barrier to collective community development and empowerment. One way of tackling this is seen in the long tradition within youth work of setting up exchanges between groups of young people from different countries and backgrounds. Being immersed in a different culture makes people aware of their assumption and norms which have been held unquestioned until then. Being exposed to different ways of thinking and acting contributes to the development of common values of freedom, tolerance and non-discrimination (EU, 2018).

Crisis

There is a strong narrative in our times that states that the causes of our various crises within our communities is due to the individual pathology of people who are in some ways lacking and defective. Therefore, overstating slightly, the crisis in schools is due to pupils not engaging properly, the crisis of poverty is due to people not developing their skills and not making the most of available opportunities, and the crisis in health is due to poor individual decisions. What comes across clearly is an explanation which is based on deficit and focuses on the individual.

Kretzmann and McKnight's (1993) classic critique of the deficit-based approach has given rise to an asset-based approach to Community Development. Mathie and Cunningham (2003) identify a variety of steps in developing an ABCD response to these local crises. These include:

- collecting stories of community successes and analysing the reasons for success
- mapping community assets
- forming a core steering group
- building relationships amongst local assets for mutually beneficial problem-solving within the community
- convening a representative planning group
- leveraging activities, resources, and investments from outside the community.

Whilst it is acknowledged that an asset-based approach enables community members to work productively together and to challenge a poverty-influenced mindset, enabling them to more effectively take responsibility for their own development by both utilising their own assets and drawing in assets from outside the community (Nel, 2018) this approach has also been criticised. MacLeod and Emejulu (2014) suggest that highlighting the role of the community has the unintended consequence of removing the state as a primary actor in social welfare thereby privatising public issues such as inequality, poverty and discrimination. We argue that ABCD has an important role to play in the empowerment of communities but that in order to maximise that possibility, it needs to operate within a context where people reflect deeply on both the local manifestations of injustice and their structural causes.

Educational Action

We hold that Community Development is essentially an educational activity where people learn as a praxis, thinking and acting together to achieve individual and social outcomes.

We discuss this more fully in our chapter on Freirean education but let us briefly revisit some central aspects that are key to supporting empowerment.

First, all good practice starts with people's lived experience. It is tempting to start with a programme or an issue, particularly if the worker is being funded for a particular purpose but it is essential to resist that temptation and locate any intervention in how people see their world, what issues they think are important and the ways in which they want things to change. This ensures that issues are not being imposed on the community and increases the levels of commitment and ownership to the process that people will have.

Second, education in this sense is collective. Social epistemology (Goldman and Blanchard, 2018) uncovers the collective nature of meaning-making. We learn what we know and who we are through multiple social interactions. If people learn a sense of powerlessness and passivity through their lived, social experience, then empowerment must similarly be learned through a collective social experience. Paula Allman (2001) describes this as an abbreviate experience of transformed social relationships, an idea borrowed from Boggs (1978), by which he meant the embodiment of the particular forms of social relations, the process of decision-making, the emerging of alternative cultural understandings, and the creative human experience, all of which are the aim of a social movement. In other words, people whose daily experience has told them that they are powerless, ignored and reliant on others to help them, explain their lives and give them answers, are given an experience of how it feels to be listened to, have an influence over the decisions which affect them and how working with others increases their ability to effect change.

Third, education is always political, it either domesticate or liberates. It either shapes people to fit into the world as it is, or it supports them to question and challenge and re-make their world.

Finally, it supports empowerment. Authentic educational experiences should result in shifts in power: a stronger sense of personal power, greater interconnections between people resulting in greater influence over the decisions that affect their lives, and moving of power from the haves to the have-nots. If some of these features are not developing out of our work, we must question the extent to which we are engaged in empowering practice.

Transformative Action

All of the above must find its expression within an overarching theory of transformative action. We draw on the work of Gramsci to set that framework: first, the role of the worker as organic intellectual, a permanent persuader and organiser, working with people in praxis, constantly thinking and acting; second, acknowledging that hegemony will tend to maintain the status quo and will favour the powerful; third, that counter-hegemony is a meta-strategy – a strategy that recognises the interconnectedness of all systems; and fourth, that civil society is the sphere within which to develop a groundswell for change.

An Empowering Worker

Finally, empowering practice is carried out by empowering workers. At the end of the day it is not policies or strategies or agencies that make the difference, it is workers who have a clear set of values, a commitment to a more just world, the ability to analyse complex issues and contexts, and the skills to work with all kinds of people. The CLD Standards Council (2019) identifies some of the ways in which an empowering worker must practice. The worker must:

- analyse and understand power dynamics and decision-making processes
- use community action as a means to achieve change

- be inclusive and involve the wider community
- interact within and across communities
- participate in decision-making structures and processes
- campaign for change
- identify and manage community assets

Multidimensional Construct

In order to grasp both the power and the nuance of empowerment, we must recognise it as a multidimensional construct or an aggregate construct. Aggregate constructs are conceptualised as functions or composites of dimensions which form into more general concepts (Peterson, 2014) and so, in order to understand the overall concept of empowerment, we must disaggregate it into its component parts. Drawing on Drysdale and Purcell's (1999) typology, we could construe those component parts as being:

- Personal Empowerment
- Positive Action
- Development of Community Organisations
- Power Relationships and Participation

Personal Empowerment

Hussain (2010: 107) draws on the work of Zimmerman to highlight three interrelated components of personal empowerment: (1) an intrapersonal component. This is concerned with issues around self-efficacy, control, motivation and competence in a particular domain; (2) an interactional component. This is concerned with the development of awareness, skills and competence, which may be specific to one domain or transferable across various life domains; and (3) the behavioural component. This is concerned with involvement in more collective activities and organisations and the development of strategies and solutions that respond to life events and issues.

All of these components operate on the level of the individual and are concerned with their increase of human capital and personal efficacy. Whilst this personal dimension of empowerment is important, it lacks crucial collective dimensions. First, it fails to recognise the socially constructed nature of people's subjectivities. If we are, at least to some extent, the product of our social environment then our empowerment will come as a result of us exorcising changes within that social environment. Second, it fails to recognise the social and political power of collective action. People are disempowered not just because of personal traits or personal choices but because they are the products of a disempowering world, expressed through politics, economics and other forces within society. To only focus on the individual is to locate the blame for disempowerment within the individual. This victim-blaming takes the focus off the structural changes, that is, the changes in social power that need to come about to produce a more just world within which people are more empowered.

Positive Action

This component of empowerment is concerned with the development of a fair and just community. It builds on a collective view of humanity which is in keeping with the concept of Ubuntu, described by Michael Onyebuchi Eze (2010) as 'an affirmation of one's humanity through recognition of an "other" in his or her uniqueness and difference ... And if we belong to each other, we participate in our creations: we are because you are, and since you are, definitely I am.' As Starratt (1994) puts it, 'isolated individuals working for themselves are but half persons. One becomes whole when in relationship with another and many others' (1994: 195). In contrast to much of our neo-liberal inspired social policies and welfare provision, this goes beyond a concern with efficiency, where people are seen as a means to some larger purpose of productivity.

Within this area of work is the exploration of identity, including class, race, gender, culture, sexuality, etc. with a view to developing a deep understanding and confidence in one's own positionality, thereby becoming more accepting of the other.

An example of this type of practice can be found in the single-identity work carried out by some practitioners in Northern Ireland as part of the process of developing community cohesion in a context typified by sectarian divides. Church et al. (2002) describe single-identity work as 'engaging individuals singularly from within one community to discuss, address and potentially challenge the causes of conflict, with particular emphasis on skills and confidence-building measures. Single identity work most commonly, but not always, occurs when cross-community contact is untenable due to fear, suspicion or physical threat.' One particular strand of this approach is the 'respect for diversity'. In this, the stated intention is that the single identity work happens either as a precursor to, or in parallel with, cross-community work and that, in particular, has an important role to play in initial introductions and explorations, identifying common issues and building sustainability and supporting mutual confidence, honesty and respect (Church et al., 2004).

Additionally, the collective development of equal opportunities statements, policies and practices could also support this component of empowerment practice.

Development of Community Organisations

This component of empowerment is concerned with developing an Organised Community. Saul Alinsky (1971) said, 'All change means disorganization of the old and organization of the new'. Empowerment, with the central idea of power, is closely linked to ideas of organisation. People may well have developed their confidence, knowledge and skills and they may also have explored their identity and culture but if there is no structure within which to express that in the impact of that learning and development is greatly diluted.

Effective and legitimate organisation within communities is based on locally initiated and locally owned research processes. An excellent exemplar of good practice in this area is the work carried out by Slum Dwellers International (SDI). The enumeration processes which are one of their central rituals provides both a comprehensive understanding of the needs and resources within the community and produces information which provides the basis for negotiations and agreements with powerholders. The work of SDI is explored in more depth in Chapter 3.4.

Within empowered communities, activities of individual organisations respond to clearly researched community needs but, and perhaps more importantly, happen within the context of networks and alliances. This approach opens up the possibility of developing holistic ways of tackling community issues, ensures that resources are best used and the effort is not duplicated and, to return to an Alinsky-inspired view of the world, makes possible the development of people power. Collective action across multiple issues, involving multiple organisations, can form the basis of an organisation that can speak on behalf of the community, shape the agenda, shift the power and hold policymakers and decision-makers to account.

Power Relationships and Participation

This component of empowerment is concerned with developing an influential community. It comprises three interlinking elements: development of organisations that are open and accountable; the development of a political literacy; and the development of strategies of influence.

Community organisations and community groups, at their best, are experiments in new ways of being. They embody what Paula Allman describes as the abbreviated experience of transformed social relationships. It is here that we experiment with new ways of thinking and acting and relating to one another that are more humanised and more empowering. This is the indispensable foundation for making any claims on the wider instruments of society.

It could be said that we live in an age where the level of political literacy has decreased, where political debate has been reduced to slogans, and political decisions are made on the cult of the personality rather than a thorough analysis of the issues. An important role for community development is the reclaiming and remaking of spaces for discourse and debate. In this age of fake news it is all the more important that people have the opportunity to develop, not only an understanding of the issues but a means of critically investigating them. How and why decisions are made, who makes them and how they can be influenced are all central questions in processes of social change.

Finally, how do community workers support communities to influence change? If we accept that what happens locally is fundamentally influenced by what happens globally, then we will have to discover ways to influence both locally and globally. Through ease of transportation and the development of information technologies, making connections with like-minded individuals and organisations across the world has never been easier. This has the potential to make influence at the local and global level similarly easier. We have seen the beginnings of global resistance in the form of anti-globalisation and occupy movements. However, connecting at the global level is likely to be successful only if it is part of the overall process described above.

Critiques and Concerns

Having outlined possible dimensions for empowering practice and considering some of its transformational power at every level from the individual to the global, there still remain some fundamental concerns for community development practitioners. As a response to these, Inglis (1997) suggests we do away with the term 'empowerment' altogether and use rather the term 'emancipation', 'empowerment involves people developing capacities to act successfully within the existing system and structures of power, whilst emancipation concerns critically analysing, resisting and challenging structures of power' (1997: 4). Whilst I am unsure if emancipation is any less susceptible to misinterpretation or co-option, keeping a clear focus on analysis, resistance and challenge is essential to any process of understanding and application of the concept of empowerment. This constant defending and defining of what we mean is indeed part of the process of empowering practice since there always exists 'the capacity of "the dominant class" to recuperate concepts like empowerment, adapt them to social demands, and thereby transform them into so much "hollow, nominal, and empty terminology"' (Lankshear, 1993: 164).

Key Learning Points

- Empowerment is a contested term
- It is built on interconnected processes of individual and collective analysis and action

- Empowering workers must have clear values, analysis and highly developed skills
- Empowerment is a multidimensional concept that interweaves Personal Empowerment, Positive Action, Development of Community Organisations, and Power Relationships and Participation

Learning Tasks

Identify an organisation in your area that claims to do empowering work. Analyse it in terms of

- Personal Empowerment
- Positive Action
- Development of Community Organisations
- Power Relationships and Participation

Where are the gaps or areas that are weak?
How could you make their practice more empowering?

Key Reading

Christens, B.D. (2019) *Community Power and Empowerment*. New York: Oxford University Press.

References

Alinsky, S. (1971) *Rules for Radicals*. New York: Random House.

Allman, P. (2001) *Critical Education Against Global Capitalism: Karl Marx and Critical Revolutionary Education*. Westport, CT: Bergen and Garvey.

Beck, D. and Purcell, R. (2010) *Popular Education for Youth and Community Work*. Exeter: Learning Matters.

Boggs, C. (1978) 'Marxism, Prefigurative Communism, and the Problem of Workers' Control', *Radical America*, 11(6), 12(1).

Church, C., Visser, A., and Johnson, L. (2002) *Single Identity Work: An Approach to Conflict Resolution in Northern Ireland*. Derry/Londonderry: International Conflict Research.

Church, C., Visser, A., and Johnson, L.S. (2004) 'A Path to Peace or Persistence? The "Single Identity" Approach to Conflict Resolution in Northern Ireland', *Conflict Resolution Quarterly*, 21, 273–293.

CLD Standards Council (2019) 'Facilitate and Promote Community Empowerment'. Available at: http://cldstandardscouncil.org.uk/resources/the-competences/facilitate-and-promote-community-empowerment/.

Drysdale, J. and Purcell, R. (1999) 'Breaking the Culture of Silence: Groupwork and Community Development', *Groupwork*, 11(3), 70–87.

Elliot, A. (2014) 'Principles of Community Engagement', in *Royal Society of Edinburgh. Advice Paper on Community Empowerment and Capacity Building*, Appendix B, 26–28.

EU (2018) *Report from the Commission to the European Parliament, the Council, the European Economic and Social Committee and the Committee of the Regions: Mid-term Evaluation of the Erasmus+ Programme (2014–2020)*. Brussels: The European Union.

Eze, M.O. (2010) *The Politics of History in Contemporary Africa*. New York: Palgrave MacMillan, 223 pp.

Fay, B. (1987) *Critical Social Science: Liberation and its Limits* . Cambridge: Polity in association with Basil Blackwell.

Goldman, A. and Blanchard, T. (2018) 'Social Epistemology', in E.N. Zalta (ed.), *The Stanford Encyclopedia of Philosophy* (Summer edn). Available at: https://plato.stanford.edu/archives/sum2018/entries/epistemology-social/.

Hussain, S. (2010) 'Empowering Marginalised Children in Developing Countries through Participatory Design Processes', *CoDesign*, 6(2), 99–117.

IACD (2018) 'The Maynooth Declaration'. Available at: www.iacdglobal.org/2018/07/04/the-2018-maynooth-declaration-on-community-development/.

Inglis, T. (1997) 'Empowerment and Emancipation', *Adult Education Quarterly*, 48(1), 3–17.

Kretzmann, J. and McKnight, J. (1993) *Building Communities from the Inside Out: A Path Towards Finding and Mobilizing Community Assets*. Evanston, IL: ACTA.

Lankshear, C. (1993) 'Functional Literacy from a Freirean Point of View', in P. McLaren and P. Leonard (eds), *Paulo Freire: A Critical Encounter*. London: Routledge, 90–119.

Ledwith, M. and Springett, J. (2010) *Participatory Practice: Community-based Action for Transformative Change*. Bristol: The Policy Press.

Macharia, D. (ed.) (2005) *Paulo Freire: Handbook for Community Youth Workers*. Durban: Umtapo Centre.

MacLeod, M.A. and Emejulu, A. (2014) 'Neoliberalism with a Community Face? A Critical Analysis of Asset-Based Community Development in Scotland', *Journal of Community Practice*, 22(4), 430–450.

Mathie, A. and Cunningham, G. (2003) 'From Clients to Citizens: Asset-Based Community Development as a Strategy for Community-Driven Development', *Development in Practice*, 13(5), 474–486. Available at: www.jstor.org/stable/4029934.

Nel, H. (2018) 'A Comparison between the Asset-oriented and Needs-based Community Development Approaches in Terms of Systems Changes', *Practice*, 30(1), 33–52.

Peterson, A.N. (2014) 'Empowerment Theory: Clarifying the Nature of Higher-Order Multidimensional Constructs', *American Journal of Community Psychology*, 53: 96–108.

Starratt, R.J. (1994) *Building an Ethical School: A Practical Response to the Moral Crisis in Schools*. London and Washington, DC: Falmer Press.

Tomlinson, K. (2018) 'How can Yoga be a Tool for Empowerment?' Available at: www.ekhartyoga.com/articles/practice/how-can-yoga-be-a-tool-for-empowerment.

Zubair, S. (2016) 'Makeup: A Tool of Empowerment'. Available at: www.kettlemag.co.uk/makeup-a-tool-of-empowerment/.

4.3 Community Capacity Building and Human Capability

Introduction

As we have discussed before, one of the key objectives of community development is to help build personal and collective empowerment, for people to be able to take more control over their lives, fulfil themselves as a human being, and for communities to become collectively more powerful and effective in helping meet the needs of their members.

Community Capacity Building

Part of the process of empowerment is building the individual and collective capacity in terms of knowledge, skills and confidence. Community capacity-building programmes and activities may be one of the ways to achieve this. However, questions need to be posed about what the capacity-building programmes include (and exclude), who decided this and for what purpose. As we will see in the case studies, some capacity-building programmes are excellent – others less so.

Most community capacity-building programmes talk about a range of positive outcomes that may include: building economic prosperity, promoting social and political inclusion, environmental protection and sustainability, enhancing personal and community self-worth, personal and public health improvements, personal and community safety and security, and social cohesion. The problem is that all of these noble objectives are themselves contested terms. Not only can their meaning be in dispute but how are these objectives to be achieved? What is, and what is not, on the agenda and whose agenda is it?

The authors have experienced programmes where community development workers hold meetings in communities to tell the local people what their needs are and the training they need to go through. Sometimes, the training simply reflects the needs and priorities of the local government and instructs people on how to work in a predefined role as part of a top-down partnership arrangement. In this context personal empowerment is not on the agenda. Some commentators (for example, Craig, 2007) argue that despite the rhetoric, capacity-building programmes are often a means to control local organisations. Capacity building is a contested area where different ideas and agendas are at play.

The United Nations issued a definition of Community Capacity Building (UN, 1996). It stated that Community Capacity Building was:

> The process and means through which national governments and local communities develop the necessary skills and expertise to manage their environment and natural resources in a sustainable manner within their daily activities. The main concepts behind this concept are the following:
>
> - Strengthening people's capacity to achieve sustainable livelihoods;
> - A cross-sector multidisciplinary approach to planning and implementation;

- Emphasis on organisational and technological change and innovation;
- Placed emphasis on the need to build social capital through experimentation and learning; and
- Prioritised developing the skills and performance of both individuals and institutions.

The UN statement is a broad definition. The following statement from Learning Connections in the UK, sees capacity building as development work that strengthens 'the ability of community organisations and groups to build their structures, systems, people and skills so that they are better able to define and achieve their objectives and engage in consultation and planning, manage community projects and take part in partnerships and community enterprises'. The second part of the statement is telling as it identifies the purpose of the work to be about engaging in partnerships. Independent activity or oppositional campaigning is not on the agenda.

Craig, in his 2007 study of capacity building, concludes that it is often

- No different from Community Development
- A catch-all for top-down initiatives
- A mechanism for incorporation

and that it

- Ignores local leaders and leadership development

He wrote,

> the experience of many communities [in the UK] is that 'community capacity-building' programmes [with a myriad of titles], have been imposed on them; with perceived needs, desired outcomes and preferred methods part of the package which they have not had the opportunity to identify, develop or agree ... the 'community' (often not self-defined) is exhorted to play its part in an environment where inequalities of resources, power, information and status are not even acknowledged, never mind addressed.

Human Capability

In contrast to the often-problematic training approach of capacity building stands the concept of human capability. The capability approach was developed initially by Amartya Sen (1985) as a revision to traditional welfare economics. The core idea is to make clear how to enable people to achieve their potential capability as a person. This is realised in part by helping build the functional capacity of a person, and second, creating what Sen terms 'opportunity freedom', that is, people being able to make choices that will improve their quality of life. In this sense, personal empowerment and developing human capability are intrinsically linked.

Sen's ideas have been influential in the development community. For example, the Human Development Index created by the United Nations Development Programme is based on the idea of human capability. The index measures the level of a country's development according to a range of indicators such as: people being well fed; having access to shelter; being physically and mentally healthy; having work and an income; receiving an education; being able to freely vote; and to participate in community life. If these factors are not in place then people will be constrained in their ability to fully develop themselves and realise their human potential.

The question here is, what in practical terms do we need to do in order for human potential to be maximised? Martha Nussbaum (2000) has addressed this question and identified ten capabilities that should be the focus of development programmes.

1. **Life** – being able to live to the end of one's natural life
2. **Bodily Health** – enjoying good health, an adequate diet, having adequate shelter
3. **Bodily Integrity** – having freedom of movement, freedom from physical assault, choice over sexual activity and reproduction
4. **Senses, Imagination, and Thought** – having access to education, religious freedom, cultural freedom
5. **Emotions** – loving and caring without fear or anxiety
6. **Practical Reason** – thinking through and taking control of one's life
7. **Affiliation**
    (a) recognising and showing concern for others
    (b) having the social bases of self-respect and non-humiliation. This entails provisions of non-discrimination on the basis of race, gender, sexual orientation, ethnicity, caste, religion, national origin and species
8. **Other Species** – having concern for and in relation to animals, plants, etc.
9. **Play** – Being able to laugh, to play, to enjoy recreational activities
10. **Control over one's Environment**

On the face of it, these do appear to be a set of challenging objectives. On the other hand, if such objectives are not included, then how far is the proposed programme of work actually developmental? It is, of course, possible to build specific objectives into any development programme, which help people to move in these directions. Maximising human capability is a lifelong task for all of us.

The idea of human capability is important as it provides a focus and ambition for community-based development programmes. It is also useful to note the similarities between Nussbaum's criteria and the UN Human Rights agenda, which we have already discussed as being fundamental in underpinning community development practice for social change. You may also have noticed that the Freire/Popular Education approach is also centrally concerned with the development of personal/collective empowerment through helping people to become 'fully human'.

Key Learning Points

Designed and implemented properly community capacity building can be very useful in developing skills and knowledge for a range of developmental tasks. However, many such programmes are heavily compromised by the top-down and banked approach adopted by agencies. This can severely limit the personal development potential of the programme. In the worst cases capacity-building programmes can simply incorporate local people into the agencies and government agendas, and in doing so disempower, rather than empower, local communities.

The human capability approach needs to be applied through creating practical and achievable objectives in development programmes. Doing so can bring real benefits in terms of human growth and empowerment. It is important to note though, that human capabilities are twofold; it is about personal growth, and the social change required to create the freedom for personal development to take place.

Learning Tasks

Review a community development programme. It may be one you are engaged in either as a worker or as a participant, o'r a programme that you research.

- Does the programme include specific objectives that help promote any of Nussbaum's criteria?
- If not, why is that?
- If it does, how effective do you think these objectives will be, and can they be improved?

Key Reading

On capacity-building programmes read the excellent overview by Gary Craig:

Craig, G. (2007) 'Community Capacity Building: Something Old, Something New?', *Critical Social Policy*, 27(3).

For human capability see Martha Nussbaum's text:

Nussbaum, M. (2000) *Women and Human Development: The Capabilities Approach*. Cambridge and New York: Cambridge University Press.

For further information about the Human Development Index and the UN assessment of various countries' development, see: http://hdr.undp.org/en/2016-report.

References

Craig, G. (2007) 'Community Capacity Building: Something Old, Something New?', *Critical Social Policy*, 27(3).

Nussbaum, M. (2000) *Women and Human Development: The Capabilities Approach*. Cambridge and New York: Cambridge University Press.

Sen, A. (1985) *Commodities and Capabilities*. Amsterdam: North-Holland.

UN (1996) *Community Capacity-building*. New York: UN Commission on Sustainable Development.

4.4   Building Community Resilience

Introduction

In this chapter we will consider the idea of resilience, which has taken a place of prominence in discussion and policy around community development in recent years, including some of the controversies that surround it. We will then consider how community resilience might be strengthened and, finally, we will discuss the concept of resourcefulness as a way of strengthening the concept and dealing with some of the concerns that are raised in current debates.

Community Resilience is a term that is used in a variety of ways within a broad range of social policy contexts. For example, Wales Council for Voluntary Action discuss the usefulness of thinking in terms of resilient communities, which focuses on how communities marshal their strengths and assets to respond to a shock or crisis but also stress the need for models which consider how the community can adapt and flourish through that change, rather than merely surviving it (Lloyd Jones, 2017). Glasgow Council on Alcohol (2018) describe resilient communities in their terms as ones where attitudes to drug and alcohol misuse are challenged and knowledge and skills are increased to enable individuals to make safer choices. Newport Council (2018) state that they support the creation of resilient communities by offering individuals advice and support on looking for employment, training, family or housing support, learning English, access to IT, volunteering opportunities and more. Finally, the UK Government (2014) put forward a number of measures to become more resilient by using local resources and knowledge to help them during an emergency in a way that complements the local emergency services. Since the spread of meanings is so wide, we now go on to think about some of the emergent strands of thinking and tensions surrounding the idea.

Resilience theory emerged in the context of a proliferation of literature under the broad heading of the 'new ecology' from the late 1960s through the 1970s (Holiday Nelson, 2014). Lerch (2017) discusses resilience as the ability of a system to cope with short-term disruptions and adapt to long-term changes without losing its essential character. This is especially important at times of crisis – environmental, energy, economic – that threaten to overwhelm the resilience of the systems we care about, particularly at the local level. Although initially focused on community responses to environmental disaster, the term has broadened out to encompass much more. Talk of resilience is now widespread in debates about how communities of place can deal with multiple, increasingly unpredictable and complex, social, economic and environmental challenges. Two main positions are emerging in discussions about resilience: (1) it is seen as the ability of a community to 'bounce back' (to normal) from adversity, shock or disaster, and (2) as the ability to innovate, transform and 'bounce forward', in response to changed conditions (Revell and Dinnie, 2018).

Drawing on the first view, resilience is defined by the Scottish Government (2012) as 'the capacity of an individual, community or system to adapt in order to sustain an acceptable level of function, structure and identity'; the focus of this definition is to maintain the continuity of a way of life or return to relative normality after any disruptive event.

However, community resilience is not necessarily about maintaining the current characteristics or the ability to 'bounce back' and 'stay the same'. Rather, the concept often suggests systemic change, adaptation and proactivity in relation to stresses and challenges. Its main feature is adaptive capacity represented through a continuous process that enables a community to thrive, despite ongoing change (Steiner et al., 2018). The Canadian Centre for Community Renewal (2000) defines a resilient community as 'one that takes intentional action to enhance the personal and collective capacity of its citizens and institutions to respond to and influence the course of social and economic change' (2000: 9). They go on to describe the fundamental behaviours of resilient communities:

- 'They take a multifunctional approach to create a sustainable (economically ecologically politically and socially) development system within the community through strategic planning, or other efforts.
- They maximize the use of a limited time and resources in those areas that will give you the greatest overall benefits.
- They develop plans that merge social and economic goals and build local capacity and are able to mobilize key sectors of the community around priorities.
- They focus their energies and mobilize internal assets, both financial and human, while also leveraging outside resources to achieve their goals.
- They have established a critical mass of cooperating organizations, through which locally based initiatives are implemented, and evaluated.'

(Canadian Centre for Community Renewal, 2000)

Others, however, point to more sinister uses of the concept of resilience. Diprose (2014) notes that the rise of discourse around residence coincided with a sustained austerity drive from government and suggests that it has been deployed as an inducement to putting up with precarity and inequality and accepting the deferral of demands for change, and as a means of relocating responsibility – those who manufacture and profit from crises are being let off the hook, whilst the burden of risk management falls disproportionately elsewhere. Resilience policies represent a failure of political will to offer substantive change for marginalised communities. Take, for instance, the suggestion that fuel-poor households should simply wrap up warm: it disregards the system that is making people unwell.

She, however, also recognises that for some, resilience connotes communitarian ideals such as autonomy from the state, skills sharing and mutual care and may indeed be the difference between a fateful or fatalistic response to social change, between hope and hopelessness.

Other commentators claim that resilience theory is being co-opted by those whose interests lie in perpetuating the neo-liberal discourses and governance that privilege existing power relations and contribute to the maintenance of the current, dominant capitalist system (Cretney and Bond, 2014). It has further been noted that resilience discourses are being widely used as a tool to implement neo-liberal ideological projects following a crisis. Broadly speaking, these projects are used to justify and motivate actions that increase inequality and disadvantage marginalised communities through the use of a market-driven rationale. In this context, disasters are seen as opportunities for furthering projects that selectively restructure urban space and social services (Cretney and Bond,

2014). An example of this process and how it is resisted by an organised and resilient community is documented in Wade Rathke's (2014) excellent book *Battle for the Ninth Ward*.

Ways to Strengthen Community Resilience

Lerch (2017) identifies six foundations that could provide a framework within which to develop resilience within communities:

People

The power to envision the future of the community and build its resilience resides with community members.

Systems Thinking

Systems thinking is essential for understanding the complex, interrelated crises now unfolding and what those crises mean for our similarly complex communities.

Adaptability

A community that adapts to change is resilient. But because communities and the challenges we face are dynamic, adaptation is an ongoing process.

Transformability

Some challenges are so big that it is not possible for the community to simply adapt; fundamental, transformative changes may be necessary.

Sustainability

Community resilience is not sustainable if it serves only us, and only now; it needs to work for other communities, future generations, and the ecosystems on which we all depend.

Courage

As individuals and as a community, we need courage to confront challenging issues and take responsibility for our collective future.

Concept of Resourcefulness

MacKinnon and Driscoll Derickson (2012) claim that current conceptions of resilience privilege established social structures, which are often shaped by unequal power relations and injustice, and therefore offer the term 'Resourcefulness' as one which is more appropriate. In addition to what we have discussed above, a resourceful community would problematise both the uneven distribution of material resources and the associated inability of disadvantaged groups and communities to access the levers of social change. They would have the capacity to engage in genuinely deliberative democratic dialogue to develop contestable alternative agendas and work in ways that meaningfully challenge existing power relations. The forms of learning and mobilisation arising from that deliberation would be based upon local priorities and needs as identified and developed by community activists and residents. In addition to capacities built at the community level, they would be outward-looking, emphasising the need to foster and maintain relational links across space to address local issues in the light of systemic challenges, and the need for alliances between community groups and broader social movements.

Resourcefulness honours indigenous and 'folk' knowledge. Alternative and shared ways of knowing generated by experiences, practices and perceptions are important spaces of knowledge production about the world. Indigenous and 'folk' knowledge produces critical 'myths' from which resourceful communities may draw explanatory frameworks that weave together normative and observational knowledge and serve as the guiding framework for shared visions.

Key Learning Points

- Resilient communities can adapt and flourish through change, rather than merely survive it
- The most progressive definitions of resilience suggest systemic change, adaptation and proactivity in relation to stresses and challenges
- The concept is criticised as a way of masking the rollback of the state and justifying inequality
- Resourcefulness draws on the ideas of resilience but sees them in the context of a structural analysis of inequality

Learning Tasks

Govan, Glasgow (UK), with whom we collaborated, mobilised the myth of past Gaelic Highlander life, and the folk ways and knowledges that emerged from that mythology, as a grounding for their alternative vision of social relations that ultimately cultivate resourcefulness.

- What are the stories that we tell ourselves about our identity, history and place in the world in order to develop and strengthen resilience and resourcefulness?

Key Reading

Canadian Centre for Community Renewal (2000) *The Community Resilience Manual. A Resource for Rural Recovery and Renewal*. Port Alberni, Canada: Centre for Community Enterprise.

Diprose, K. (2014) 'Resilience is Futile: The Cultivation of Resilience is not an Answer to Austerity and Poverty', *Soundings: A Journal of Politics and Culture*, 58, 44–56. Retrieved 29 March 2019, from Project MUSE database.

References

Canadian Centre for Community Renewal (2000) *The Community Resilience Manual. A Resource for Rural Recovery and Renewal*. Port Alberni, Canada: Centre for Community Enterprise.

Cretney, R. and Bond, S. (2014) '"Bouncing Back" to Capitalism? Grass-Roots Autonomous Activism in Shaping Discourses of Resilience and Transformation Following Disaster', *Resilience*, 2(1), 18–31, doi: 10.1080/21693293.2013.872449.

Diprose, K. (2014) 'Resilience is Futile: The Cultivation of Resilience is not an Answer to Austerity and Poverty', *Soundings: A Journal of Politics and Culture* 58, 44–56. Retrieved 29 March 2019, from Project MUSE database.

Glasgow Council on Alcohol (2018) 'Resilient Communities'. Available at: www.glasgow councilonalcohol.org/resilient-communities/.

Holiday Nelson, S. (2014) 'Resilience and the Neoliberal Counter-revolution: From Ecologies of Control to Production of the Common', *Resilience*, 2(1), 1–17, doi: 10.1080/21693293. 2014.872456.

Lerch, D. (ed.) (2017) *The Community Resilience Reader: Essential Resources for an Era of Upheaval*. Washington, DC: Island Press.

Lloyd Jones, S. (2017) 'Resilient and Empowered Communities: A Discussion Paper', Wales Council for Voluntary Action, Cardiff.

MacKinnon, D. and Driscoll Derickson, K. (2012) 'From Resilience to Resourcefulness: A Critique of Resilience Policy and Activism', *Progress in Human Geography*, 37(2), 253–270.

Newport Council (2018) 'Resilient Communities'. Available at: www.newport.gov.uk/en/About-Newport/Resilient-communities.aspx.

Rathke, W. (2011) *Battle for the Ninth Ward: ACORN, Rebuilding New Orleans and the Lessons of Disaster*. New Orleans, LA: Social Policy Press.

Revell, P. and Dinnie, E. (2018) 'Community Resilience and Narratives of Community Empowerment in Scotland', *Community Development Journal*, bsy038. Available at: https://doi.org/10.1093/cdj/bsy038.

Scottish Government (2012) *Preparing Scotland: Resilience Guidance*. Edinburgh: Scottish Government.

Steiner, A., Woolvin, M., and Skerratt, S. (2018) 'Measuring Community Resilience: Developing and Applying a "Hybrid Evaluation" Approach', *Community Development Journal*, 53(1, January), 99–118. Available at: https://doi.org/10.1093/cdj/bsw017.

UK Government (2014) 'Resilience in Society: Infrastructure, Communities and Businesses'. London: UK Government. Available at: www.gov.uk/guidance/resilience-in-society-infrastructure-communities-and-businesses.

4.5   Leadership in the Community

Introduction

It is sad but true, that much community activity fails. It fails for many reasons, but these include the inability to organise effectively, to develop the skills and knowledge necessary for the tasks at hand, to embrace creativity and flexibility, and to own the problem and see the community at least as the partial solution to the problem.

One of the critical factors in building success and avoiding failure is effective leadership. The question of leadership is a contentious issue within community development. Interestingly, this debate on the importance and nature of leadership appears to be country/culture based. In the USA there are extensive routes to develop leadership from youth programmes through community programmes, and support for leadership development within community organisations themselves. In the UK, very little of this training and support infrastructure exists. In fact, in some quarter's leadership is seen as anti-democratic, something for the external world but not for community groups. The community training that is available is, as we have discussed, often focused on capacity building, and based around local people fulfilling a role in local government-run partnership structures. In this setting, local people are defined as representatives not leaders. Why would you need strong leaders of independent community organisations when your pre-defined role is to sit on a partnership sub-committee?

In the UK, many local leaders themselves place a low value on training. One CEO of a voluntary organisation that supported a range of community organisations told the authors that 'leadership cannot be taught, you either have it or you don't!' This attitude is usually the result of their poor experience of schooling and previous community-based courses. Much of the training that is offered is often boring and irrelevant. How often is it said that the best part of the training course was the informal conversation in the coffee breaks?!

It is naïve to think that by not having formal leadership positions in an organisation, or by simply saying we do not believe in leadership, that there are no leaders. Within any group setting there will be people who exert more influence than others, who are deferred to by some (or all) of the group membership. In effect, *informal leadership* fills the vacuum where there is no *formal leadership*. Informal leaders can rise through talent, force of personality, manipulation, bullying or simply seizing the position in a demoralised and under-functioning organisation. This is less democratic and transparent than actually having formal elected leadership positions in the organisation.

To be clear, leadership in the community context is not about an individual's role, status, and personal power. Rather, it is about ensuring that the organisation is focused, effective and moves forward, building the capacity of its members to act. Leadership can be through an elected individual or a collective group. It needs to be democratic and accountable. One of the key roles of a leader is to develop the leadership potential of other people. It is also important to say again that the community development worker is not the leader, but that one of their key roles is to help develop community leadership within organisations and to support leaders in their activities.

Purcell (2005) explores the characteristics of good leadership. He identifies the following factors.

Self-discipline: This is manifested through a sense of purpose and a commitment to meeting the needs of the community, owning personal actions and decisions, constantly working to improve the organisations' collective knowledge and learning from experience, working co-operatively with others, and always trying to lead by example.

Being effective: The fundamental purpose of working in the community is to promote personal and collective change. We know that to achieve change, we need effective planning. This, in turn, is based upon acquiring and assessing accurate information. Taking action follows the planning stage. We can contrast this with what can be termed 'mindless activism' where people are very busy rushing from one meeting to the next, but without any sense of purpose or objective. Effectiveness is based on the quality and purpose of your action not the quantity of activity.

Taking your opportunities: Speed, flexibility and innovation are the keys to success. Most organisations that the community campaigns against are large, bureaucratic and slow. The community's advantage is their small size and the potential to respond quickly to opportunities. Do not throw this away by waiting for the next monthly meeting to make a decision.

Helping people to commit themselves to the organisation: It is important to know who supports you and who does not (this takes us back to effective asset mapping). People and organisations are either committed to your side or they are not. There should be no grey areas here. People are motivated by a number of factors: the importance of the issue (this depends on how you present it); the expectation that you will win; personal interest (or family, community, career); enjoyment and fun.

Being creative: When campaigning, or simply organising a community event, always think and act creatively. Nothing fails more quickly than doing the same old things in predictable ways. Creativity does not require genius. It is based on learning from experience, doing simple things better, trying new ideas and approaches and aiming to improve all the time.

Training for action: When reviewing case studies of community organisations, it is astounding to see how local people are expected to manage resources, develop services, undertake campaigns and constantly put themselves in challenging situations with little or no preparation. It is to the credit of community leaders that they constantly subject themselves to these pressures with little real support. However, without adequate preparation it is hardly surprising that so much community activity is unproductive.

Creating surprise: Sun Tzu in *The Art of War* said '*what does it matter if the enemy has greater resources? If I control the situation, he cannot use them*' (emphasis added). In essence, this sums up effective organisation; analyse the situation, see the opportunity, plan for action, respond with the unexpected, do it well.

Power: leadership is also about the effective (and appropriate) use of power both within the organisation and by the organisation. It is helpful to re-read Chapter 4.2 Promoting Empowerment.

Let's further unpack what we mean by collective leadership. There is a useful quote from Amical Cabral who said, '*to lead collectively is not and cannot be, as some suppose, to give all and everyone the right to uncontrolled views and initiatives, to create disorders, empty arguments, a passion for meetings without results*' (quoted in Hope and Timmel, 1984, emphasis added). Cabral went on to say '*collective leadership must strengthen the leadership capability of all and create specific circumstances where full use is made of all members ... To lead collectively, in a group, is to*:

- Study questions jointly
- Find the best solutions
- Take decisions jointly
- Benefit from the experience and intelligence of each person
- Create the opportunities for thinking and action
- Demand that people take responsibility within their competence
- Require that people take initiative
- Co-ordinate the thoughts and actions of those within the group.'

(quoted in Hope and Timmel, 1984, emphasis added)

Hope and Timmel develop this theme and identify three types of leadership: authoritarian, consultative and enabling. This overlaps with the definition of community group types we discuss below in the section on group-work (Chapter 4.6). Often there is a symbiotic relationship between the style of leadership influencing the nature of a group – as well as the nature of the group producing a similar style of leadership.

> **Authoritarian leadership** therefore, is where the leader takes the key (or in some cases all) decisions and presents it to the group. Discussion may be invited but only in the knowledge that the decision will stand regardless of what is said.
> **Consultative leadership** is based on the group discussing options and recommending courses of action. However, the leader has the final say on what is to be done.
> In community development only **enabling leadership** is acceptable where the group itself has the power to make the final decision. Here the role of the leadership is to facilitate the discussion and ensure that an informed decision is reached.

We can also learn from business models, in particular the VCM leadership model. This sees leadership as having three essential components: *vision*, *commitment* and *management skills*. Ideally, leaders or a collective leadership will have a balance of all three components. The benefits of collective leadership are that it is more likely to find these three skills within a group than in any single individual.

Another useful concept in leadership is the idea of authenticity (Northouse, 2015). This style of leadership is particularly relevant for community organisations. An authentic leader is one who is trusted by members of the organisation, as well as those external to it. It involves personal honesty, as well as actions that reflect a value base, and a commitment to live by those values.

We all have imperfections, so this discussion is in some sense aspirational rather than an expectation of perfection. However, if community development is about social change to make the world a better place, then is it unreasonable to ask people who take leadership positions to try and live up to the values of community development?

Key Learning Points

In this section we have discussed how:

- Good leadership is essential for effective community development to take place
- The nature of the leadership will impact on the nature of the community organisation, and vice versa
- The role of the community development worker is to support and help develop community leaders
- The nature of community leadership needs to reflect the principles and values of community development
- Leaders in community organisations have an essential role in focusing the work of the organisation, setting an example of good practice, supporting group members and promoting leadership potential in others

Learning Tasks

Identify a community-based organisation of your own choice.
    Examine how leadership operates within that organisation. In particular:

- Who is/are the leader/s?
- How were they selected?
- What is their official role, and what else do they do?
- What is the leadership model, does it reflect the values and principles of community development?
- Is it authentic leadership?
- How far are other people supported and encouraged to develop their leadership potential?
- How could leadership in this organisation be improved?

Key Reading

The Community Tool Box has online materials, including on leadership. See: http://ctb.ku.edu/en/table-of-contents/leadership/leadership-functions/become-community-leader/main.
To explore in fuller detail the various conceptualisations and current research around leadership, see: Northouse, P.G. (2015) *Leadership: Theory and Practice*. London: Sage.

References

Hope, A. and Timmel, S. (1984) *Training for Transformation Vols 1–3*. London: ITDG Publishing.
Northouse, P.G. (2015) *Leadership: Theory and Practice*. London: Sage.
Purcell, R. (2005) *Working in the Community: Perspectives for Change*. Morrisville, NC: Lulu Press.
Sun Tzu, 'The Art of War'. Available at: www.sonshi.com.

4.6   Working with Groups

Introduction

In this chapter we discuss why people join groups, the various styles of working that groups might adopt, the process and life cycle of groups and the learning needs of groups.

The first question though, given the increasingly individualised nature of developed societies, is why have community groups at all? After all we are continually encouraged to 'be all we can be' and make the most of individual talents.

There are many reasons why people join community groups. For example, Henderson and Thomas (2001) suggest it may be:

- to protect their personal and/or family interests
- for social and cultural activities and support
- to improve the quality of life within their community
- to preserve or create community assets
- to examine opportunities or repel threats whether real or perceived

It may sound obvious, but success in working with community groups comes from responding to the above needs. This is why, as we have stressed, successful community development work comes from putting peoples expressed needs and desires at the heart of what we do. If we simply organise around an agency or our own agenda it will be hard to build and sustain a group. The nature of a community group is also important.

As with leadership, there are three types of groups, generally described as:

- Authoritarian
- Consultative
- Enabling

Purcell (2005) summarises the nature of these groups.

First, **Authoritarian** groups tend to have a fixed dominant leadership based around an individual and may include family members or a small clique of supporters. Often these groups have been in existence for many years and the current leadership may see themselves both as the embodiment of the group's history and the arbiter of what should happen. Group members are usually told what to do and little open discussion and sharing of ideas and feelings take place. If the leadership is competent then authoritarian groups can be effective in delivering routine tasks. However, the rigid nature of these groups inhibits personal and collective development.

Purcell suggests that **Consultative** groups appear more open and may have free-flowing debates. Consequently, the means of decision-making may appear more accountable and open than authoritarian groups. However, the leadership in such groups may still dominate decision-making and what happens. These groups may appear friendlier and can be effective in recruiting members.

Finally, **Enabling** groups, in contrast, use their leadership to create an environment where open and supportive discussion can take place. This approach is more democratic, but has the danger of the group drifting into conflict over decision-making or simply becoming indecisive and ineffective. Effective leadership is required to facilitate the proper working of these groups. Purcell argues that the group leadership needs to:

- make all members feel they are accepted and valued by the rest of the group
- create an environment where ideas, concerns and feelings (both positive and negative, happy and sad) can be openly shared
- work productively to identify needs, plan action and learn the lessons from experience without recrimination and egotism

An important consideration here is the formal structure of the group. In the UK, for example, many community groups operate on a formal structure of office bearers (chair, secretary, treasurer, etc.) being elected at an annual meeting and in accordance with a formal written constitution. Sometimes this is the way to go. However, this arrangement can be more formal than necessary and constrain rather than enable the working and development of a group. Community groups can be run as a collective, or in a more open and fluid way. It all depends on what you are trying to do, and the preference of local people.

The Life Cycle of Groups

Many community groups are created to meet a specific need (for example, to deal with road safety issues), or to represent members of the community over a broad range of concerns as well as provide a mechanism for improving social activities (for example, community associations). A single-issue group may dissolve itself once the issue has been resolved, it may refocus its activities and take on new challenges, or it may just carry on without any real focus, with its members slowly drifting away. The challenge for a broader representative organisation is to keep itself dynamic and relevant, rather than repeat itself year by year.

Because community groups have an inherent social function, and for many people become the focus of their social life, there is often a desire to keep organisations going when the group's purpose and energy has gone. Community development workers can also try to maintain a community group whose effective life has come to an end. Agencies and workers themselves can often view the ending of a group as a failure, rather than the natural conclusion to a group's life cycle.

Purcell comments that 'it is important to see a community group as a living entity. They are born, grow, may encounter life-threatening crises, have high points and low points. Eventually they die, hopefully after a successful life that can be acknowledged and celebrated. They may also be reborn as a new group.'

Tuckman (1965) (see also Benjamin et al., 1997) created a team development model that explores the development process of a group, through the stages of 'Forming', 'Storming', 'Norming' and 'Performing'. The model was later elaborated to include 'Mourning' and' Reforming' stages. As all groups go through a variation of this model it is useful to consider Tuckman's work for community-based groups.

Tuckman identifies the first stage as the **forming** stage, where people are coming together for the first time. People are getting to know each other and are making decisions about whether they wish to be involved in this collective activity. There will be initial conversations exploring what the nature and purpose of the group might be, and beginning to determine which objectives are most important. The key role for the community development worker here is to help the new group members set an open, inclusive and reflective tone to the group.

The second **storming** stage unusually comes soon after the formation of a group. This is where initial tensions are acted out, the nature of the group becomes set and decisions made, such as who holds the power in the group (both formally and informally), who are the emerging leaders within the group, how will the group be organised, what is the work programme? There may be conflict around gender issues and roles, age differences, race, religion and individual attitudes, for example lone parents or people from a particular part of the community. It is important to acknowledge that storming happens and the role for the community development worker is to assist people through it, with as little interpersonal and group damage as possible. However, it is a mistake to try and avoid storming. The tensions that come out at this stage are real. If they are not dealt with openly and effectively then they fester below the surface and break out later in more destructive forms.

The third stage is **norming**, and this is where the group develops a sense of togetherness at both personal and organisation levels. Purcell points out that it is important that the group achieves something at this stage otherwise the positive feelings can quickly turn to disappointment. It does not matter what is achieved – a small gain is often all that is required. It is the symbolic message that we can do things together that is important. Understandably, group members and community development workers often make the mistake of going straight away for the big (and challenging) objective. Attempting the very difficult at too early a stage before the group has the knowledge, skills, and resilience to succeed will only undermine (sometimes with dire consequences) the development of the group. The group needs an initial success of some kind at the norming stage to give it the confidence to tackle the difficult tasks.

The next stage is **performing**, where the real work of the group is done. To perform, the group needs experience, resilience, clarity of purpose and a clear sense of self-belief and trust in each other. They will only have this if the early stages of group development have been handled effectively. It is important to remember that all groups will encounter one or more crises during their life cycle. A strong and well-founded group will survive these crises. A group that never really resolved the storming issues can easily collapse under the pressure of a crisis.

Eventually, all groups will come to the end of their natural life cycle. At this point the group can be refocused or restructured to new ends (the **reforming** of the group). Alternatively, the group can enter the **mourning** stage. Success, as we have said before, needs to be celebrated. A thriving community group should be fun, not just hard work and misery. Workers need to know when a group is coming towards the end of its natural life and to help group members consider if this is the time for a decent burial. A wake that celebrates the past history of the group, its success, and brings people back together is critical for sustaining community activity.

The Learning Needs of Groups and Learning Circles

Purcell points out that community groups are essentially a learning environment. Community groups, if they are to function effectively, have an increasing need to acquire new knowledge and learn new skills both on an individual and a collective basis. Also, if we are committed to promoting personal and collective empowerment as a key outcome of community development, then community groups are the place where much of this knowledge, skills, experience and determination for change take place.

Often, this learning occurs invisibly, and people just pick up information and learn how to do things on a day-to-day, trial and error basis. This approach is not good enough, and community development workers need to be more conscious and active in facilitating the learning experience. How learning in groups happens is important because, as Freire pointed out, education can be either a tool of domestication or liberation. It all depends on what is learned and how it is learned. The participatory approach to learning can take various forms, and Purcell suggests that one common and successful method is through the use of learning circles.

At their core, learning circles are simply about people sitting down together sharing knowledge and experience, and collectively working to understand some aspect of life in more depth. This is a practice that is found in many cultures, for example the 'wisdom circles' of native councils of elders. Learning circles also reflect the basic principles and practices of adult learning, being flexible and participatory, with the worker facilitating the process rather than undertaking the role of teacher/expert.

In many ways learning circles are like the Freirean groups that we have discussed elsewhere. The educational process and learning environment are indeed similar. The main difference being that learning circles are less dependent upon the generative theme which is central to the Freirean approach, and more focused on immediate tasks, issues that need to be explored, and the action to be taken.

Critical Questions for Community Workers

Community development workers face a number of personal and practice issues that need to be understood for effective group work. This can be explored through the COMPASS model developed by Kelly and Sewell (1989). The model raises questions whether we are *inside or outside of the group process* and if we are acting on our *own or on the people's agenda*.

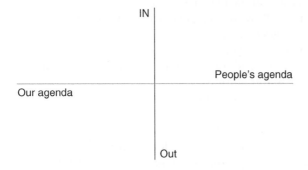

Figure 4.1

The *In/Out* continuum (Figure 4.1) explores the degree of trust granted to the community worker by the community group. We need to recognise that, due to their education and training, community development workers are different in many social and cultural ways from the members of the communities within which they work. This is true even of those who were born, and continue to live, in those communities. Workers can become 'honorary' insiders through being open, honest, transparent, reliable and committed. It is a position that has to be earned through work on the ground. Workers have to accept that they need to achieve this position with local groups and they should chart and reflect on their progress to this end. With any group, the worker should ask where they sit on this continuum, where do they want to be, how do they get to that position?

The other axis, *Our agenda/People's agenda*, confronts the issues we have explored above about the possible conflict between social planning agendas and the identified needs of local people. It can also concern debates over value positions between the worker and the group and questions over the formal and informal power of the community worker. Seldom does a worker completely locate themselves on the people's agenda side of the continuum. It is important though, that the worker identifies where they are on this continuum; is it where they wish to be, where does their employer want them to be, where does the group think they are? Whatever the answers to these questions, what is important is the transparency with which the worker conducts him or herself, and the way in which potential conflict of agendas are openly discussed and dealt with.

It can be helpful for workers to regularly map themselves out on these criteria for each of the groups they work with.

Working successfully with community groups is fundamental to achieving the goals of community development. It is a complex and multifaceted undertaking. To summarise this endeavour, it is helpful to refer to this checklist for effective practice by Drysdale and Purcell (1999, 2000).

Positive practice: *these are things we must do*
- Really listen to what is being said, instead of being preoccupied on what we are going to do next
- Stay the course and be seen to be impartial
- Draw out the quieter group members
- Offer personal support when required – either in the group or outside it
- Be explicit about the values and principles of community development
- Challenge discrimination within the group
- Use open questions to encourage discussion
- Help to keep the group focused on the key tasks and issues
- Help the group to make, and follow through, democratic decisions

Negative practice: *these are things we must avoid*
- Letting the group treat you as the expert
- Letting the group 'dump' routine work on you, for example minute-taking
- Backing out from asking the hard questions
- Ignoring conflict rather than exploring and trying to resolve issues
- Having a hidden agenda
- Not being open about your employer's agenda
- Not being honest when you don't know, or can't do, something

Effectiveness of groups: *key questions for both the community development worker and group members to collectively work on*
- Does the group share common objectives?
- How far is the group involved in, and committed to, achieving these objectives?
- How well does the group work together?
- How well does the group make decisions?
- How well does the group support new members?
- How well does the group care for its members?
- How does the group deal with internal conflict?

- Does the group celebrate success?
- Does the group analyse failure?

Practical issues for groups: *things to be solved*
- Does the group meet at a convenient place and time for everyone?
- Can transport to and from the meeting be improved?
- Is the location and travel safe for everyone?
- Are roles equally shared between men and women, young and old, etc.?
- Are the meetings fun?
- At the end of a meeting does the group feel it has made progress?
- How does the group advertise its activities – and does this work?

Key Learning Points

In this chapter we have explored the following:

- People join community groups to meet specific and identified personal, family and community needs
- Community groups take various forms, not all of which are enabling and empowering
- Groups have their own life cycle
- Groups go through stages of 'Forming', 'Storming', 'Norming', 'Performing', Mourning' and 'Reforming'
- The learning needs of groups need to be recognised
- Community groups should identify their own learning needs
- Learning circles provide an informal and flexible approach to meet group learning needs
- The key role for workers in community groups is facilitation
- Community groups have a range of tasks that they have to deliver to be effective
- Workers need clarity about their own position in the group
- There are critical questions community workers need to keep in mind to ensure good practice with groups

Learning Tasks

Select an established community group and consider the following questions:

- Is this an Authoritarian, Consulting or Enabling group?
- Where is this group on the Forming – Storming – Norming – Performing – Mourning – Reforming process?
- What is the community development worker's role(s) in the group?
- How does the group learn to do new things?
- Look at the summary checklist at the end of this chapter – what does this tell you about the group and the way it is being run?
- If you were the local community development worker, what would you do in light of the above points?

Key Reading

Skills in Neighbourhood Work by Henderson and Thomas (2001), gives a very thorough exploration of the process model of community work, which includes many insights into working with groups.

The discussion of the stages of group development can be found in Tuckman (1965).

Once again the work of Freire is made accessible though the *Training For Transformation* volumes by Hope and Timmel (1984 and 1999). These books contain many exercises that can be useful to help build group cohesion and development.

References

Benjamin, J., Bessant, J., and Watts, R. (1997) *Making Groups Work. Rethinking Practice.* St. Leonards, Australia: Allen and Unwin.

Drysdale, J. and Purcell, R. (1999) 'Breaking the Culture of Silence: Group Work and Community Development', *Groupwork*, 11(3), 70–87.

Drysdale, J. and Purcell, R. (2000) *Reclaiming the Agenda: Participation in Practice.* Bradford: CWTC.

Henderson, P. (2012) *Skills in Neighbourhood Work.* London: Routledge.

Kelly, A. and Sewell, S. (1989) *With Heads, Hearts and Hands, Dimensions of Community Building.* Brisbane: Boolarong Press.

Purcell, R. (2005) *Working in the Community: Perspectives for Change.* Morrisville, NC: Lulu Press.

Tuckman, B.W. (1965) 'Developmental Sequence in Small Groups', *Psychological Bulletin*, 63.

4.7   Evaluating Your Practice

Introduction

In this chapter we look at the purpose of monitoring and evaluation, and how it is an essential element of community development practice. In particular, we discuss logical frameworks as a tried and tested method of creating a monitoring and evaluation framework. We go on to give an illustrative example of a logical framework.

In this book we argue that monitoring and evaluation is a core part of effective community development practice. Not everyone agrees with this position. Many years ago, the author (Purcell) was part of a team delivering a large training programme on evaluation in community development (Barr et al., 1996), and was frequently told by community development workers that community development is something that cannot be measured, success is intangible (you just know it when it happens), and that community development is an 'art form', not a professional activity. For others, evaluation is something you do at the end of a project to satisfy funders, and all that is required is some statistics, letters and testimonials from local people saying how good it all was. This is simply not good enough.

Monitoring and evaluation have to be embedded in community development activity from the start. It is not a luxury, an add-on, or an afterthought. As we explore below, setting up an evaluation framework is a rigorous process that imposes clarity on what you are trying to do. Crucially, it enables you, through periodic monitoring, to know if things are going to plan and creates checkpoints where the programme and focus of work can be rethought if required. Overall, evaluation helps you understand what works and what doesn't, and to know if you have succeeded or failed.

There are many ways of evaluating community development. Here, we discuss the most popular model, known as Logical Frameworks. In the literature, there are many versions of 'logframes' but they all have the same underlying process. The logical framework model was originally developed by the US Agency for International Development (USAID) and is extensively used in the international development context. Jensen (2013) describes a logical framework as:

> an approach [which] enables the main elements of a project to be concisely summarised and brings structure and logic to the relationship between project purpose and intended inputs, planned activities, and expected results. If used with flexibility this approach to planning encourages creative thinking and promotes participatory engagement between all parties throughout the project life-cycle.

The final sentence is crucially important. Evaluation in community development should be a participative process that includes staff, volunteers and users. It is not something done by experts to local people.

At its heart, a logical framework is a matrix that helps us to know in detail:

- What are the **objectives** of the work
- What **activities** you need to undertake to meet the objectives
- What **resources/assets** you need to complete the activities
- What **assumptions** you have made about the work
- What are the planned **outputs**
- What are the intended **outcomes**
- How you can **measure** what is/is not achieved compared to the starting baseline

An Example of a Logical Framework

The first point is that creating a logical framework is part of community development practice. It is not something bolted onto practice, or an activity given to external experts. Local people are fully able, with some training and support, to undertake this work. We have discussed elsewhere about community development being a process that follows the *Reflection – Planning – Action – Reflection* cycle. If we work through this cycle with local communities we find that:

> **Reflection** – helps people develop a fuller understanding of their current situation (the **baseline** from which change takes place). It also includes taking stock of current and potential community and organisational assets that can be used to enable change to take place. See the above discussions on Understanding the Community and Freirean practice for suggestions on how to promote reflective community activities.
>
> **Vision** – is the process through which people identify **goals** that broadly describe the changes they wish to make. Generally, the goals will emerge from facilitated discussion on the reflection process.
>
> **Planning** – should be a participative process that turns these goals into specific SMART **objectives**.
>
> **Action** – is the collective work to deliver the objectives.
>
> **Reflection** – is where, using data collected in the action phase, we can collectively *evaluate* whether the objectives have been achieved.

Generally, it is helpful if the planned objectives are SMART. This means that we are trying to define objectives that are:

Specific
Measurable
Achievable
Realistic
Time-bound

Using SMART objectives helps us to be focused in what we are trying to achieve. For example, we may have a broad goal such as wanting to improve the quality of life of elderly people in the community. From this goal we have to create objectives that are specific and identify what this actually means: changes to day-care provision, volunteer home visitors, summer day trips, Christmas parties, and so on. Running the possible objectives against the SMART criteria prevents us from setting objectives that are vague and/or cannot be achieved.

In the vision/objective-setting phase it is important to also explore external factors that may impact on the deliverability of the objectives. It is useful to consider the local political, cultural and economic environments. If the focus of the work includes a variety of ethnic groups, what extra consideration needs to be made? Is there potential opposition to the work from vested interests, or from other sectors of the community? Where possible, solutions to these factors need to be included in the setting of objectives.

A fundamental consideration in setting objectives is ensuring the basic principles of community development are incorporated in an effective way. It is useful to discuss how far the objectives:

- Are genuinely participative
- Promote personal empowerment
- Promote community empowerment
- Are gender sensitive
- Are inclusive of various ethnic groups, LGBT communities, etc.
- Challenge oppression
- Promote social justice
- Move decision-making and power to the community

The relative importance of these principles will vary according to the nature of the work. However, it is important to ask the question to ensure the basic underlying principles are not forgotten. The principles that are relevant to the work need to be specifically written into the objectives/outputs/outcomes with appropriate measures. It is not enough to simply claim these things will automatically happen.

Definitions

Before we move on to create the logical framework, we need to put down some definitions.

      Baseline – the measured conditions at the start of the project as explored in the reflection phase. The outputs and outcomes are measured as changes from the baseline. Without knowing the baseline situation it is impossible to accurately know what changes have taken place.

      Goals – the broad definition of what you are trying to achieve. *For example, support for children of working parents.*

      Objectives – as discussed, the objectives are the specific things you want to do to meet the goals. *For example, the provision of after-school care, summer playschemes etc.*

      Outputs – objectives you are directly responsible for delivering. *For example, the positive experience for children in the local after-school project.*

      Outcomes – the broader impact that comes from the outputs. *For example, what parents do when children are in day care.* It is important to note that often it is the outcomes that can make the most significant change for the community. However, outcomes are also determined by a variety of factors outside of your control. It is reasonable therefore, to include outcomes in your framework as long as you recognise that you may not be able to deliver them due to external factors.

What we are looking for here are *Intended* Outputs and Outcomes, However, unexpected things happen and there are often *Unintended* Outcomes and Outputs. Sometimes, the unintended results can be beneficial, but often they are detrimental. Either way, such effects should be recorded and analysed with the lessons built into the work plan.

Indicator – a way of measuring/demonstrating what has happened. Such measures can be:
Quantitative – the numbers involved
Qualitative – the quality of provision
Often it is helpful to use both statistics and quality-related measures.

Monitoring – collecting data to inform progress with the outputs and outcomes. Reviewing this data and making decisions (if necessary) to make changes to the work plan. Depending upon the nature of the project, monitoring should take place every six and 15 months.

Evaluation – the final overall assessment of the project and drawing the lessons learned from the analysis of the work. The evaluation process uses the data collected from the monitoring exercises and looks at the changes from the conditions as identified in the baseline.

Logical Framework Matrix

There are various ways of constructing the matrix. We suggest this version as it includes a column for assumptions/risks. This is useful as it makes explicit some of the underlying ideas behind the rough the monitoring exercises.

Specimen Matrix

	Narrative	*Indicators*	*Verification Data*	*Assumptions (inc. Risks)*
Vision/Goal				
Inputs/ Resources				
Inputs/ Processes				
Inputs/Activities				
Outputs				
Outcomes				

Narrative – the description of what you are trying to do
Indicators – the information you need to see what is being delivered/achieved
Verification Data – the source of data for the indicators
Assumptions – the underlying ideas behind each row of the matrix
Vision/Goal – what you are trying to do
Inputs/Resources – your own resources being used for this work
Inputs/Processes – things you need to do to deliver the work
Inputs/Activities – specific activates that are essential for the process to take place
Outputs – what is achieved for which you are directly responsible
Outcomes – what is achieved for which you are partly responsible

To fill the boxes in the matrix you have to have clarity about what you are trying to do and how you are going to do it. Collective discussion is often the best way to undertake this task. It does not need to be, and in community development should not be, a process done for a group by an outside 'expert'. The community development worker should be able to facilitate this process.

To illustrate the kind of information that fills the boxes, let us take the example of a local childcare provision. The matrix as completed here is illustrative, not comprehensive.

	Narrative	*Indicators*	*Verification Data*	*Assumptions (inc. Risks)*
Vision/Goal	Improved childcare, reduced local poverty through parents working, improved child health and school performance	n/a	n/a	The work is a product of a developmental process with the local community. Parents need and want this service.
Inputs/ Resources	Staff, accommodation, equipment Funding	Each requirement is itemised	List of what is available under each heading	Support from school, funding bodies, other agencies
Inputs/Processes	Informal learning Healthy eating	New learning by children Nature of food provided	Observation of children Interviews with parents Analysis of menus, and actual food consumption	Activities will be appropriate and delivered correctly Children will want the food provided
Inputs/Activities	Recruit and train staff and volunteers Homework support	Staff in post Volunteers recruited Training programmes delivered Numbers attending	Records Interviews with staff	Training will reflect childcare values and principles Parents and children want this service
Outputs	50 breakfast club places 25 after school places Children are happy in the project	Attendance levels Children participating in activities	Attendance records Interviews with parents/children	Parents and children want this service Children will enjoy participating in the project
Outcomes	More working parents Improved educational performance in school	Increased number of parents in employment School reports	Survey of parents Interviews with teachers	Jobs are available and parents want them Dependent upon other factors affecting school performance

Once constructed a logical framework needs to be tested. One way to do this is through a logic test:

- If the stated activities take place, and the assumptions are true, then the outputs will be created
- If the outputs are delivered, and the assumptions are true, then the objectives will be achieved
- If the objectives are achieved, and the assumptions are true, then the goal will be delivered

As said, once the project is underway, monitoring should take place at agreed intervals. For this to happen, identified data needs to be collected for each indicator. This needs to happen at the start of the work to create the baseline, and at each monitoring point to show what is happening. If things are not going to plan then the indicators will identify the nature of the problem, and appropriate changes can be made.

At the end of the project a final evaluation can be made using the collected data to identify the difference between the original baseline situation and the end position. In addition, time should be made to clearly identify the broader lessons for practice from the work. Evaluation questions to be explored include:

- What worked and why?
- What didn't work and why?
- How well were resources used and how could this be improved?
- Could participant learning have been improved?
- Was there personal and collective empowerment?

Finally, it is important to note that logical frameworks are simply a tool to manage the process of change. As such they *need to be used flexibly and to reflect what the community organisation is trying to do, rather than dictate what is happening*. As circumstances change, and the underlying assumptions change, the objectives/outputs/outcomes and the associated inputs should change. The monitoring point is also a time to review the suitability of the logical framework as it is currently written. As in all community development processes, success is only likely to be achieved if the work is a genuine product of local needs and desires.

Key Learning Points

- Monitoring and evaluation are an essential part of community development
- Monitoring and evaluation should start with a baseline study at the beginning of a community development process
- A useful approach to creating a framework for monitoring and evaluation is through using a logical framework
- Logical frameworks make you think through what you are trying to achieve (goals and SMART objectives), how you are going to achieve it, the resources/activities/processes required and how to recognise if you have succeeded or not
- A community development-focused logical framework should make reference to (appropriate) community development principles and these should be built into the framework
- Producing and managing a logical framework and the final evaluation that is derived from it should be a participative activity

- Local people can, and should, undertake their own evaluations. The community development worker's role is to facilitate this process and access expert support when necessary
- Logical frameworks need to be applied flexibly, and should be changed as circumstances change

Learning Tasks

- Identify a community development activity to use as a case study
- Within this case study, identify a key goal and develop a set of objectives
- Are these SMART objectives?
- Make a logical framework template and populate the matrix
- Does this matrix incorporate principles of community development, if not, build in appropriate principles as objectives linked to outputs and outcomes

Key Reading

Greta Jensen, *How to Write a Logframe*: www.theguardian.com/global-development-professionals-network/2015/aug/17/how-to-write-a-logframe-a-beginners-guide.

References

Barr, A., Hashegan, S., and Purcell, R. (1996) *Evaluation and Monitoring in Community Development.* Northern Ireland: Northern Ireland Voluntary Activities Unit, NI DHSS.
Jensen, G. (2013) 'The Logical Framework Approach'. Available at: www.bond.org.uk/data/files/resources/49/The-logical-framework-approach-How-To-guide-December-2013.pdf.

Section 5

Case Studies of Practice

Introduction

In this section we discuss 12 case studies of practice, which have been commissioned directly for this book. The studies have been written by practitioners and academics on current aspects of their daily practice. These studies also appear in a special 2019 edition of the Radical Community Work Journal.

The nature of practice evolves over time to reflect the broader social, cultural and economic changes. A generation ago a cross section of practice would have focused on such issues as working in community centres to build networks and social capital (although it would have been called 'creating a sense of community' back then), organising around poor social housing conditions, children and play, support to mothers and unemployed men. The growth of feminism, awareness of ethnic minority communities, the growth of the LGBT movement, and environmental concerns have all shifted the focus of practice.

Each case study in this section stands in its own right as a distinct description and analysis of practice. The studies also have a key role in the book. Specifically, the **purpose of these case studies** is sixfold:

1. To demonstrate some of the many ways of conceptualising, understanding and writing about community development practice
2. To provide snapshots of some of the diverse contexts within which community development takes place, as well as different ways of writing about practice
3. To illustrate some of the issues that community development addresses
4. To illustrate some of the real-world challenges that practitioners have to overcome
5. To explore some of the differing practice models and theoretical perspectives that underpin that practice
6. To make direct links between chapters in the book and some of the ways that values/ models/theories are applied to practice

We have added a short introduction to set the scene in each study. At the end of the case study we provide suggestions to link the practice to relevant parts of the book for **further study**.

In addition, there are **key learning points and learning tasks** offered to the reader. In any practice setting there is a range of choices available to the community development worker on how to procced: what do they want to achieve, what do local people want to achieve, how might this be done, which ideas/theories underpin this analysis. For each case study it is useful for the reader to consider the following questions in order to think through *their* approach to practice. Specifically:

- What is your analysis of power relationships in the study?
- What do you think it is possible to achieve in this practice context?
- Of the range of possibilities, which are the most important, and why?
- Which models/theories would you wish to apply, and why is this your choice?
- How do your choices here relate to the values of community development?
- If you took over this piece of work, what would you do in the first month?

The case studies are:

1. A Statement of Hope, by Andy Turner
2. Community Impact of an Australian Aboriginal Art Centre, by Trudi Cooper
3. Popular Education and Neighbourhood Centre Work, by P. J. Humphreys and Peter Westoby
4. Spinning Rubbish into Gold: A Community Development Route to Environmental Social Enterprise, by John Stansfield
5. Play Sufficiency as an Organising Principle of Community Development, by Ben Tawil and Mike Barclay
6. Creative Nottingham North: Arts-based Community Development, by Frances Howard
7. When Young People, Resident Artists and Curators Work Collaboratively on a Community Arts Project, by Tina Salter
8. The 'JOY' Project, by Clive Sealey, Ruth Jones, Joanne Lewis and Danny Gregory
9. Show Racism the Red Card, by Luke Campbell and Nicola Hay
10. The Bengali Women's Programme 2011–2014, by Rick Gwilt and Rehana Begum
11. Developing a New Generation of BAME Community-based Leaders: Lessons from an Ongoing Journey, by Yvonne Field
12. 'Peas & Love'. A Case Study in Kindness and the Power of Small Actions: Incredible Edible, Todmorden, by Martin Purcell

A short biography of the case study authors can be found in the List of Contributors.

Case Study 5.1

A Statement of Hope

Andy Turner

Voice 4 Deptford: Empowerment and Change – Reality or Rhetoric?

Community work can feel complex, frustrating and untidy, amplified by the rhetoric of empowerment by state and private sector, and the realities of people overwhelmed by obstacles and inertia, unable to enable change.

Working for Change

In June 2014 at Deptford Library, the Convoys Wharf Community Group organised their first public meeting. The agenda brought together residents, agencies and groups living and working in and around Convoys Wharf, an area of land bordering the Thames to the North of Deptford High Street. Attendees shared concerns about the proposed development of luxury apartments on the Convoys Wharf site, the last remaining riverside development in London. Outline planning permission for a massive scheme had been granted by the Mayor of London earlier in March 2014 – a controversial decision undermining local planning procedures, the views of residents, local councillors and planning officers, who were all opposed to the scheme.

Attendees were concerned about the implications of the development, some indignant at a perceived absence of consultation, including a proposed allocation of £50 million of S106 Agreement monies. A consensus emerged from the meeting, which focused on legal action, and a possible process, challenging the statutory public consultation by the developer, Greater London Authority and the local authority around the use of S106, a legal agreement between an applicant seeking planning permission and the local planning authority.

As the meeting concluded people lingered, sharing ideas, solidarity and support. Many of the 47 attendees agreed to meet again, following up the initial gathering with a proposed series of community meetings to build awareness of, and organise opposition to, the development.

Convoys Wharf Community Group (CWCG) continued to meet throughout 2014 and early 2015. Meetings were advertised using street posters, flyers and encouraging word of mouth. The agenda aimed to update attendees of news, information and developments – a continual request from attendees – and explore emerging issues, consulting and making decisions about the campaign. A smaller core group was established to plan the agenda and help progress actions.

Actions, Inertia and Failure

Maintaining the momentum of the group proved challenging. Attendance was low, between four to ten people, and wildly inconsistent, leading to repetition of previous discussions to update those absent from earlier meetings – frustrating for those who attended regularly.

Occasionally individuals could dominate, either determined to share inappropriate detail, or discredit the contribution of others, which demanded careful management from the meeting facilitator.

It was agreed early on that an effective meeting would generate 'useful' actions to progress the group. Actions were decided – though as attendance ebbed and flowed tasks may or may not have been followed up, and at times this generated inertia. One example involved submitting a legal challenge to the S106 agreement – regarding funding provided by the developer to finance infrastructure associated with the scheme, from schools to transport and public art. A plan to challenge the GLA over a perceived lack of consultation helped to define the purpose of the group, leading to frustration and failure early in 2015. The group's lack of success in organising and completing an essential task to challenge the S106 highlighted the vulnerability of the group, which was overdependent on a solitary volunteer to achieve a key task, whose absence finally put the plan at risk.

Reorganise and Regroup

After a pause, the small working group responsible for planning CWCG meetings met in early 2016 and decided to change the name from a passive 'Convoys Wharf Community Group' to 'Voice 4 Deptford'. This name better communicated the group's intentions – to facilitate residents in voicing their views about Convoys Wharf and the changing community of which they were a part.

A second step change was a successful request to the Big Lottery 'Awards for All'. The small grant provided income to fund hiring of venues and printing costs for promotional material as well as essential crèche, childcare and refreshment costs for meetings. The grant ensured work was better resourced to engage more fully with the local community.

The group prioritised consultation – community engagement that would generate insights about the proposed development and frame the concerns of local residents. Students from Goldsmiths were recruited alongside local residents to undertake street interviews, researching local opinion about the development, and promoting a series of regular Voice 4 Deptford meetings.

Following 12 months of successful community engagement activities with local residents in 2016 and early 2017, and hosting five well-attended community meetings; feedback from the meetings highlighted that the group – with regular attendees of around 15 to 20 – needed to be clearer about its aims and priorities, and express these publicly on a public forum, for example, a website.

Two key priorities emerged, focusing the ambitions of Voice 4 Deptford. First, to establish a development trust, a community-owned and community-run asset, which could work with residents to establish local enterprise, develop sustainable employment and, with children, young people, parents, carers and older people, host and promote community activities and resources, funded in part by S106 monies.

The second objective focused on housing – matching the frequent and intense concerns expressed in street surveys and Voice 4 Deptford for the need to significantly increase the numbers of social housing in Deptford. Residents noted that 'affordable' housing was clearly unaffordable to those on an average salary in South East London.

Becoming Seen and Heard

Residents also spoke at length about Deptford as a forgotten community, swallowed up by Lewisham local authority. In this context, where exploring notions of community and identity came up in discussion regularly at initial meetings, themes emerged related to collective confidence and the process of speaking out and working effectively for change. If the identity of the area was ignored or forgotten – particularly by Lewisham local authority and adjacent London boroughs – what hope was there that residents would be heard and their concerns taken seriously?

Alongside perceptions of antipathy towards communities in Deptford was the awareness that residents needed to compete more effectively to be heard in what was seen as an overcrowded market place, with lots of voices competing for attention. The group – and discussions – concluded that residents needed to synchronise local voices more effectively in order to be heard. It is perhaps no surprise that 'Voice 4 Deptford' emerged after exploring the concerns and objectives of the group – combining them into a single named organisation.

People Power

Whilst residents described the experience of feeling powerless – being ignored or discredited collectively – they spoke less about notions of empowerment, if and how they could empower themselves. However, for some involved, the process of participation did generate trust, a feeling of comfort through sharing insights, concerns and ideas, of being listened to and able to join with others, that did lead to comments about 'people power', and a sense of loyalty and attachment towards the work of the group and solidarity with its members.

Yet, despite this acknowledgement of 'people power', the process did not engender a transfer of power, nor did it enable change in specific policy. The experience links to extensive debates about how empowerment is defined, either as a subjective experience or an objective shift in power.

Page and Czuba (1999) argue that empowerment is a process occurring in sociological, psychological and economic contexts at various individual, group and community levels. A social process or journey that occurs in relation to another person, empowerment is a:

> Multi-dimensional social process that helps people gain control over their own lives. It is a process that fosters power in people for use in their own lives, their communities, and in their society by acting on issues that they define as important.
>
> (Page and Czuba, 1999: 5)

This relates to the use and impact of empowerment practice, and the extent of empowerment rhetoric deployed. One underlying assumption behind many interventions is that those who are excluded wish to be included in consultations, development and society as it currently stands. However, Shanahan and Ward (1995) assert that many of those 'excluded' do not want to be included or incorporated but would rather, if able, reflect and act collegiately: 'to change that system and "to make it their own" by addressing structural issues of their choice' (Shanahan and Ward, 1995: 72). In practice, empowerment of communities remains a challenging test for those in power, who perceive they have the most to lose – in the case of Voice 4 Deptford, this was the local authority and the developer.

Craig and Mayo (1995) refer to the limitation placed on empowerment strategies by the 'wider requirements of profitability and viability within the increasingly global market'. This is regardless of what individual or community gains can be negotiated locally. As an alternative, Craig and Mayo state that if a fixed amount of power exists, increasing the power of one group will cause reduction in the power of another.

> The empowerment of the powerless would involve gains which would, of necessity have to be achieved from the powerful ... negotiated as part of wider strategies for social reform.
>
> (Craig and Mayo, 1995: 5)

The practical political and commercial realities of this transaction were discussed at Voice 4 Deptford meetings, the group fragmenting with some participants enthusiastic for direct action as opposed to lobbying, or others expressing concerns that ideas were abstract and theoretical. Here the agenda frequently shifted to concerns about tactics and effective organisation, and how the group could extend power and influence from its own assets and resources, rather than influence the transfer of power with those outside the group.

One of the key outcomes of empowerment is an experience of working together, exercising skills and nurturing individual confidence (Solomon, 1976; Zimmerman, 1990; Zimmerman and Rappaport, 1988; c.f. Parsons, 1991). These 'individual participatory competences' (Kieffer, 1984), can be observed explicitly in the development of self-confidence, accumulating knowledge and skills amongst participants. Empowered individuals take their own initiative, creating change through participation, learning various strategies, collaborative joint ventures and occasional confrontation to accomplish goals. This was and remains evident with Voice 4 Deptford, as individuals felt safe to participate.

Process and Product

Throughout the development of Voice 4 Deptford, the agenda of the steering group, made up of core members, was routinely divided between those concerned with a robust process and those focused on the end product, that is, empowerment and change. As the relationship between members of the group grew and deepened, some perceived as priorities the process of planning and organising meetings, engaging residents, spending grant funding effectively and reporting to funders. An example of the latter was the administration and spending of Big Lottery 'Awards for All' funding and the impact of the grant on the group.

For some members of the group, including those managing the grant, administrative competence associated with full grant spending and reporting back to the funder, influenced the choices the group considered. This was perceived by other group members to undermine opportunity for specific strategies – including direct action approaches, or deployment of tactics – including political engagement. Here the anxiety was that of the funder, and by default, the impact that deploying these tactics would have on future funding. Whilst the terms and conditions associated with grant funding were never undermined, the independence of the group at times felt questionable, as members deferred decisions and actions to 'the funder'. This raises questions about the influence of funders – even those keen to promote independence of grant recipients – and the independence of community groups like Voice 4 Deptford.

For Dunham (1970) effective practice involves a combination of product and process objectives, involving individuals and a facilitator agreeing and striking a balance between task and process. Both objectives can be achieved through participating in community activity, whilst the degree to which one achieves these objectives will vary according to the practice employed by the facilitator.

In the case of Voice 4 Deptford, when the group was funded by an Awards for All grant, anxiety was frequently expressed by some members about aspects of the process – including the appropriateness of proposed strategies in relation to the presence of the grant. Here, facilitators promptly challenged concerns, referring to grant conditions, working to move the group towards decisions and actions. At times, the absence of a perceived level of progress and development generated reflection, frustration and – often, but not always, away from the meeting in the nearby pub – confrontation. Here discussion focused on product and outcome. The revisiting of the circumstances, as a reminder of why Voice 4 Deptford was established, alongside an appeal for action, at times generated a renewed sense of urgency, and willingness from those more focused on or motivated by task and process, to act.

This example highlights the impact of funding and the potential erosion of independence, arguably resulting in the further de-politicisation of community development (Gaynor, 2011). Referring to the global south, Meade et al. (2016) note how the goal of empowering is undermined by a wider imperative – to ensure the compliance of the funded programme.

> Here, community development roles are often constructed around technical procedures involving evaluation, audit and reporting systems designed to suit the requirements of funding bodies, rather than facilitating community initiatives.
>
> (Meade et al., 2016: 54)

Within literature related to community empowerment, questions of which objective – the product or the process – is more significant, remain contested. For Voice 4 Deptford the debate was at times characterised by those concerned either about grant spending, reporting and administrative competence, or community engagement and need to change policy towards housing development on Convoys Wharf.

Going through the Motions

Despite the rhetoric of 'localism', the practice of empowerment by local and central government or housing developer is at best elusive. Here, empowerment is frequently interpreted as consultation. One example is via a neighbourhood forum meeting. In Deptford, members of Voice 4 Deptford would learn about and could attend the quarterly meetings of the Evelyn Ward neighbourhood forum.

In one meeting, an agenda that included the opportunity for residents to select their preferred choice of community projects to be funded, also included consultation on the redevelopment of Convoys Wharf. When challenged about the absence of affordable or social housing in the proposed scheme, the council officer blamed legislation and external agency, stating that housing requirements had been agreed in the outline planning application. Here the forum seemed to be about council management trumpeting modest examples of 'empowerment' via a type of participative budgeting and deploying language of community engagement and consultation, whilst effectively platforming council policy, avoiding responsibility to engage dialogue and consider resident concerns.

Newman and Clarke (quoted in Meade et al., 2016) raise questions about the function and practice of community development and the capacity and space for antagonism and autonomous agency – in short, the 'privileging' of the local community in a context of depoliticised participative governance (Newman and Clark, quoted in Meade et al., 2016).

> From this perspective, the emphasis on community engagement in many government programmes can be viewed as a way of tutoring citizens through forms of participative governing, rendering potentially unruly populations compliant through the production of new forms of self-governing subjects.
>
> (Newman and Clark, quoted in Meade et al., 2016)

The small number of residents attending the neighbourhood forum meeting and participating in discussion betrays a perception articulated at Voice 4 Deptford meetings, that much of the process was about 'going through the motions', and that 'decisions have already been made'. According to Craig and Mayo this conclusion reflects limited possibilities under a capitalist system, dominated by market forces:

> The poor and relatively powerless may become empowered to participate more effectively in particular development projects and programmes … But however valuable, or even vital, this may be in terms of particular gains and specific projects in certain places, these are all confined by the constraints of the wider requirements of profitability and viability within the increasingly global market.
>
> (Craig and Mayo, 1995: 5–6)

Even if the debate about process and product at times divided the group, members of Voice 4 Deptford worked hard to continue to maintain a sense of momentum and progress, nurturing participation and community engagement. Regular street interviews, outreach and frequent use of posters helped to raise awareness of the plans being proposed for Convoys Wharf and the regular bi-monthly Voice 4 Deptford meetings. Each meeting typically saw new attendees, who had heard about the meeting via word of mouth or had seen one of the posters displayed.

Dialogue and Action

A key aim was to move the agenda from dialogue, and an 'exchange of information' and 'awareness raising', to action. The Brazilian educationalist Paulo Freire (1972, 1976) argues that dialogue, group conscientisation and consciousness raising are critical principles and key components of an empowerment process (Ledwith, 2016). According to Freire, dialogue is not about a question followed by an answer; rather, dialogue is a tool for empowerment embracing social learning and raising consciousness (Ledwith, 2016), involving a two-way interactive process between the person actively listening, and the facilitating worker encouraging the person to talk about their experience, ideas, concerns and hopes. The process includes description, clarification and explanation. Dialogue provides freedom to express perceptions, reasoning and expectations as to how the world is perceived. Reflection nurtures a state of consciousness about the experienced reality of a community or neighbourhood (Blackburn, 2000).

In the example of Voice 4 Deptford, local people with expertise were invited to contribute insights, with other attendees questioning and scrutinising explanations and information and contributing their own knowledge. This mutual information typically generated a range of data – from names to follow up, to agencies and networks to connect with. Sharing became an essential component of each meeting, allowing time for deep thinking and reflection about the changes going on and the deeper, wider issues at stake, with attendees frequently disclosing associated anxiety and feelings. Becoming more conscious of a situation enables transformation from passive or false consciousness to a critical consciousness. This critical consciousness encourages awareness of context and the potential to influence or bring about social change (Blackburn, 2000; Freire, 1976;

Ledwith, 2016). This is about 'the right to name one's reality' (Breton, 1994), nurturing the opportunity for people to 'name the world' (Freire, 1972, 1976).

Facilitating a process of dialogue enables experience to be shared and problems to be understood, helping transform ideas into new knowledge for people (Ledwith, 2016). Freire's emphasis on critical reflection provides a theoretical framework through which to respond to the approach of 'manipulative' activists or facilitators. Significantly, Freire notes that reflection without action is verbalism, encouraging a passive 'armchair revolution', whereas action without reflection is 'pure activism', that is action for action's sake. This presented challenges for Voice 4 Deptford and its members.

Talk to Action

One Voice 4 Deptford meeting involved identifying key actions that targeted specific power groups or planned further outreach. This was about a range of key actions, from setting up and meeting with local council officers and developers to meeting with politicians to voice concerns. Of the 20 attendees and three small groups working together, a range of actions was agreed and responsibilities allocated. At the following meeting, little work had been completed about which to report back and minimal progress had been made – in part due to the lack of availability and commitment of participants, volunteering their time. The theory that critical reflection leads to consciousness of conditions, and subsequent involvement in the struggle for liberation, assumes a fixed reality that people can discover and which everyone will understand and respond to in the same way, leading to a collective, homogeneous response (Blackburn, 2000). In practice, individuals and groups become stuck and work stops.

In practice, not everyone attending Voice 4 Deptford meetings shared a 'false-consciousness' about the proposed development and changes to their neighbourhood or a feeling of disconnect to local government institutions, or felt liberated as meetings concluded. Instead the impact and complication of different views, perspectives and interpretations of reality about Convoys Wharf, as well as contrasting ideas of how to act, or not in response to what is perceived, generated a wide range of responses – from action frustrated by institutional inertia or opposition to people leaving, and doing nothing. Despite this, the principles and practice of participation and empowerment, and the theoretical concepts of Freire: 'the processes by which the oppressed can become subjects of their own histories' (Blackburn, 2000), remain a valuable community development tool for communities working together to bring about social change.

Development and Challenges

Voice 4 Deptford has evolved slowly, without the resources of staff or paid professionals. Members have navigated complex challenges related to the behaviour of multinational corporations and large administrative bureaucracies, even as each refer to community engagement and consultations. Since starting in 2015, activity has become prioritised around emerging themes, with participants confronting practical issues related to power and privilege. The stakes for residents remain high with the possibility of a vast housing development transforming a corner of Deptford for generations.

The work of Voice 4 Deptford has, in part, been sporadic, ineffective, undisciplined, delayed by internal conflict or contrasting approaches. Like many community groups, Voice 4 Deptford represents a reality of skill and capacity which, whilst inconsistent, has worked effectively for change. After a dormant period following outline planning permission being granted in 2014, a full planning application from the developer was anticipated in 2018. Voice 4 Deptford has hosted large-scale meetings confronting developers, planning officers and politicians, used the Freedom of Information Act to obtain documents evidencing apparent financial risk to the proposed scheme, and at the time of writing was recruiting a solicitor to take forward plans to engage legal processes. Outcomes involving the reworking of a scheme that will generate more social housing and investment in local infrastructure for residents remain hugely challenging. As local people develop their knowledge, ideas and skills, the energy and commitment continues to grow.

Further Study

We suggest looking back through the book to further explore these specific issues from the case study:

- *Other organisational models that would lead to a greater number of active people*
- *Asset analysis to identify possible allies and resources*
- *Funding*
- *The potential of Freirean methods to build group vision and cohesion*
- *The group-work process*
- *The importance of setting clear and realisable objectives*

References

Blackburn, J. (2000) 'Understanding Paulo Freire: Reflections on the Origins, Concepts, and Possible Pitfalls of his Educational Approach', *Community Development Journal*, 35(1), 3–15.

Breton, R. (1994) 'Modalités d'appartenance aux francophonies minoritaires. Essai de typologie', *Sociologie et Sociétés*, 26(1), 59–69.

Craig, G. and Mayo, M. (ed.) (1995) *Community Empowerment – A Reader in Participation and Development*. London: Zed Books.

Dunham, A. (1970) *Community Development*. New York: Thomas Crawell Company

Freire, P. (1972) *Pedagogy of the Oppressed*. Harmondsworth: Penguin.

Freire, P. (1976) *Education: The Practices of Freedom*. London: Writers and Readers Publishing Co-operative.

Gaynor, N. (2011) 'Associations, Deliberation, and Democracy: The Case of Ireland's Social Partnership', *Politics & Society*, 39(4), 497.

Kieffer, C. (1984) 'Citizen Empowerment: A Developmental Perspective', *Prevention in Human Services*, 3(2/3), 9–36.

Ledwith, M. (2016) *Community Development in Action – Putting Freire into practice*, Bristol: The Policy Press.

Meade, R., Shaw, M., and Banks, S. (2016) *Politics, Power and Community Development*. Bristol: The Policy Press.

Page, N. and Czuba, C. (1999) 'Empowerment: What Is It?', *Journal of Extension*, 37(5, October), [online]. Available at: http://joe.org/joe/1999october/comm1.html, accessed 9 March 2005.

Parsons, R.J. (1991) 'Empowerment', *Social Work with Groups*, 14(2), 7–21.

Shanahan, P. and Ward, J. (1995) 'The University and Empowerment: The European Union, University Adult Education and Community Economic Development with Excluded Groups', in G. Craig and M. Mayo (eds), *Community Empowerment, A Reader in Participation and Development*. London: Zed Books, 70–85.

Solomon, B. (1976) *Black Empowerment – Social Work in Oppressed Communities*. New York: Columbia University Press.

Zimmerman, M. (1990) 'Toward a Theory of Learned Hopefulness: A Structural Model Analysis of Participation and Empowerment', *Journal of Research in Personality*, 24, 71–86.

Zimmerman, M. and Rappaport, J. (1988) 'Citizen Participation, Perceived Control, and Psychological Empowerment', *American Journal of Community Psychology*, 16, 725–750.

Case Study 5.2

Community Impact of an Australian Aboriginal Art Centre

Trudi Cooper

Introduction

The central question explored in this case study is how a grant-supported social enterprise can have an impact on the well-being of a community, beyond the immediate financial benefits. This chapter draws upon research conducted by Cooper et al. (2012) in 2011. The research documented the community effects of the establishment of the Wirnda Barna Aboriginal Art Centre in a remote area of Western Australia. The case study outlines how the Wirnda Barna Art Centre manager used community development methods within a social enterprise framework that specified commercial goals. Although this case study occurred in a particular context, the lessons learned have applications to community development beyond this setting.

The case study illustrates four aspects of community work. First, that community benefits often extend beyond the initial target group. Second, whilst there are advantages to the social enterprise model, there are also disadvantages, and the realistic assessment of project establishment and development time frames and costs are essential to the success of this approach. Third, when setting budgets, competitive tendering sets up conditions that reward overly optimistic estimations of costs and progress of projects, and this can lead to real risks with implementation. Finally, the case study illustrates strengths and limitations of a social capital model of community work in a racialised community context, and the concluding discussion considers the implications of these observations.

Background

The Wirnda Barna Art Centre is located in Mount Magnet in the Mid-West region of Western Australia, 573 km north of Perth. The area is sparsely populated and is classified as very remote, according to the ARIA index (Australian Institute of Welfare, 2004). Wirnda Barna was established in 2009 with support from the Department of Indigenous Affairs in Western Australia (DIA) and the Mid-West Development Commission (MWDC) (Cooper et al., 2012), following feasibility studies by Pearn (2007) and Acker and Cosgreve (2009). It was intended that Wirnda Barna would service Aboriginal Artists in Badimia and Wadjarri country, in the remote communities of Mount Magnet, Cue, Meekatharra, Yulga Jinna and Yalgoo. These communities are widely spread over several hundred square kilometres and have populations varying from less than 50 people to 1300 (Mulholland and Piscicelli, 2006). According to the 2006 census, the proportion of Indigenous people in these townships ranged from 20 per cent to 40 per cent (Australian Bureau of Statistics, 2006) but it is likely that the census underestimated the Aboriginal population, possibly by as much as 16 per cent (Taylor and Biddle, 2010). All the townships are classified in the lowest socio-economic decile according to the SEIFA index (Australian Bureau of Statistics, 2011).

Prior to colonisation, Aboriginal people had lived in this area for millennia as semi-nomadic hunter-gatherers. They were forced off their lands when white townships were established in the nineteenth and early twentieth centuries after gold was discovered and Aboriginal country was allocated to white settlers for pastoral enterprises. Most of the townships have now been depopulating over an extended period of time (Mulholland and Piscicelli, 2006). Historically, inland Mid-West towns had been racially segregated (South West Aboriginal Land and Sea Council, 2015), and Aboriginal children had been subjected to forced removals (Human Rights and Equal Opportunity Commission, 1997), which disrupted cultural transmission. There is a legacy of institutional racism in all these settlements, with unemployment amongst the Aboriginal population at over 50 per cent in several towns. Aboriginal children were in the majority at local schools, but at the time of this case study, few completed the final year of high school, partly because they saw no prospects for future employment. Alcohol abuse was another community concern. The target group for Wirnda Barna comprised Aboriginal artists who had been commercially active prior to the establishment of the art centre, as well as new and emerging Aboriginal artists. The community development methodology meant that many others became involved in the project, either directly or indirectly.

Method and Model

The project did not have an explicit model or theoretical framework. The approach used had evolved from successful practices developed when previous Aboriginal Art Centres were established in remote communities and the proposed project process and milestones are summarised in Acker and Cosgreve (2009). In community development terms, the overarching framework was social enterprise moving towards becoming an unsubsidised collective/co-operative operation, which was self-sustaining from commissions on art sold. The main non-profit objective was cultural preservation and transmission. The initial plan relied on government grants from multiple sources, none of which were more than three years in duration and most of which were annual or less. No grants were available that offered longer-term support, and no single grant scheme encompassed the full remit of the project. The methods used combined community work to build social capital, with commercial and business knowledge transfer to facilitate the social enterprise elements of the project.

The academic literatures on both social capital theory and social enterprise are extensive and contested. According to Young and Lecy (2014: 1309) social enterprises are 'organizations or ventures that combine a social purpose with pursuit of financial success in the private marketplace'. Social capital is defined by the OECD as 'networks together with shared norms, values and understandings that facilitate cooperation within or among groups' (OECD, 2001: 41). Social capital is considered necessary for groups of people to be able to act collectively to solve problems they face, or to work collectively for the common good (Cox, 2002).

Modern social capital theory usually begins with Putnam (2000) who asserted, on the basis of his research into civic organisations, that social connection had declined in American society. The relevance of Putnam's theory to Australia has been discussed by Cox (2002), who affirmed that the main conclusions of Putnam's analysis applied to communities in Australia. Putnam's work has been criticised from a number of perspectives. The most relevant for this case study is the question of whether social capital theory adequately considers the effects of institutional and intercultural barriers to social connection based upon race (or gender or class). Jennings (2007: 10) argues that many of the civic organisations that Putnam applauds acted in exclusionary ways towards people of colour and women, and their existence perpetuated racial (and gender) exclusion from community power. This illustrates the importance of avoiding uncritically romanticising the benefits of strong community organisations without analysis of context. Similarly, Vinson (2004), in his study of an Australian housing estate, found that strong interpersonal bonds could be negative for some people in some contexts. Revisiting Cox's analysis of social capital in Australia, these objections apply. There is only one mention of Australian Indigenous communities within Cox's chapter, and no extended discussion. Accepting these caveats, this case study will show there are some elements of social capital theory that can be useful for understanding the operation of community development in the Wirnda Barna case study.

In social capital theory, two types of social connection are usually differentiated, bonding connections and bridging (and linking) connections. Bonding capital is characterised by personal relationships, shared social background and access to similar resources. Bridging capital is characterised by social connections between people from disparate social networks, who have access to different resources and different social connections. Community development pays special attention to bridging linkages between people who have very different access to resources. These linkages may facilitate access to organisational governance by people who are members of social groups who have been previously excluded from positions of community influence and power (Pope, 2005).

Pope (2005) developed a diagnostic measure for social capital in community development. She used it both to inform initial resource allocation and for evaluation. The strength of bonding capital was assessed through questions about whether, in an emergency, people could borrow $1,000 from family or friends and whether they would receive practical assistance. More distant bonding links were assessed through membership of community clubs and organisations, participation in community events, and parental involvement in schools. Bridging networks were assessed through involvement in governance networks and community activism that require interactions beyond a participant's usual social network. These measures were used as part of the assessment of the success of the Wirnda Barna project in terms of community development, and the Wirnda Barna project will be used to reflect on the limitations of these measures in this particular context.

Intended Outcomes

The criteria for participation were that participants had to be Aboriginal; they had to live in or be culturally connected to the specified geographic region; and they had to be artists or aspire to become artists. The main explicit purpose of the project was to establish a self-sustaining organisation that was able to provide a commercial outlet to improve the quality and volume of Aboriginal art produced and sold in the region. The project would support the development of Aboriginal artists in the region, promote the work of Aboriginal artists and help artists achieve better financial returns on their work. This intended outcome was considered important for many reasons. There was little employment available in the region for Aboriginal people without accredited skills. There was a good commercial market for high quality Aboriginal art, but new and emerging artist had little support, and access to art materials was difficult because of the remote location, which meant that some artwork was produced with inferior materials. In the past, artists had been exploited by unscrupulous art dealers because there was no exhibition or gallery space in the region. There was hope that this initiative would contribute to cultural preservation and transmission as well as increased prosperity for the artists and their dependants. The intention was that the Art centre would become an Aboriginal controlled and collectively managed organisation. This would require transfer of business and governance skills to the artists and those within the community who might manage Wirnda Barna in the future.

What Happened

The evaluation was conducted during the first year of the project, and the methodology and findings are reported in detail in Cooper et al. (2012) The project was staffed by a non-Aboriginal full-time Art Centre Manager (ACM), and a part-time Community Liaison Officer, who was a local Badimia man. This section summarises the main project achievements and how methods were applied.

Within a year of commencement, the project had established a gallery and a website. Wirnda Barna was supporting artists' secure workshop premises in three locations, providing supplies and selling artwork and had run art development courses. Forty-five Aboriginal artists of various ages were actively involved in the project. The artistic benefits mentioned by artists included better access to materials, improved sales, better access to markets and improved technique. This Wirnda Barna Art Centre case study provides an example of how an Aboriginal Art centre facilitated bridging links and financial benefit. The ACM mediated between the artists and the marketplace, a relationship which, when unmediated, has resulted in poor financial outcomes for Aboriginal artists (Acker, 2008; Altman, 2003). According to the artists, even in its first year, Wirnda Barna had begun to realise the intended outcomes for cultural preservation and transmission.

When the ACM arrived he quickly involved himself in community life, and fostered relationships with other social and community agencies across the town. This was necessary for both his acceptance in the town and for establishing the centrality of Wirnda Barna within the community. At the same time he had to gain the trust and acceptance of local Aboriginal artists and elders, and find time to establish and develop the Art Centre. He was expected to support the artists to extend their artistic skills, find markets for their work and prepare Aboriginal people to assume the business and governance roles after he left the organisation. He had to find time to keep applying for new funding as existing multi-sourced funding was mostly from one-off grants of short duration. He also had to spend time dealing with existing funds gained from different sources, each with their own reporting requirements. The ACM had a renewable one-year contract. He was under huge time-pressure, and the heavy demands and relentless competing pressures were evident even during our first visit. These pressures were as a result of the short-term funding derived from multiple sources, combined with the 'stretch objectives' for the project, which included a likely maximum three-year time frame to make the project economically sustainable, but with no assured funding even for that period of time. The project was also socially complex because the ACM acted as a bridge between the local white population and various Aboriginal artists and Aboriginal elders, whose families had been dispossessed, and who had had children stolen from them in living memory.

Two areas of concern emerged. First, financial viability and second, staff retention. In the first year of operation, art sales had generated less revenue than originally projected, and project operations had resulted in a small deficit by the end of the first year. Despite the best efforts of all involved, some bills could not be paid. In a small organisation any deficit threatens the continued existence of the organisation, because it is illegal to trade whilst insolvent. First, the Community Liaison Officer resigned and then the ACM decided not to renew his 12-month contract when it expired. These departures allowed the organisation to survive by cutting expenditure. The project avoided bankruptcy, but had lost people (or in social capital parlance, human resources) who were needed for the continued development of the project. The personal cost was also heavy for the two staff members, who both moved away from the area. A remarkable outcome of this evaluation had been the universal positive regard for the ACM amongst the stakeholders, artists and community members we interviewed. The ongoing financial struggle to try to keep the project afloat financially, and the heavy workload of managing complex demands in a remote location with little formal back up, had taken its toll. The project has survived, but at a human cost to those who had been instrumental in its establishment.

Unintended Outcomes

The project did not have any explicit community development goals. Community development was a means to achieve the project goals but not an intended outcome. However, many non-Aboriginal people who were interviewed commented upon the changes to the broader community that had come about as a result of the establishment of the Wirnda Barna Art Centre. In community development terms, there were three major unintended outcomes of the project. The first was improved respect for Aboriginal culture within the immediate community, the second was improved self-respect for the artists and for their families, and the third was the beginnings of community healing between the local white community and Badimia and Wadjarri people.

Many people attributed the increased respect for Aboriginal culture and improvement of community relationships to the work of the ACM and the community-building strategies he used. He involved Aboriginal people in other organisations as representatives of Wirnda Barna, and he modelled respect for Aboriginal culture. Tourism was a high priority for the local council. The ACM linked Aboriginal art to council strategies to promote tourism, and this helped gain broader acceptance of Aboriginal culture. In terms of social capital theory, the ACM had strengthened the bridging capital by linking the Aboriginal artists to other groups with different resources outside their usual social connections. Less prominent to outsiders was the work of the Community Liaison Officer who strengthened bonding capital within the local Badimia community. Positive regard for Aboriginal culture was also supported by the prominent position in Wirnda Barna in the centre of Mount Magnet. Local people (both Aboriginal and non-Aboriginal) could see tourists and others stop to view and purchase the artwork. This provided a positive public acknowledgement of Aboriginal culture, which Aboriginal people found affirming, and which caused some non-Aboriginal people to view Aboriginal culture more positively.

'Aboriginal artist', is a social identity that is highly valued. When someone sees themselves as an artist, it is easier for them to see themselves positively, as someone who is skilful and valued, and who contributes positively to cultural maintenance and cultural transmission through their artwork. Some artists saw themselves as providing a useful positive role model to young people in their community, and actively mentored emerging artists. Artists' self-respect was increased as they assumed these cultural leadership roles, and also as others purchased their work and acknowledged the value of Aboriginal art from this region. Art provided them with a respected social identity, where previously, as unemployed Aboriginal people, they had no social respect. Even artists who rarely sold their artwork began to see themselves differently, and could see a pathway to respect that had not been previously possible. This had translated into greater optimism for the future, for themselves and for their families.

Public recognition of their work and greater recognition for individual artists and their culture had begun to heal some of the divisions between the Aboriginal community and the non-Aboriginal community, and this could be seen in a number of ways, including that some white townspeople asked to attend art development workshops offered at the centre. Wirnda Barna had also improved relationships within the Aboriginal community by providing a neutral gathering space that was not owned by any particular group.

Learning

There are several things that can be learned from this case study that have applications beyond the context of this project. First, projects that are complex and address entrenched social issues require long-term funding certainty. This project was ambitious, complex and long-term. It addressed community reconciliation, self-respect and well-being outcomes, and would have benefited from secure funding over an extended period of time. A limitation of the social enterprise model was that the survival of the project depended upon generating a certain amount of income that could not be assured. The budget required for this project was not high, especially compared with saved health and social costs. If the salaries and running costs were underwritten recurrently by another organisation, preferably for an extended period of time, it would have been possible for the ACM to focus on the long-term work of community development, capacity and skill building and development of social capital, governance and business expertise. This would have aided the long-term development of the project and prevented staff burnout. It would also have avoided the disruption, cost and loss of trust incurred by repeated recruitment in circumstances where positions of this type are difficult to fill. A lesson from this project is that the social enterprise model is difficult to implement in projects where income cannot be reliably forecast and assured. Under these conditions, it is necessary for costs to be fully underwritten over a sufficient time period, to ensure viable projects do not fail before they have time to become fully established.

Second, the budget projections of revenue from sales were overly optimistic, given the proportion of new artists within the group, and the lack of established markets for art from this region. The most likely reason for this was to increase the likelihood that the project be supported by grant funding. A less optimistic projection would have risked the project being rejected as unviable. Within competitive tendering funding arrangements, therefore, overly optimistic outcomes are systemically preferred. In this project, a consequence of this approach was understaffing and instability. A lesson from this observation is that competitive tendering is problematic for community work because it tends to reward overly optimistic, well-written tenders that underplay risk, rather than similar projects that are more cautious and realistic in their risk assessment. This bias has human costs when it comes to implementation.

Pope's (2005) framework was developed for use in suburban communities and had some limitations in a racially divided remote context. Pope's measures make useful distinctions between different types of social connection, and the special relevance of relationships that promote bridging capital. However, the findings of this case study affirm the argument of others, that methodologies need to be adjusted to the context in which they are applied. In the communities Wirnda Barna served, many participants had strong personal connectedness and bonding capital, but few of these social connections were cross-racial. Racism meant that despite a strong personal connection between individuals, the communities were deeply divided and most Aboriginal people had very little involvement in governance or 'bridging' relationships beyond the familial social circle. A lesson from this finding affirms the observation of Jennings (2007) that unmodified social capital theory does not adequately consider how community organisations may perpetuate exclusion from social power. Nor does it consider how strong personal bonds may be beneficial to some individuals but detrimental to others within a community.

Further Study

We suggest looking back through the book to further explore these specific issues from the case study:

- *Social capital*
- *Inequality and exclusion*
- *Promoting empowerment*

The case study also raises questions about the advantages and difficulties in developing self-sustaining social enterprises as a vehicle for community development activity. This question is discussed in Section 6.

References

Acker, T. (2008) 'Aboriginal Art: It's a Complicated Thing', *Artlink*. Available at: www.artlink.com.au/articles/3144/aboriginal-art-its-a-complicated-thing/.

Acker, T., and Cosgreve, S. (2009) 'Wirnda Barna Artists Development Plan', *2006 Census Data*. Perth: Australian Bureau of Statistics. Available at: http://abs.gov.au/websitedbs/censushome.nsf/home/historicaldata2006.

Altman, J.C. (2003) 'Developing an Indigenous Arts Strategy for the Northern Territory: Issues paper for consultations', CAEPR Working Paper 22. Available at: www.anu.edu.au/caepr and www.arts.nt.gov.au.

Australian Bureau of Statistics (2011) 'Socio-economic Indexes for Areas (SEIFA)'. Available at: www.abs.gov.au/ausstats/abs@.nsf/DetailsPage/2033.0.55.0012011.

Australian Institute of Health and Welfare (2004) 'Rural, Regional and Remote Health: A Guide to Remoteness Classifications', *Rural Health Series (Australian Institute of Health and Welfare)*, 1448–9775. Available at: www.aihw.gov.au/publications/phe/rrrh-gtrc/rrrh-gtrc.pdf www.aihw.gov.au/publications/index.cfm?type=list&id=0&criteria=rural+health&requestTimeout=1000 www.aihw.gov.au/publications/phe/rrrh-gtrc/rrrh-gtrc-c00.pdf.

Cooper, T., Bahn, S., and Giles, M. (2012) 'Investigating the Social Welfare Indicators of Regional Art Centres: A Pilot Study'. Available at: www.dia.wa.gov.au/en/Publications/.

Cox, E. (2002) 'Australia: Making the Lucky Country', in R.D. Putnam (ed.), *Democracies in Flux: The Evolution of Social Capital in Contemporary Society*. New York: Oxford University Press. Oxford Scholarship Online. Available at: http://dx.doi.org/10.1093/0195150899.001.0001.

Human Rights and Equal Opportunity Commission (1997) *Bringing them Home: Report of the National Inquiry into the Separation of Aboriginal and Torres Strait Islander Children from their Families*. Canberra: Human Rights and Equal Opportunity Commission. Available at: www.humanrights.gov.au/sites/default/files/content/pdf/social_justice/bringing_them_home_report.pdf.

Jennings, J. (2007) *Race, Neighborhoods, and the Misuse of Social Capital*. New York: Macmillan.

Mulholland, T., and Piscicelli, A. (2006) 'Western Australia Tomorrow', *Population Report No. 7, 2006 to 2026*.

OECD (2001) 'The Well-Being of Nations: The Role of Human and Social Capital'. Available at: www.oecd.org/site/worldforum/33703702.pdf.

Pearn, T. (2007) 'Mid West Indigenous Arts Industry Strategy (MWIAIS)'. Available at: www.mwdc.wa.gov.au/indigenous%20arts%20industry.aspx.

Pope, J. (2005) 'Indicators of Community Strength at the Local Government Area Level in Victoria'. Available at: www.dvc.vic.gov.au/spar.htm.

Putnam, R.D. (2000) *Bowling Alone: The Collapse and Revival of American Community.* New York: Simon & Schuster.

Vinson, T. (2004) *Community Adversity and Resilience: The Distribution of Social Disadvantage in Victoria and New South Wales and the Mediating Role of Social Cohesion.* Richmond, Victoria: Jesuit Social Service.

Young, D.R. and Lecy, J.D. (2014) 'Defining the Universe of Social Enterprise: Competing Metaphors', *Voluntas: International Journal of Voluntary and Nonprofit Organizations*, 25(5), 1307–1332.

Case Study 5.3

Popular Education and Neighbourhood Centre Work

P.J. Humphreys and Peter Westoby

Introduction

The purpose of this case study is to share the story of a community-based learning initiative called Building Better Communities (BBC). In a time of increasing de-politicisation of community development, much of the work of Australian neighbourhood centres has also been co-opted by the dominant service delivery paradigm (Burkett, 2011) whereby community work is considered to be providing services *to or for* people. This story shows how neighbourhood centre work drawing on the adult and popular education tradition can be revitalised.

The BBC course has a long history, designed by the Community Praxis Co-operative in the late 1990s. Since then, working in partnership with many local partners (neighbourhood centres and other local government and/or civil society actors), the Community Praxis Co-operative has delivered over 100 such courses. The BBC aims to support a particular kind of community leadership, building the skills and confidence of local residents to work together, make sense of their world through collective deliberation, and be more active in their communities.

Background

Community Plus+, the key local partner in this case study, is a community development organisation that operates neighbourhood centres to strengthen communities across the inner-south side of Brisbane. In doing this it provides spaces for people to meet their neighbours and work together to create positive change.

The inner-south side suburbs of Brisbane are about seven kilometres from the innercity CBD (Central Business District) and include the suburbs of Annerley and Yeronga. The geography of these two suburbs is distinctly different, with Yeronga situated on the picturesque Brisbane River (known as *Maiwar* in indigenous language), and Annerley is split by a major arterial road, frequently congested with heavy traffic. Yeronga has an aging population and a high school with a strong multicultural focus. Annerley has a high multicultural population, in particular those who are refugees and asylum seekers. The main stressors identified through the neighbourhood centre work across Annerley and Yeronga are social isolation, barriers to employment, homelessness and housing affordability.

Community Plus+ has been working in Annerley and Yeronga for a short period of time: three and five years respectively. In Yeronga, the neighbourhood centre emerged from a disaster-response to the 2011 Brisbane floods (West End Community House, 2011) and most activities were service-based. In Annerley, much of the neighbourhood centre work involved crisis response to appropriate and affordable housing. The core neighbourhood centre funding is provided by the Queensland Government, which in turn calls such centres 'service providers' (Department of Communities, Child Safety & Disability Services, 2015). Yet, the organisational vision is to support people to be active citizens in their communities and to create positive social change in the places where they live, work and play. Therefore, in 2017 Community Plus+ partnered with Community Praxis Co-operative to deliver the BBC course.

Conceptual Framing

The BBC course is conceptualised as an adult education initiative in the popular education tradition. Popular education is a form of adult education that encourages learners to examine their lives critically and take action to change social conditions (Kerka, 1998). It is 'popular' in the sense of being 'of the people'. This is in contrast to the elites of a community, such as big business, political parties and ruling classes. Rick Flowers (2004) refers to this as the distinction between 'education *for* the people' and 'education *by* and *with* the people'.

The goal of popular education is to develop 'people's capacity for social change through a collective problem-solving approach emphasizing participation, reflection, and critical analysis of social problems' (Bates, 1996: 225–226). Brookfield (2005) has provided a useful summary of how critical theory informs liberating education. The task of critical theory is to challenge ideology; confront hegemony; unmask power; overcome alienation; learn liberation; reclaim reason; and practice democracy. Thus, popular education explicitly works for empowerment; it aims for social change and has political action as an integral part of its intention (Arnold et al., 1985; Mackenzie, 1993; Wagner, 1998). The intention is for people alienated from their own cultures to become self-aware political subjects (Freire, 1970; Hernandez, 1985 cited in Hamilton and Cunningham, 1989: 443). It is this use of critical theory that firmly locates popular education at the crossroads of politics and pedagogy.

Flowers (2004) attests that popular education practice in the Freirean education sense does more than promote active participation – as adult learning might do. It fosters robust debate, encourages questioning, hopes to foster a sense of indignation and anger, and at times supports confrontation. Popular education does more than help people feel more informed, responsible and self-reliant. It helps people to take action and actively pursue alternative visions for the future. It helps people to not just feel empowered but actually to strive for *more* power.

Perhaps the most well-known expression of popular education lies with Paulo Freire and his literacy work in Brazil in the 1960s. *Pedagogy of the Oppressed* (1970) announces the main themes of Freire's career: the non-neutrality of education; the power of knowledge; the coercive force behind rote learning and 'banking' education; the need for dialogical pedagogies; empowerment of the learner and the importance of co-constructing knowledge based on the experience of learners. These themes lead to a 'consciousness-raising' or 'conscience awakening'; helping people to see their positionality in the world and to recognise how their knowledge gives them the power to act and to change that world.

Freire's work had provided the basic pedagogical concepts and methodologies necessary to stimulate 'critical consciousness' and the transformation of worldview. However, *Pedagogy of the Oppressed* is written in both strongly Marxist and patriarchal language which can alienate some readers. Freire himself suggests that no one can fully understand his ideas from that single text, given that his thinking has continued to develop over 30 years. In 1998, Freire wrote *Pedagogy of Freedom: Ethics, Democracy and Civic Courage*. Although he returns to many of his perennial themes, here his vision is wider and more holistic in terms of connecting learning with the wider world; to ethics, globalisation, and civil society and in social change. His vision is also more hopeful, reiterating that through critical, reflective pedagogies the world can be transformed to be a freer and more just place.

Although Freire's published work did not appear in English until the 1970s, this kind of educational approach has an impressive lineage, most notably Myles Horton's work with the Highlander Folk School during the American Civil Rights Movement, one we focus on as their work reflects some of the BBC aspirations.

Horton created the Highlander Folk School (now Highlander Research and Education Center) in the Appalachian Mountains of Tennessee in the 1930s and worked continually for social justice and transformation until the early 1990s. His lifetime of work played a key role in the American Labor Movement of the 1930s, the American Civil Rights Movement of the 1960s and the environmental and land rights struggle in the Appalachian region in the 1980s. Despite vastly different life paths, Freire and Horton shared remarkably similar views and practices on educating for change. Their joint work provides a dialogue (see Bell et al.'s *We Make the Road by Walking*) that alternates between Freire's conceptual understandings of the connections between education and social change, and Horton's straightforward descriptions of how such ideas have been practised in reality over six decades (Bell et al., 1990). Horton emphasises the importance of storytelling for allowing people to share knowledge and build from a collective knowledge base to address their own problems without being dependent on outside assistance.

Alongside Freire and Horton, a third author who has been important for the BBC pedagogy, is the African American feminist theorist bell hooks. hooks has become a pre-eminent pedagogue in her own right. Whilst embracing Freire's work, hooks (1994: 49) also offers a critique of the sexism of Freire's language and of his patriarchal model of liberation, which she read as equating liberation with manhood. hooks brings a black feminist perspective to critiques of education, and also to the way teaching and learning should be re-visioned.

Building Better Communities in Yeronga and Annerley

Twenty-five participants attended with 20 completing the course. The participants were made up of people who lived, worked and volunteered in Annerley or Yeronga, as well as three participants from the neighbouring suburb of Moorooka. The participants were mostly residents and/or volunteers in Annerley or Yeronga. There were three participants who did not fit one of the categories. One participant was a Community Plus+ employee working in another Brisbane neighbourhood centre and two were students undertaking their social work placements with Community Plus+. Of the 25 participants, 16 were female and nine were male. Their ages ranged from 25 years to 65 years with an even spread across the decades.[7] The participants were predominantly Anglo-Saxon with three participants from a culturally and linguistically diverse background.

Inviting People In …

The participants were predominantly invited to join the course through Community Plus+ existing networks across the two neighbourhood centres in Annerley and Yeronga. This consisted of approaching people in person about the course, distributing a flyer through Facebook, email lists, newsletters and community noticeboards. Only three participants were not known prior to the course commencing – that is, most participants had a pre-existing relationship with the workers within the two centres. Motivation and interest in community was the priority. Other factors such as age, gender, socio-economic status and cultural diversity were not. As part of this 'inviting in' process we also made it clear that during the course we would be encouraging people to *do something* in their community. These actions could be around: forging new relationships, linking to an existing project or starting a new initiative. We would then use the course to reflect on these 'actions' and share our learning. The aspiration was to move into praxis, as per action/activity and reflection.

Structure and Content

An open information session was held initially to introduce the BBC course, ensuring people had both enough information to know what they were 'signing-up for', and also to negotiate with people the best times (day of the week/time of the day). Almost everyone who came to that convivial information session, which included the normal rituals of community building – tea/coffee, cake and so on – agreed to continue. There was an exciting energy to be felt immediately. The course consisted of six three-hour workshops conducted on a Monday evening over a six-week period with two follow-up sessions.

The content and format of the course was intentionally relational with a circle check-in and reflection at the beginning of each session. A break was also taken during each session to share supper together, and as it was during winter months, a lovely warming soup was enjoyed by all. These intentional relational processes created a shared experience and enabled the weaving of social ties within the group. Many of the participants reported how meeting and getting to know others in their community was a highlight from the course.

The first three sessions built the foundation for the course exploring:

- *'the kind of community that we would like to live in'*. This explored participants' experience of community and the values and characteristics that enable 'community';
- *'what are the things that block us'* and *'how to overcome them'*. This session considered the difficulties people face in trying to build communities under the contemporary conditions of hyper-capitalism, with its accompanying ways of living (mobility, labour flexibility, technology and so on); we also explored positive ways to increase our power;
- *'some skills and methods around connecting with others in our community'*. This core session develops, with participants, a framework for community building, inclusive of dialogue, forming small groups, sustaining work through appropriate community structures, and then 'moving beyond the local' through coalitions, networks, and federations.

Then, as a group, we chose the topics that were most helpful to us at this point in the development process. Examples of topics covered included:

- How to motivate people to get involved
- Working inclusively (culture/class/gender etc.)
- Starting and sustaining a group
- The contribution of introverts and extroverts (can an introvert be a good community worker?)
- Managing conflicting
- Entrepreneurial change vs. collaborative-collective efforts
- Dealing with difficult people or difficult organisations.

Outcome Aspirations

As per popular education and community development, the intended outcomes were for participants to *both* increase their skills, confidence and knowledge to do community work, *and* to participate in actual collective analysis and action – that is, moving towards praxis. Of note, the two facilitators – the authors of this chapter – made it clear that the collective did not have to be 'a group formed from this course'. People could pair up, form threes, or join with others not in the course. The main point was, 'don't go it alone – work with others as per the community work tradition'. Overall, the course aimed to provide a platform to meet others who want to create change. Restated again, and in a slightly different way, one of the crucial ideas communicated is that people do not have to create change alone as per the heroic or entrepreneurship model (which was discussed a lot) – and that, instead, people can be active citizens together.

An evaluation was conducted one year on from the course whereby 13 participants took part in semi-structured interviews. The findings show that the intended outcomes were met in terms of increased confidence, skills and knowledge.

Actual Outcomes

Participant Confidence

During the course, there was evidence of increased confidence. People would come to sessions willing to share stories of their experiments, often just a new kind of conversation with someone in their neighbourhood; or some idea they had been pondering during the week. But, during the evaluation, it was clear that participants reported an increase in confidence in how to go about being involved in their local community. For example, some of the comments included:

> I was hesitant to ask people. I have a lot of ideas but now I feel that I can do it and people can help me.
> The main thing is confidence and I have put it in my work.

In a socio-political context, where people's habituate response to difficulties or concerns is individual action or 'waiting' for the state, confidence to approach others to initiate group or community-oriented activities is significant.

Skills and Knowledge

However, initial confidence, without enough skills, will soon wain. Probably, the main outcomes of the course were people's sense that they'd learned many skills, concepts and frameworks relevant to everyday life and also community work. Examples included a framework known as '0-1-3' (Westoby and Owen, 2010) which signifies the idea that if you are alone with a dream you have zero relationships; if you are with one other person there's one relationship, but if there are three people, there are also three relationships. The course facilitators argued that for community development, three was the minimal structure to make it 'a community process'. This differentiated a community praxis clearly from a heroic or entrepreneurial approach. Evaluations also showed that the idea of 'holding your own agenda lightly' was powerful for people. This idea supported participants to rethink their habitual way of thinking – away from 'yell my idea loudly, and try to convert or recruit people', to a more conversational approach in which people would enter into conversations with others lightly and create 'shared agendas'. It was not so much about recruitment to 'my idea', but building energy around 'shared ideas'.

A tangible example of a community project emerging from BBC is the Share Shed,[8] a 'library of things' initiative. A participant shared this idea with the other course participants. As a result of this, a fellow participant shared a Facebook post on a community page regarding an overseas 'library of things' example and there was energy for the idea from others who worked together to make it happen.

Unintended Outcomes

We should add that there were also many unintended outcomes. There are many examples of ongoing connections between the participants. For example, personal friendships have been formed – two participants are now exercise buddies and are sharing a house together. A few people have regular coffee catch-ups and others share food from their culture over neighbourly meals.

Moving towards 'the Political'

Whilst most of the initiatives could be described as socially oriented (e.g. Share Shed) there were also some experiments in more politically oriented work. For example, Create Annerley, started by one of the BBC participants, and now joined with other residents, is a place-making experiment that is trying to deal with many issues linked to a large main road cutting through the neighbourhood of Annerley.

One of the outcomes of the Create Annerley group was a town hall meeting in October 2017, to which 80 people turned up. The meeting was a space for residents to share their concerns around issues of safety, pollution (noise and fuel), and city planning. Actions from the town hall meeting have been to provide input into the City Transport Plan and initiate a petition and other tactics were being considered into 2018. The group has lots of energy, although there are challenges around sustaining and structuring the group to 'last the distance'.

Conclusion

How do Neighbourhood Centre Workers Support Ongoing Community Action?

Linked to the final point above, one of the questions within neighbourhood centre work drawing on popular education initiatives such as the BBC, is that things get started, but who is there to support citizen action over the long haul? From the perspective of the community worker, there is little or no time to support such politically oriented citizen activities, or more importantly provide mentoring, nurturing or reflective support to some of the key animating citizens. People have skills, confidence and knowledge, but we have observed that people do still need extra support to sustain and structure the action.

Our analysis is that the paid community workers of such neighbourhood centres as Community Plus+ need to *be given some space* from 'service provision' (the requirements of the funding). This space would be used to support community-oriented and citizen-led political work and therefore also needs supportive managers to act as buffers between funders and citizen action.

Closer Linkages to Social Movements

Intriguingly, the people who did the course and who initiated more politically oriented collective activities, were also connected to broader social movements. Some were linked to sustainability movements (urban and waste), and others to anti-coal campaigns. This appears to be important when a neighbourhood centre is resourced to work in a geographically oriented place. It is all too easy for issues to become local, and even self-interested (e.g. NIMBY). Citizen and worker connections to broader social movements ensure that the local activities (which are crucial) are understood within a broader, or even global, frame (e.g. 'think globally, act locally' etc.).

Further Study

We suggest looking back through the book to further explore these specific issues from the case study:

- *Popular education*
- *Building and sustaining groups*
- *Active citizenship*
- *Leadership*
- *Empowerment*
- *Monitoring and evaluation*

References

Arnold, R., Barndt, D., and Burke, B. (1985) *A New Weave: Popular Education in Central America and Canada*. Ontario: CUSO Development Education and Ontario Institute for Studies in Education.

Bates, R.A. (1996) 'Popular Theatre: A Useful Process for Adult Educators', *Adult Education Quarterly*, 46(4), 224–236.

Bell, B., Gaventa, J., and Peters, J. (eds) (1990) *We Make the Road by Walking: Conversations on Education and Social Change, Myles Horton and Paulo Freire*. Philadelphia, PA: Temple University Press.

Brookfield, S. (2005) *The Power of Critical Theory: Liberating Adult Learning and Teaching*. San Francisco, CA: Jossey-Bass.

Burkett, I. (2011) 'Organizing in the New Marketplace: Contradictions and Opportunities for Community Development Organizations in the Ashes of Neoliberalism', *Community Development Journal*, 46(2), 111–127.

Department of Communities, Child Safety and Disability Services (2015) 'Community Investment Specifications'. Available at: www.communities.qld.gov.au/resources/funding/investmentdomains/investment-spec-community.pdf.

Flowers, R. (2004) *Defining Popular Education* [Online]. Available at: www.uni-due.de/imperia/md/content/eb-wb/defining_popular_education.pdf, accessed 12 February 2018.

Freire, P. (1970) *Pedagogy of the Oppressed*. New York: Herder and Herder.

Hamilton, E. and Cunningham, P.M. (1989) 'Community-based Adult Education', in S.B. Merriam and P.M. Cunningham (eds), *Handbook of Adult and Continuing Education*. San Francisco, CA: Jossey-Bass, 439–450.

hooks, b. (1994) *Teaching to Transgress: Education as the Practice of Freedom*. New York: Routledge.

Kerka, S. (1998) 'Popular Education: Adult Education for Social Change', *ERIC Digest 185*. Ohio: ERIC Clearinghouse on Adult, Career, and Vocational Education.

Mackenzie, L. (1993) *On Our Feet: Taking Steps to Challenge Women's Oppression: A Handbook on Gender and Popular Education Workshops*. South Africa: Centre for Continuing Education, University of the Western Cape.

Wagner, P.A. (1998) 'Popular Education in the Philippines: To Make Ready to Risk', *Popular Education Notebook*, 4(1), 20–22.

West End Community House (2011) *Strengthening People and Places: The Role and Value of Neighbourhood Centres*. Brisbane, Australia: West End Community House.

Westoby, P. and Owen, J. (2010) 'The Sociality and Geometry of Community Development Practice', *Community Development Journal*, 45(1), 58–74.

Case Study 5.4

Spinning Rubbish into Gold: A Community Development Route to Environmental Social Enterprise

John Stansfield

Ki te kahore he whakakitenga ka ngaro te iwi

Without foresight or vision, the people will be lost

Whilst the post-war period might be thought of as the era of social reform, the neoliberal period that followed was about economic reform punctuated by an emerging disquiet about our environment. Rachel Carson's (1962) seminal work *The Silent Spring* was a clarion call to environmental concern that drew a sharp focus to the poisoning of the planet. Today's environmentalism poses a powerful critique and in the contemporary lens of sustainable development addresses social and economic as well as environmental concerns. The separation of people from planet, as a locus of concern, has not served either well. Nor are the realms mutually antagonistic or exclusive (Bradshaw and Winn, 2000). The bringing together of these two themes is evident from the time of the Brundtland Commission (1987) and thereafter through the major international governance conferences and resolutions such as Agenda 21 in 1992, and the Kyoto Protocol in 1997. In this case study, I will relate how an enterprising community achieved social, economic and environmental goals building their community capacity and having a lot of fun in the process.

Context

Waiheke Island (pop. 9,000), the jewel in the crown of the Hauraki Gulf, lies just 35 minutes by fast boat from Auckland, New Zealand's largest city. The community, in common with other islands, has a strong sense of place or what we now call 'islandness' (Conkling, 2007).

Until 1989, Waiheke was locally governed by the Waiheke County Council. To the chagrin of Islanders, it was amalgamated to Auckland City Council. The first thing the good burghers of Waiheke could tangibly see change was the loss of their fledgling recycling scheme. The tip, or transfer station, a favorite scavenging point, was declared off limits to the public and ever-increasing volumes of perfectly reusable material were consigned to landfill.

Waihekeans, in common with many island communities, are sensitive to loss of sovereignty (Prescott, 2003), and were demanding a bit more say over the place in which they live. This desire for self-determination is a recurrent theme throughout the islands' history and many of the problems experienced in Government relations can be sheeted home to this value. This makes for fertile ground for community development.

Organising and Learning

With the City Council now in charge, the recycling scheme was abandoned. The islanders' renowned talent for protest died away and the community began to organise. Informally, a group formed to pursue the community's interest in sustainable waste management. The Waiheke Waste Resources Trust (WRT) was later incorporated and thrives 20 years on.

The first thing WRT did was to recognise a need to learn a great deal more about waste, waste economics, and waste in the environment. They developed a Wānanga or study group and got together every few weeks to share research and learnings. Convivial meetings always centred around a shared 'pot-luck' meal, reinforcing local community development lore and our first community development principle for this case study.

'The Community Sector Marches on its Stomach'

The meetings were also useful opportunities to recognise expertise and try out working with each other. The organisation had high ambitions and would need a seasoned crew.

During this period, WRT was informed by meetings with:

- Other communities and organisations concerned about waste
- Community waste operations such as the Kaitaia Community Business and Environment Centre CBEC
- Community waste campaigners and their experience from campaigns as far afield as Scotland and Wales
- Dr. Google and social media groups

Consolidating Learning and Building Constituency

Over the period of about 18 months, the trust gave itself a Master's level education in sustainable waste management (Seadon, 2010) and developed its key principles and strategies for the road ahead. Central to this was the development of a community consensus on a 'Waiheke way' in which Waiheke could manage the waste stream and use the enterprise to provide sustainable jobs, an improved environment, and investment in waste reduction through innovation and public education.

Building that consensus involves a range of creative strategies to inform and engage community members (Eichler, 2007). In this case extensive use of visiting local groups, holding a stall at the local markets, feeding local media and events and stunts, such as the shopping trolley dolly entry to the local Santa parade to draw attention to the issue of waste and an island approach. These speak to the second principle of Waiheke community development.

If you are fun to be with, there will always be people with you.

The first lucky break was the adoption of a new law that required local councils to consult with communities in developing local waste management plans. In its usual fashion Council arranged for a couple of consultants to talk to the community of Waiheke at a public meeting. A process that had been budgeted to take two hours then ensued over the coming six weeks. The well-informed and articulate advocates of the WRT were successful in advocating for a radical waste plan which strongly reflected the community consensus that had developed over the previous 18 months. This plan was then adopted by Council and formed the basis for new tenders in waste contracting for Waiheke. The strategy was to set the bar high for environmental performance so that groups with strong environmental credentials could compete with the waste Moghuls.

An Enterprise of Our Own

In 2000, the WRT began meeting with the Kaitaia group CBEC to plan a joint bid for the waste contract. The WRT partner had significant knowledge of the challenges of Island logistics, the fragile road system and precarious infrastructure as well as a strong support from the local community; CBEC had several years' experience both contracting with Council and delivering kerbside waste collection and recycling. The parties came together incorporated as Cleanstream Waiheke Ltd and developed the successful bid for the contract. The company was incorporated in May 2001 and commenced operations on 1 July 2001.

The day before operations were due to commence, with all the contracts having been executed, the directors were aghast to find the council was requiring a further one hundred thousand dollar bond in addition to all of the bank and personal guarantees which had already been supplied. The company had never operated and had very modest capital. Seeing no other options, the directors, all volunteers, took personal loans against their homes, and in one case against his parents' home, to ensure the operation could start on time.

This was a terrifically exciting time with a very steep learning curve for those involved. The company commenced operations with an experienced community waste operator managing operations and a board with both commercial and community development experience.

The first big surprise was how jubilant the community was at having regained control of their waste stream. The second was how little Council really understood about the operation. For example, Council had been relying upon the previous operator to faithfully record the tonnage of green waste converted to mulch and compost. This was sold at the gate and, as the transactions were largely cash and there was no audit process there may have been some under-reporting. Council estimated process and sales to be up to 200 ton p.a. of green waste, but this was, in fact, over 800 ton in the first year rising to over 2000 tons.

As soon as operations commenced, WRT started to get real and reliable data on waste volumes. In the first year refuse volumes dropped by 250 tons, recycling was up by 530 tons and all this looked like good news. However, combined weights were increasing and, with the construction boom and growing local industry, an impending rubbish explosion loomed. In response, the company, which had been severely undercapitalised and was scrambling to keep on top of unpredicted volumes, invested in its parent organisation, WRT, and developed a waste education and community engagement programme. They backed community development to reduce the problem ahead of expensive plant to manage it. WRT engaged a pair of community development leaders to build a volunteer army fit for the task.

The waste education team had some highly innovative strategies for community engagement and were constantly challenging the company to innovate further than the waste stream – for example, the successful biodiesel plant harvested 25,000 litres of waste cooking oil and converted this to diesel fuel which ran the company's trucks and machinery. This was the result of a small piece of research conducted by the waste educators and a successful partnership with the University of Auckland Engineering School, Engineering Projects in Community Service (EPICS).

The education team developed the much-loved annual festival Junk to Funk, which showcased the island's creative talent and produced wearable art from the waste stream. This event involved 1200 in a population of just 4000 at the time.

The team also used opportunistic strategies where existing events, such as the local market and the music festivals, provided opportunity for community engagement. These events were the forerunners of the sustainability festival which most recently saw ten days of sustainability focus and over 50 events, and involving many other clubs and environmental organisations.

Another initiative of the team, which has now gone Auckland-wide, is the zero-waste (Song et al., 2015) approach to large community events. From the environmental disaster of previous years, a crowd of 5000 at the Onetangi beach races can now produce as little as 20 litres of waste to landfill. Half a dozen community groups staff zany waste reduction stalls with volunteers growing engagement and earning grants for their clubs. The undeniable success of this programme, which vastly outperformed both commercial and Council events, has now become mainstream. In its later years, the WRT company was contracted by commercial event organisers and zero waste events are now part of the Waiheke way.

WRT won awards for innovation both nationally, from the glass packaging Council, and internationally, at the Green Globe awards. It had a strong research and development ethos, which informed its innovations. In the case of glass, changes in the New Zealand economy meant the glassworks were flooded with clear glass and the market price plummeted from $78 a tonne to just $12 a tonne. Freight costs alone were $60 a tonne and it was clear the company would need to develop either a higher value product from the glass or find ways of using it domestically. Investigations with the engineering school led us to explore glass-processing options and eventually import specialised machinery from the United States. This gave a domestic aggregate at $35 a tonne with no freight cost (down-cycling) and some much higher value products for export to the mainland (up-cycling).

Over the nine years of operation, the population grew by 11 per cent whilst waste to landfill fell by 20 per cent. Figure 5.1 illustrates the process of the Waiheke Way model.

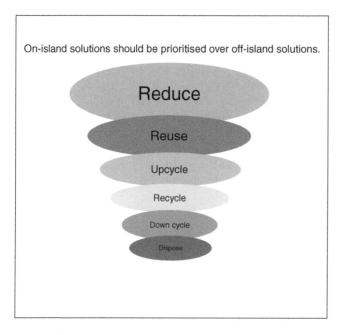

Figure 5.1 'This experience prompted us to develop our own model of waste management'

Learnings from the Front Line of the Waste War

Operations are a Transport Business

Waste operations are transport businesses. Most of the big waste companies have grown out of the transport industry. This is because most of what they do is not transforming waste or influencing in any way how much waste there is. It is the much simpler task of picking up waste from one place and taking it to another. There is nothing inherently evil about a transport business but we need to understand the limitations of its worldview. It understands that its job is to put things in trucks and drive them around and that it makes the most money by driving the most stuff for the biggest distance.

This is not a worldview which has any sense of the waste hierarchy and the need to reduce waste. Waste education, where it is conducted by the big waste companies, is not sophisticated. The real innovators in the waste sector around the world have been small committed communities that are values-driven. These communities understand that we are on a trajectory of complete unsustainability in unaffordable waste practices.

A more sophisticated approach to waste begins with the waste hierarchy and whilst everybody understands it, it is seldom at the forefront of operational design. Whilst the hierarchy identifies *reduce and reuse* as the highest order actions it is *dispose and mitigate* which receive all the resources. Unsurprisingly, then, waste volumes grow and little real attention is paid to *reduce and reuse*.

There are some things about Waiheke and transport that are unique. We are a small island surrounded by an expensive piece of sea. Our road network is narrow, fragile and expensive to maintain. Big trucks might be efficient to cart waste, however their impact on quality of life and the fragile road system must be considered. Savings by using big trucks accrue to the waste operator but the burden of road repair costs and decreased quality of life become the burden of the residents.

Given the Consistent Opportunity, People will do the Right Thing

The community development approach used by the WRT and Cleanstream emphasises the importance of the relationship with households in the community because no sustainable change can be made without the primary work being done at the household level. This is our third community development principle.

> *Trust the people, only the community can make real and lasting change.*

Sometimes this approach brought WRT into conflict with Council. When it began in 2001, WRT instituted the kerbside collection of recyclables and then demanded that recycling bins were placed alongside public litter bins wherever they appeared. Council disagreed, they did not use public recycling bins in Auckland until 2008. WRT insisted and went ahead, arguing that you must give the public a consistency of opportunity if you are going to make sustainable long-term change. You cannot, for instance, train people to do one thing at home and another thing when they are out because the dissonance this causes has a corrosive effect on a commitment to sustainable waste practices. The company's investment in community engagement and community waste education built a consistency of approach that enabled real conversations about long-term change. WRT's not-for-profit status and visible investment in their own community gave it a legitimacy that private sector operators and Council would struggle to achieve.

Waste is not an Engineering Problem, it is a Problem of Human Behaviour

This is a most important lesson because, although the company invested in all kinds of clever engineering innovations, the biggest changes are made at the household level. If you cannot make sustainable changes at the household level you cannot solve it through engineering. George Blanchard, a long-time WRT board member who was himself a senior lecturer in engineering, once told us as a board 'I love machines. I've spent my life around machines they have been my life work, yet I can tell you, as proficient as I am in the world of machines, there is no machine built which can outperform the human ability to learn and adapt and change processes.' The very best performance internationally, in communities whose demographics and density resemble ours, are systems where the householder is the primary sorter and the secondary sorting happens at a kerbside vehicle. These are very low-tech solutions but they are enormously flexible. They can, for instance, add a new product to the recycling stream with minimal re-engineering and, with good measurement and appropriate communications, can build success and share this with the communities that enable this success. One of the real failures of the typical industrialised system is that it does not report to households or acknowledge their place in the system. Waste reduction is an ideal community development project because community developers know this communication is their most powerful tool.

It Is All About The Sorting

In the materials flow economy, the first thing we do to add value to a commodity is to sort and grade it. I learned this as a very young boy helping on a tomato farm. A case of tomatoes would be worth so many shillings a pound, and my job was to sort these into four grades. The lowest grade struck the rate per pound of the entire case and every grade higher attracted a premium. It is pretty much the same with rubbish. One of the problems with the co-mingled collection system is its outcome is a bigger problem than its inputs. Picture this: I have on one hand an empty egg carton and in the other hand a used sauce bottle. They are separated. I now put them into a single receptacle so they can be carted first to the industrialised Materials Recycling Facility (MRF) where a machine separates them, sometimes successfully, one from the other. We have taken what was separate, mingled it, compressed it, carted it, and we are now processing it to re-separate it. That is engineering madness. There are other problems with a centralised co-mingled system. Principal amongst these is that, to achieve the transport efficiencies required, the co-mingled recycled material is compacted at a higher than ideal density and the glass tends to shatter. Glass slivers then contaminate the cardboard and paper which can then no longer be recycled in New Zealand. Moreover, machinery is not available to sort the small particles of glass into the constituent.

The Waste Hierarchy

It may be time to revisit the waste hierarchy. A more sophisticated waste management system must now identify opportunities for up-cycling materials as well as down-cycling. However, the basic principle of the waste hierarchy is very sound and is largely ignored. Reduce is at the apex of the hierarchy, followed by re-use, and third is recycle. The point of the hierarchy is that we only recycle materials that we have failed to reduce and failed to reuse. There has been too much celebration about the increased recycling volumes, particularly where the result is degraded materials with limited markets and are essentially down-cycled. The only sustainable long-term solution to reducing Waiheke's waste costs is to reduce Waiheke's waste. This means the waste operation must be governed by an organisation that is committed to waste reduction first, reuse second and recycling third. Given the transport costs Islanders face, recycling is appropriate only where it is unfeasible to reduce and reuse. This freight cost creates a tariff barrier which means as freight costs increase local reuse becomes increasingly attractive.

The Winning Formula

Above all, WRT learned in its island environment, given the transport problems and costs, that the rule is:

> *We should never move anything away from the island until it is at its highest value, greatest density and we have extracted from it as much as we can use or earn locally.*

An examination of the domestic refuse found that, after removal of organics, various non-recyclable plastics, multimedia plastics, and waste fibre constitute around 60 per cent of the waste stream. Research and development, initially with the University, developed a prototype plastic fibre composite board made entirely from waste materials. This was then further refined with a private sector partner and an engineered composite board (ECB) was developed. This board has the capacity to utilise a significant part of the waste stream which is destined to landfill and to incorporate waste, including hazardous fibre such as chipped treated timber which can neither be burned nor buried because of the absorbed toxins. ECB was developed into domestic and building products. Both the process and business plans for the product were refined by two further university studies and the initiative gained international recognition in the Green Globe awards.

The Company employed, along with the Trust, up to 26 workers at its peak; many staff had suffered from long-term unemployment or irregular work. Intensive training and a 'skills'-based pay system were introduced and workers were encouraged up a promotion path and into qualifications. Two positions were created for severely disabled workers and workflows were adjusted to meet their health and rehabilitation needs. The company earned most of its money off-island and spent almost all its money on-island. The manual sorting system was more labour intensive than the City plant but produced much better quality and higher earning recyclables. These better-quality recyclables continued to find markets during the Global Financial Crisis when poor quality recyclables from the city machine-sorted plant became valueless.

The sharing of opportunities has been a deliberate strategy to broaden the WRT base and has resulted in its gradual ascendency to the most prominent of the islands, with NGO's frequently acting as mentor and umbrella to other organisations. Its waste project supported community gardens, childcare centres, adult literacy, the schools, local environmental restoration initiatives, our local marae and many other community causes.

Key Outcomes

- Improved training and employment for locals, one even took her waste mission to parliament, becoming the first spokesperson for waste in the House of Representatives
- Improved environmental outcomes

- Strengthened community organisations
- A strong sense of local ownership, community capability, and connectedness
- Strengthened community identity and civic pride

Prologue

In 2009, the WRT lost the contract for rubbish and recycling services to a multinational firm now owned by the investment arm of a Chinese municipality. The community was outraged. By 2015 waste to landfill had increased by over 30 per cent, the support of community organisations had shrunk, as had the workforce. I am tempted to offer a fourth community development principle:

No good deed goes unpunished

But I am a believer and am sure the community will rise again to recapture its rubbish after all as the WRT leaders are wont to say 'controlling the rubbish is an imperative, we have to grab all the rubbish for the poor before the rich find out how valuable it is!'.

Further Study

We suggest looking back through the book to further explore these specific issues from the case study:

- *Identifying local assets*
- *Group building and sustainability*
- *Coalition building*
- *Building mass local involvement through a community-based education programme and public events*
- *Social enterprise as a development model*

References

Bradshaw, T.K. and Winn, K. (2000) 'Gleaners, Do-Gooders, and Balers: Options for Linking Sustainability and Economic Development', *Community Development Society Journal*, 31(1), 112–129.

Brundtland, G. (1987) *Our Common Future, from One Earth to One World. World Commission on Environment and Development.* New York: United Nations. Available at: www.undocuments. net/our-common-future.pdf.

Carson, R. (1962) *The Silent Spring.* New York: Houghton Mifflin Harcourt.

Conkling, P. (2007) 'On Islanders and Islands', *The Geographical Review*, 97(2), 191–201. doi: 10.1111/j.1931-0846.2007.tb00398.x.

Eichler, M. (2007) *Consensus Organizing: Building Communities of Mutual Self-Interest.* Thousand Oaks, CA: Sage.

Prescott, V. (2003) 'A Geography of Islands: Small Island Insularity', *The Professional Geographer*, 55(2), 294–295.

Seadon, J.K. (2010) 'Sustainable Waste Management Systems', *Journal of Cleaner Production*, 18(16–17), 1639–1651.

Song, Q., Li, J., and Zeng, X. (2015) 'Minimizing the Increasing Solid Waste through Zero Waste Strategy', *Journal of Cleaner Production*, 104, 199–210.

Community Development and Social Enterprise Resources

Organisation: www.wrt.org.nz/
                 http://cbec.co.nz/
Engagement: www.youtube.com/watch?v=KDT3FsZIKkI
                 www.youtube.com/watch?v=TyY7Ko5SZaQ
                 www.youtube.com/watch?v=6hkbIMntUiw
Innovation: www.youtube.com/watch?v=5HUAJDT_Yyc&t=89s
                 www.youtube.com/watch?v=_hzlNKFrxw4
                 www.nzherald.co.nz/nz/news/article.cfm?c_id=1&objectid=10464715

Case Study 5.5

Play Sufficiency as an Organising Principle of Community Development

Ben Tawil and Mike Barclay

Children playing out in their neighbourhoods can be considered as an indicator of community well-being. Research in Wrexham has shown that children and parents recognise that improving opportunities for play can make an area a better place to live. In particular the amount of free-time children have to play in their neighbourhood is directly linked to levels of place attachment and that more people playing outside more of the time in more places can improve community cohesion and strengthen intergenerational relationships (Hartshorne, 2014). Communities that work for children and adults are places that value children enough to ensure their rights are met alongside those of adults, recognising that children and their play are not separate from other aspects of community life but instead are an essential part of it. Where communities answer this description, we find children enjoying their childhoods despite their experiences of financial and social disadvantage (Long et al., 2014).

Diversity of environmental resources and access to play and exploration have been regarded as two central criteria for child-friendly environments, or as we might like to consider them, communities (Kytta, 2003). However, children's ability to find time and space for playing is often dependent on adults. Perhaps the most significant change for childhoods today compared to those of previous generations is the increasing degree to which children are living, and therefore playing, in environments designed, built and supervised by adults, whose tendency is to prioritise the interests of other adults over those of children. Play has been trivialised, colonised, commercialised and designed out by adults (Gray, 2013).

The fact that play matters so much to children but has received so little attention from adults presents an opportunity to do things differently. By prioritising play alongside other adult agendas and positioning play as central to our thinking, we can ensure children and their way of engaging with the world have a much greater influence over how we govern and over the design of environments we create for people. In 2012, the Welsh Government introduced the Play Sufficiency Duty, making Wales the first country in the world to legislate specifically in support of children's play. This duty places a responsibility on all local authorities in Wales to carry out an assessment of children's opportunities for play every three years, and between times, to take action to secure sufficient opportunities for play based on their findings.

'Wales – A Play Friendly Country' is the Welsh Government's (2014) statutory guidance for local authorities on assessing and securing the sufficiency of play opportunities for children living in their area. The guidance begins by stating that children have a fundamental right to be able to play, going on to recognise that play is central to children's enjoyment and well-being, can help mitigate the negative effects of poverty by building resilience, has value for children's holistic development, and also contributes to the well-being of families and the wider community.

In 2013, the United Nations Committee on the Rights of the Child published General Comment 17 on Article 31 of the UNCRC. The purpose of this 'General Comment' was to clarify and emphasise the responsibilities of countries within the United Nations in terms of children's right to play:

> The Committee, in its reviews of implementation of the rights of the child under the Convention, is concerned by the poor recognition given by States to Article 31 rights. Poor recognition of their significance in the lives of children results in lack of investment in appropriate provision, weak or non-existent protective legislation and invisibility of children in national and local level planning. In general, where investment is made, it is in the provision of structured and organised activities. Equally important is the need to create time and space for spontaneous play, recreation and creativity, and the promotion of societal attitudes that support and encourage such activity.
>
> (UNCRC, 2013: 3)

Both the Welsh Government's play sufficiency guidance and General Comment 17 are clear that securing sufficient play opportunities for children is not just about designated provision but is dependent on the ability of local authorities to cultivate the temporal, spatial and psychological conditions needed for children to play (Barclay and Tawil, 2013). This, in turn, highlights the need for changes to be made across national and local government, within local community practices and adult run institutions, and within people's own homes to create an environment that is more supportive and considerate of children's innate playful behaviour, leading Lester and Russell (2013: 64) to conclude:

> The PSA (play sufficiency assessment) has set local authorities on a road that pays increasing attention to the ways in which adults (both in a professional capacity and through their everyday encounters with children) may adopt a more caring role that acknowledges the importance of children finding time and space, with and without adults, in their immediate environments. It requires adults to begin to pay more careful attention to the multiple ways in which adults and children are connected, directly and remotely in co-creating conditions for playing.

The Welsh Play Sufficiency Duty legitimises play as an outcome, justifies time spent supporting play, requires a broad range of professionals to give consideration to play, and elevates the status of play alongside other strategic priorities. However the beauty of this legislation can be found in its ambiguity and the Welsh Government should be commended for resisting the temptation to define what is enough. As a consequence the duty raises more questions than it answers: What is sufficient in terms of play? How can we know and how do we find out if children are getting enough? As Professor David Ball (2011) suggested when talking about the Health and Safety at Work Act, it is this ambiguity that encourages a more thoughtful approach.

Factors affecting the sufficiency of opportunities for play include but are not limited to: parental permission, influenced by their fears and values; other obligations on children's time; the amount and proximity of public open space; the layout of residential roads; the amount and speed of traffic; the availability and quality of play provision; the attitudes of other residents; the visibility of other children; practices within adult-run services and institutions; local and national media coverage; planning, transport, housing and education policies; and public liability concerns. The concept of play sufficiency provides a lens through which we can examine a wide range of factors to consider how they impact on the rights of children and explore how they might be reimagined and rearranged to create more favourable conditions for playing. This process requires adults to account for the ways in which we impact (both positively and negatively) on children's ability to find time and space for play. Play sufficiency is therefore a process of critical analysis that involves scrutinising adult assumptions, attitudes and practices to identify ways in which we can improve our collective ability to better respond to children's right to play. Play matters to children but their right to enjoy it fully is co-dependent on the availability of environmental resources, their ability to access those resources, having enough time to do so, and the permissions and supportive attitudes of adults. Working with the entanglements of this interrelationship is the work of play sufficiency as an organising principle for community development.

For this to be an organising principle for community development two things must happen. First, a play sufficiency assessment must be carried out. This assessment informs the second aspect, the play sufficiency action plan. This action plan informs engagement and participation in targeted areas identified through the assessment stage. The outputs of this action will be assessed during the next sufficiency assessment. In essence then, what is happening is a continuous process of community engagement, participation and development through twin processes of research and evaluation, action and re-evaluation with children and adults as key stakeholders in this process, developing an evidence base for community development (evidence-based practice). These two aspects: research and action, should not be considered as independent of one another. The research without the action accounts for a moment in time, whilst action without the research is merely 'another' community project. Committing to play sufficiency as an organising principle for community development means researching with children and adults as a continuous process that influences action that will then be the subject of further research. Play sufficiency is an ongoing interrelational co-constructive practice, operating at micro, meso, macro, and ecosystemic levels, the results of which will be changes in practices, procedures and policies within and across communities. This will be explored further as we consider the methodological approach carried out and the resultant outputs and outcomes.

Doing Play Sufficiency

In 2012/2013 in our respective roles as local authority play sufficiency lead (Mike) and university lecturer (Ben), we took an innovative approach to the challenge of completing Wrexham's first play sufficiency assessment (PSA) and developing the associated action plans. Adopting a principled approach, we used mixed research methods to capture both quantitative and qualitative data, involving more than 850 people to develop local, credible and trustworthy information enabling us to identify how people's level of satisfaction is affected by localised social and physical conditions, and how they are affected by wider social and policy contexts. What follows is an overview of this process.

In 2013, the first sufficiency assessment aimed:

- To establish a baseline in terms of the percentage of children and young people who report satisfaction with their ability to access time and space for play as part of their daily lives
- To identify representations of play sufficiency and the social and physical conditions that support this
- To identify geographic areas lacking in sufficiency and the possible reasons for this

- To use the data generated to develop indicators for the assessment of play sufficiency in other areas
- To identify opportunities to promote time and space for play, in those areas lacking sufficiency, and recommend appropriate interventions
- To support children's informed participation and ensure that their opinions were given at least equal weight to those of adults

In order to provide a theoretical framework for our research, we adapted Bronfenbrenner's (1979) ecological systems approach to consider the affordances for play presented by the home/family environment, how these are affected by, and in turn affect, the affordances within the child's local neighbourhood, and how all of this is affected by the wider context within which the community exists. At each level we investigated how the following physical and social factors coalesce to affect children's day-to-day play experiences. The lines of enquiry were as follows:

- Time – how often and how much time children spend playing
- Space – that exists within children's locality and the 'quality' of that space
- Access – children's independent mobility, the permission they are granted and the physical accessibility of space
- Attitudes – of children, parents, other community members, and people who work with children

These lines of enquiry were taken from those identified in UNICEF's (2007) report on children's well-being in developed countries. Drawing on the work of Kytta (2003), we applied the concept of constrained, promoted or free fields of action to each of our lines of enquiry to consider how these affect children's ability to actualise (make real use of) the potential affordances for play within a local community. In this model:

> **constrained field** refers to time, space, access or attitudes that prevent children's self-directed action
>
> **promoted field** refers to time, space, access or attitudes that regulate children's self-directed action, and
>
> **free field** refers to time, space, access or attitudes that allow for children's free action.

Children involved in the research came to understand these as red, amber or green fields of action. Children could readily see that each of the four lines of enquiry were influenced by the three fields of action, as could the adults we worked with.

The following research tools were used to explore people's experiences of play:

- Facilitated group work in schools using a mosaic approach – class of children from a primary school in each of six case study communities covering a total of ten LSOAs. These communities were selected to represent varying levels of deprivation, population density, urbanisation, open space and play provision;
- Online questionnaires – for children, young people, parents, and playwork and childcare professionals. Questions mirrored the lines of enquiry explored in the facilitated group work in schools;
- Focus groups – with parents, professionals and other marginalised groups;
- Community auditing of spaces for play – audit tool to consider accessibility and play value carried out at 49 sites across the six case study communities by playwork professionals. Twelve of these sites were then cross-checked by children to compare results;

- Semi-structured interviews – with lead professionals associated with policy areas identified in the play sufficiency statutory guidance;
- Mapping of demographics, spaces and service – data collected from across: Performance & Development, Planning, Education, Family Information Service, Environment and Leisure.

When analysing the data an emphasis was placed on the information provided by children, starting with facilitated group work from schools, comparing that with the results of children's online questionnaires. The themes developed were then cross referenced, corroborated and added to from the data produced by parents and other adults. These were then considered in relation to the audits and policy mapping data to develop findings and recommendations for action. It is important to reinforce here that this research phase is itself an action phase, the process of engaging with people and people participating in a conversation about play and childhoods, thinking differently about their work or experience and how that is influenced, or influences, was itself a developmental process for all concerned. A process that fostered much goodwill and potential for future partnership working and, perhaps most importantly, perception shifting. This approach resulted in 12 strategic priorities cut across the three interrelated issues of time, space and attitudes identified, based on local, credible and trustworthy information:

Priority 1: Increase object playtime during term time
Priority 2: Enhance opportunities for playing in winter
Priority 3: Secure safer streets for play
Priority 4: Secure a wider range of spaces for play
Priority 5: Secure spaces for play in close proximity to children's homes
Priority 6: Ensure quality design for play value
Priority 7: Secure a greater range of provision for young people
Priority 8: Improve children's subjective experience of time and space
Priority 9: Increase parental permission for play
Priority 10: Improve support for disabled and marginalised children
Priority 11: Improve generalised negative attitudes towards children and their play
Priority 12: Improve people's perception of young people

Taking Action

What follows is a representative but non-exhaustive list of examples of actions that were developed to address the priorities:

- The co-production between the Play department and a community group made up of between 10 and 15 local residents of an example plan demonstrating how the design and accessibility of existing public spaces within a community wide area could be enhanced to improve play value, naturalness and connectivity.
- Research comparing conditions for play in two neighbouring communities where children reported very different levels of satisfaction with their opportunities for playing, focusing on the variables influencing community play sufficiency.
- Adoption by Executive board of a county wide Risk Management policy for settings in which children play, incorporating a risk benefit approach thereby better enabling staff in their work with playing children.
- Production of guidance to support professionals and other community stakeholders in managing risks associated with children's self-built play structures including the

development of guidance for the construction and maintenance of rope swings in public spaces.

- A comparative study, comparing children's experiences of playing in two neighbouring communities focusing on the interrelationship between play sufficiency and place attachment.
- County-wide mentoring programme for schools, supporting the development of policies and practices that enhance opportunities and experiences of play throughout the school day.
- Provision of storage boxes for loose parts street play in communities across the county, including a detailed risk-benefit assessment and briefing paper identifying how these boxes would be managed, addressing any potential concerns. This initiative is now also being rolled out in a number of primary and secondary schools across the county.
- Re-augmentation of play delivery services from seasonal universal provision in centralized locations to place a greater focus on the delivery of high quality, community focused, year-round provision in close proximity to children's homes.
- A spatial development borne out of a developed relationship with the owner of a local industrial estate where they have leased a piece of woodland (on a 'peppercorn' rent) to the community council so that they may open it up to children for playing.
- A video of Wrexham's play sufficiency assessment has been produced: https://youtu.be/ftxo054jCfE. To date the video has been viewed nearly 2000 times and is being used as a training tool by the play development team.
- A three-month art project including 398 children focusing on raising public awareness of article 31. This artwork formed the centrepiece for a broader campaign aimed at raising the profile of children's right to play.
- Delivery of play awareness sessions for parents with young children in various communities across the county.

2016 PSA – A Time for Refinements and to see if the Work was ... Working

The year 2016 saw the advent of the second PSA. As a result of our experiences over the previous three years we took the opportunity to refine the way we carried out the assessment. In 2013 the six case study communities covering a total of 10 LSOAs were selected based on existing socio-economic, demographic data to represent varying levels of deprivation, population density, urbanisation, open space and play provision and in parallel made the questionnaire available for all children across the county. One of the findings from that PSA was that there isn't a strong correlation between the socio-economic data and levels of play sufficiency. We knew from experience the questionnaires provided a good indication for identifying areas of sufficiency or lack thereof. However, whilst the number of questionnaires completed for the original assessment was sufficient to establish general levels of satisfaction across the county borough, it was not enough to identify differences in satisfaction levels across communities within the county borough. To address this issue, we refined the methodological approach.

For the 2016 PSA, all primary schools in Wrexham were offered a small amount of money as an incentive to support children in Year Five to complete the satisfaction questionnaire. This provided for a much greater density of responses per community than our 2013 approach. Data from these questionnaire responses enabled us to identify case study communities for facilitated group work with children. Identifying those communities where children report the lowest levels of satisfaction and the highest, and recorded the children (who were now in Year Six) talking about their opportunities for playing both in and out of school. This revised approach enabled us to focus specifically on communities based on play sufficiency data rather than relying on sociodemographic data. We also revisited children from communities studied as a part of the 2013 assessment to gain an understanding of their experience of any changes since that initial assessment. Other than this, the research methodology and research tools used remained unchanged.

Importantly, as a result of this systematic and rigorous approach to sufficiency assessment in 2016, after three years of work with communities the levels of those rating satisfaction with their experience of play rose by 7 per cent. The evidence developed ensured sparse resources were spent effectively; where material changes needed to be made, they were actioned; where human resources were the instrument of change, they were put into effect; and where institutional structures and shifts of attitude and perception were what needed to be addressed, they were addressed. Broadly speaking, the 12 priorities for 2016–2019 remained similar in focus but were developed in their specificity given the increased granularity of the research data generated. What follows is a list of examples of the kinds of work that were then carried out as a result of the 2016 PSA:

1. Research exploring the social return on investment for playwork in Wrexham in terms of employability.
1. Production of a Playful Communities Toolkit to provide those interested in supporting children's play in their local communities with low cost ideas and examples of what has been successful elsewhere.
2. Research commissioned mapping the layout of houses and public spaces in four case study communities reporting different levels of satisfaction with their opportunities for play. This research provides detailed examples of community planning that directly influences levels of play sufficiency and as such provides exemplars for the local authority in assessing future planning application or in carrying out community re-developments.
3. Play Development Team's involvement in helping to draft new planning policies relating to the provision of public space and neighbourhood design.
4. Signage around a community centre making drivers aware that this is also a place where children ride their bikes and scooters.
5. Converted shipping container to provide shelter and storage as part of a pilot project exploring alternative models of play and youth provision.
6. Installation of play equipment enhancing existing provision but specific to community need at multiple community sites across the county.
7. Work with a group of teenagers to develop age appropriate designs and secure funding to enhance their local community play area.
8. A practice-led research project involving young people in the creation of a temporary play structure in Wrexham town centre.
9. Production of an e-learning module encouraging practitioners within the Local Authority to consider potential impacts on children's ability to access time and space for play
10. Support people to consider the rights of children when completing both health and equalities impact assessments.
11. A professional development programme aimed at exploring the way in which adults think about children, their childhoods and their play. Attendees included strategic directors, service managers and front-line staff, resulting in the development of a set of shared values aimed at promoting a more positive view of children and their childhoods across the children's workforce.
12. Delivery of play awareness sessions for parents with young children in various communities across the county.
13. Short film produced to promote playwork to be released prior to the summer holidays to help raise awareness of the free and open access staffed play provision available across the county borough.

14. Working with the local community heritage group to develop their vision for supporting children's play.
15. Adoption of a county-wide play pledge requiring the Local Authority department to give consideration to departmental responsibilities and how they impact on children's play and identify representatives to form a strategic play sufficiency partnership.

Finally, whilst a significant amount of research with children, parents and other community stakeholders had been undertaken since Wrexham's first PSA, less attention had perhaps been paid to developing and maintaining the professional partnerships and understanding needed to progress this agenda across the county borough. The 2016 PSA therefore placed a greater emphasis on facilitating conversations with professionals whose roles potentially impact upon children's ability to find time and space for playing. To this end, representatives from across 48 different local authority departments and partner agencies were identified who had previously been involved in the play sufficiency agenda or would ideally be involved in this assessment (and beyond). These individuals were then offered the opportunity to take part in a development programme aimed at supporting the professional development of those involved in the play sufficiency process, generating further 'collective wisdom'. This series of workshops resulted in the cross departmental development of a set of key systems that were being developed and that needed to develop further to enable the Local Authority to work towards securing sufficient opportunities for children's play across the county borough:

- **Planning for Play** – embedding consideration of the ways in which children use and move through space into planning processes and making greater efforts to avoid inadvertently removing or constraining access to features that currently support children's play.
- **Playwork as Community Development** – giving greater recognition to the role of playwork, as a distinct profession working to cultivate more favourable conditions for children's play and securing the sustainability of these services.
- **Professional Development for Play** – establishing a more coherent and consistent approach to developing the play workforce, providing a wider range of professionals with access to play-based training and qualifications.
- **Play Development Team** – ensuring the team that leads on the play sufficiency duty is sufficiently resourced to do so and can work proactively with communities where children report low levels of satisfaction with their opportunities for play.
- **Policies for Play** – developing more child-centred policies that work with, and in support of, children's innate playfulness and paying greater attention to the potential impacts of different policy initiatives on children's ability to find time and space for play.
- **Partnerships for Play** – bringing people together to further develop their 'collective wisdom' as to how adults might better embed consideration of children's ability to find time and space for playing (with and without adults) into their own and other people's everyday practices.

Concluding Remarks

As illustrated, the resulting range of interventions made has been broad and fairly complex but includes work at a strategic level to change policies and procedures, work at an operational level to improve practitioner's consideration of and responses to play, and work at a neighbourhood level to improve parental confidence and develop play provision. This has involved working across departments within the Local Authority including planning, environment, housing, economic development, health and safety, social care, education, childcare, youth services, arts and workforce development. It has also been dependent on the support of several partner agencies, including third sector playwork organisations, the local university, Public Health Wales, Play Wales and those leading on play sufficiency in other local authorities. The result is a detailed, strategic and rigorous approach to assessing and securing play sufficiency, which has enabled Wrexham Council to evidence a significant improvement in children's satisfaction with their opportunities for play across the county borough since the Welsh Play Sufficiency Duty was introduced. Most importantly it has, and continues to include, children as full participants in the process, ensuring their rights to action and participation in the creation of communities that work for them.

Further Study

We suggest looking back through the book to further explore these specific issues from the case study:

- *Human Rights (with focus on children)*
- *Identifying assets (for children's play)*
- *Planning, monitoring and evaluation*
- *Slum Dwellers International for their women-focused and local information-driven development model*

References

Ball, D.J. (2011) *The Feeling of Risk: New Perspectives on Risk Perception*. London: Multi-Science Publishing Co. Ltd.

Barclay, M. and Tawil, B. (2013) *Wrexham Play Sufficiency Assessment 2013*. Wrexham: Wrexham County Borough Council and Glyndwr University.

Bronfenbrenner, U. (1979) *The Ecology of Human Development: Experiments by Nature and Design*. Cambridge, MA: Harvard University Press.

Gray, P. (2013) 'Free to Learn: Why Unleashing the Instinct to Play Will Make Our Children Happier', in *More Self-Reliant, and Better Students for Life*. New York: Basic Books.

Hartshorne, M. (2014) *Neighbourhood Attachment and Subjective Experiences of Children's Play: A Comparative Study in North East Wales*. Wrexham: Glyndwr University.

Kytta, M. (2003) *Children in Outdoor Contexts. Affordances and Independent Mobility in the Assessment of Environmental Child Friendliness*. Helsinki: Helsinki University of Technology, Centre for Urban and Regional Studies.

Lester, S. and Russell, W. (2013) *Leopard Skin Wellies, a Top Hat and a Vacuum Cleaner Hose: An Analysis of Wales' Play Sufficiency Assessment duty*. Cheltenham: University of Gloucestershire.

Long, A., Delorme, M., and Brown, F. (2014) *Developing a Culture of Play*. Leeds: Leeds Beckett University.

UNCRC (2013) General comment No. 17: The right of the child to rest, leisure, play, recreational activities, cultural life and the arts (Article 31).

UNICEF Report (2007) 'Report Card 7, Child Poverty in Perspective: An overview of child well-being in rich countries'. The United Nations Children's Fund.

Wood, J. (2017) *Planning for Children's Play: Exploring the 'Forgotten' Right in Welsh and Scottish Policy*. Edinburgh: Heriot-Watt University.

Case Study 5.6

Creative Nottingham North: Arts-based Community Development

Frances Howard

Introduction

Creative Nottingham North (CNN) is a two-year Arts Council England funded programme run by the Rebalancing the Outer Estates Foundation in partnership with Nottingham's Creative Quarter. Its vision is to support its six wards – Aspley, Basford, Bestwood, Bilborough, Bulwell and Bulwell Forest – to become 'creative places' where residents are confident in turning ideas into action that creates real change for the area. Nottingham ranked 8th on the 2015 government index of deprivation and the political constituency of Nottingham North scored particularly poorly on education and income deprivation, particularly affecting children.

A key vision for Creative Nottingham North is that spaces can be developed for creative and entrepreneurial use. It aims to develop a 'creative community' that is well networked, with members well connected to each other, where the assets of the area are shared and used widely by people of all ages (https://creativenottinghamnorth.com). The desire is that CNN develops its own identity, a strong brand that people can use as a badge or as an umbrella for their own groups or projects. Another part of CNN's strategy is engaging with the arts as a tool for reimagining the political boundary of Nottingham North, creating a sense that it is not a deprived area but it is where people can come and experience arts and culture.

This case study presents two key projects from the programme – *The Bulwell Connectors* and *Three Doors Down* and engages with them in order to analyse the shift in funding and policy rhetoric away from the social impacts of the arts towards an economic focus, which is propped up by the cultural and creative industries. In response, this study seeks to emphasise the value of arts-based community programmes for building relationships, place-based pedagogy and community empowerment.

The Bulwell Connectors

The Bulwell Connectors group live locally and are already engaged in some way with the arts – as local artists, retired musicians, parents of young children with whom they create artwork. A key aim of this group is in encouraging these people to work out what being an 'Arts Champion' means to them as individuals. They might want to sit on an interview panel or promote the cinema screenings to people where they live or post leaflets in their independent living scheme, whereby each person has a different role to play. Members of the Bulwell Connectors group expressed pride and belief that Bulwell is not a negative place – there's lots of positivity, and argued that there can be a mismatch in perceptions. The process of this group coming together is notable as alongside working on the development of public art commissions, the group enjoys visits to arts and cultural venues as well as participatory workshops. The group is experiential, with an emphasis on talking and making. One member stated that

> since being part of this group whenever I drive through a place I take more notice of the public art and it gets me thinking about Bulwell. I am able to learn something about that place just by passing through it and I think that's good for the community – to tell the story of that area.

A key objective for the Bulwell Connectors group is the commissioning of public art for the local area of Bulwell. The main commission that the group had been working towards throughout the year had been a set of new gates for the market area. Following the recruitment of the successful artist fabricator, the group enjoyed a visit to his studio and were able to try out metalworking and designing shapes for the commission, which was influenced by the designs of a local artist. Reflecting during their one-year anniversary of the group, members commented that being part of the group had challenged them to think in new ways about public art and engage with contemporary art of all kinds. They also reported an increase in confidence and commitment to leading activities for their local area. The Co-ordinator for CNN stated that:

> They are key individuals in Bulwell now who are absolutely committed and passionate about developing the group on … I wasn't surprised that they wanted to carry the group on … the next decision will be around the format of those meetings. As a group of people, I think they will want to be more public now. Up until now it's been about bonding as a core group and now they'll be thinking up new things and developing other projects.

Three Doors Down

Three Doors Down is a project for Minver Crescent in Aspley – built between the wars as part of a colossal house-building programme that was the envy of Europe. It aimed to develop conversations between people who live together but who may not know each other; and to explore ways in which a local building, the Aspley Community Training Centre (ACTC) – which has a theatre studio with a full technical rig inside of it – may become of use to the community in which it is based. A Community Theatre Director worked with individuals and groups of all ages to gather stories and memories of the estate, as well as working with local photographers to document the crescent as it is now. A series of events held created films and animations, and there was a series of performances where the stories were shared. The Theatre Director stated that:

> Unless local people get involved we can't make the work. It doesn't happen unless people do it. These projects are always about dialogue – trying to get to the truth of a place. As an outsider you can provoke and ask questions that insiders can't … I want the project to feel like a celebration of people's lives and an affirmation of the power of the collective – bringing people together will help in making connections and throwing different things in, provoking a debate on what is the potential of the collective experience.

As well as making connections between people, the Three Doors Down project created a sense of connection to place through evoking the history of Aspley and Minver Crescent. One of the aims of the project had been to explore the use of the ACTC centre as a creative space. During this six-month project there was an increase in the use of the space for arts-based activities, not only around Three Doors Down, but also other projects starting to happen there – a hairbraiding course, supported by a local Councillor, and a weekly Sewing Workshop. A key success of this project was the development of the ACTC centre in terms of collaboration and sharing resources. For example, the Sewing Group has just received their first paid commission to create the interactive gallery space for children and the ACTC centre hosted a children's theatre production. There was evidence that the connections created through the initial project are growing and becoming more established.

The Festival Model

Arts festivals are a key area of work for the CNN Programme, as the format of festivals is deemed accessible for people who haven't engaged with them before. Festivals can be responsive to the local community and within Nottingham North they are growing and becoming more sustainable each year. Bulwell has an established Arts Festival and further festivals have begun to spring up in the neighbouring wards. CNN Co-ordinator stated:

> festivals are such a fab vehicle as a way of bringing lots of different community organisations together under one umbrella to promote the value of the arts in that community. To promote what is already going on as well as taste sessions to have a go at something new. And that whole sense of place – there is definitely an expectation now. People are already saying 'what's going to happen for the arts festival next year'.

The festival 'model' has been a key success of the CNN programme through offering the volunteers involved a planning framework, expectations of how to programme the festival and knowing practical requirements such as when to give marketing copy. However, the strength of the arts festivals was in the responsiveness to the differences in their local communities and due to their reliance on volunteers, each held different features. The future potential of the festivals is the partnership work with arts organisations who can see the value of connecting with local communities as a way of getting to know a new audience and a way of engaging people in their programmes. Having a hub for the festivals was another factor of success, which brought new and unexpected connections. For example, in one location the community centre and library were the key spaces and the food bank came in to run a workshop and, following problems with their regular venue, were able to transfer to the community centre as a result of making those connections.

Creative Nottingham North – The People and the Place

The arts-based community projects explored above have been evaluated under two key themes: The People and The Place. The Bulwell Connectors, Three Doors Down and the Arts Festival elements have resulted in the building of connections and relationships between people and place and have represented a celebration of the uniqueness of people and place and the turning of ideas into action by the people for the place. Drawing on place-based pedagogy, the approach of CNN to community development clearly invests people with a sense of agency (Rodriguez, 2013) that also acknowledges them as producers rather than consumers of knowledge (Smith, 2002). With a focus on the local, as opposed to the global, the notion of place is offered as something in the making, with education through hands-on, community-engaged learning that provides residents with relevant experiences to participate actively in democratic processes (Smith and Sobel, 2014).

The particular experience of the Bulwell Connectors group in relation to learning about and commissioning public art in their locality, as well as the approach of the Community Theatre Director, highlighted a relational approach to the arts. Relational art engages in a form of social interactiveness that encourages collaboration, participation and community-based projects into both the form and content of the work. Focusing on socialisation, relational art represents artistic practice that is concerned with producing relationships between people and their surroundings. Bourriaud (2002) argue that relational art practices produce radically 'new models of sociability' that exist 'beside or beneath a real economic system' and have, in turn, political repercussions in the broader social sphere. Exploring the learning of the CNN programme through this particular framework enables a questioning not only of 'public art' but also of the broader representation of 'the public', which is often political.

A Political Shift?

'Place', as McInerney et al. (2011) argue, is a divisive and ideological construct whereby placing-making is inherently political. Historically, place has been a barrier to Nottingham North, where there has been a history of things 'going wrong', people being over-consulted and commitments not happening. This has led to a fear of risk, a lack of trust in the community and a concern that anti-social behaviour will negate any positive impacts of community programmes. This tension has played out at the level of local politics and this programme was successful in re-engaging and re-educating local politicians in terms of trusting the community. It was felt that there was a need to change the sense that things are 'done to' the community and a key objective of CNN was working towards reimagining this sense of place for Nottingham North, by working with local people, groups and councillors. The Co-ordinator for CNN reported a sense of the need for this project to 'give permission' to local people, whether that be through encouragement to say 'let's do this' or 'let's do something a bit differently'. She argued that *'the success is the relationships that we've now got with people that are able to make things happen and want to do things together'*. The successes include getting funding, working with local Councillors and creating opportunities to support local groups. The wider impact of her role has also been acknowledged by the MP for Nottingham North. In an interview, he commented upon the community values and long-term sustainability developed through the programme, and has been able to talk about some of the projects, such as the Aspley Sewing Group, in parliament in order to lobby for further support for this kind of approach to community development.

When the place is political, its people become politicised and there had been previous tensions with the tokenistic outreach work of arts organisations in Nottingham North – parachuting in, lack of long-term programming and prolonged engagement with arts activities. However, the approach of CNN has enabled the creation of strong links identifying community groups to work with and to steer organisations towards new groups and new partners with whom they had not worked before. The co-ordinator re-iterated the importance of

> knowing that these sorts of things take time, knowing that you are not going to solve the poverty and knowing that you are not going to protect every child or give every child access to a wonderful arts education. But ultimately that is what you want.

This programme has demonstrated that the negative conceptions of the place did not resonate with local residents. They were a myth and they were damaging to the people due to engendering feelings of hopelessness and isolation. Arts-based community engagement programmes, such as CNN, can re-engage local people to take ownership of their spaces, building up trust at the political level and empowerment within communities.

Conclusion

In the age of 'austerity', arts-based community development work struggles to find funding to continue and often its claims of social impact are no longer recognised. Community development projects that engaged people in cultural opportunities were seen to be addressing social inequalities (Jermyn, 2004) based on the assumption that sport, arts and other cultural activities may be seen to be, in and of themselves, a good thing (Long et al., 2002). However, recent research (Belfiore, 2010; Oakley and O'Brien, 2016) has questioned these assumptions. The marked political shift from social rhetoric to economic focus and the funding of programmes such as this, based on their contribution to the cultural and creative industries, overlooks the strength of these projects in building and repairing relations at the community level. The learning from this programme demonstrated that the foreground of social relationships was a key mechanism for reimagining a sense of people and place for Nottingham North.

Further Study

We suggest looking back through the book to further explore these specific issues from the case study:

- *Building social capital and a sense of place*
- *Freire and popular education*
- *Augusto Boal and radical theatre*
- *Building capability*
- *Identifying local assets*
- *Building alliances*

References

Belfiore, E. (2010) 'Art as a Means of Alleviating Social Exclusion: Does It Really Work? A Critique of Instrumental Cultural Policies and Social Impact Studies in the UK', *International Journal of Cultural Policy* , 8(1), 91–106.

Bourriaud, N. (2002) *Relational Aesthetics*. Dijon: Les presses du réel.

Jermyn, H. (2004) 'The Art of Inclusion', Research Report 35. Available at: http://thamesvalleypartnership.org.uk/somethingbrilliant/wp-content/uploads/art-of-inclusion-jermyn.pdf, accessed 1 March 2015.

Long, J., Welch, M., Bramham, P., Hylton, K., Butterfield, J., and Lloyd, E. (2002) 'Count Me In: The Dimensions of Social Inclusion through Culture and Sport', Report. Available at: http://citeseerx.ist.psu.edu/viewdoc/download?doi=10.1.1.466.2996&rep=rep1&type=pdf, accessed 1 March 2015.

McInerney, P., Smyth, J., and Down, B. (2011) '"Coming To A Place Near You?" The Politics and Possibilities of a Critical Pedagogy of Place-based Education', *Asia-Pacific Journal of Teacher Education* , 39(1), 3–16.

Oakley, K. and O'Brien, D. (2016) 'Learning to Labour Unequally: Understanding the Relationship between Cultural Production, Cultural Consumption and Inequality', *Social Identities*, 22(5), 471–486.

Rodriguez, G.M. (2013) 'Power and Agency in Education: Exploring the Pedagogical Dimensions of Funds of Knowledge', *Review of Research in Education*, 37(1), 87–120.

Smith, G.A. (2002) 'Place-based Education: Learning To Be Where We Are'. *Phi Delta Kappan*, 83(8), 584–594.

Smith, G.A. and Sobel, D. (2014) *Place- and Community-based Education in Schools*. New York: Routledge.

Case Study 5.7

When Young People, Resident Artists and Curators Work Collaboratively on a Community Arts Project

Tina Salter

Introduction

Westminster Academy places an emphasis on 'international business and enterprise' (www. westminsteracademy.org.uk). As part of this focus, Year Ten students are encouraged to secure work experience placements and are given dedicated time to do this within the Year Ten academic year. However, some students found it challenging securing multiple work experience opportunities, particularly those whose first language was not English. The Youth Forum was designed as a work experience opportunity with a difference. The Cockpit Theatre, based just over a mile away from the school, was hired by Serpentine Galleries as a venue for the project. Each Youth Forum cohort had a different arts focus and therefore drew on the expertise of resident artists who worked with the education curators to support the young people to collaborate together to co-produce art that drew on community-based issues where artists supported young people to generate co-authored change.

The first two Youth Forum cohorts each lasted for one term where the group would meet weekly alongside an artist or artists working with a cohort of around 12 to 15 young people. The Year Ten students were expected to spend each Wednesday during the term at work experience placements held at the Cockpit Theatre from 11am to 3pm. The format changed for the third cohort (made up of 16 Year Ten students) due to changes in the way student internships were facilitated through the school. The internship was delivered as a two-week block placement.

As well as providing students with the opportunity to work alongside an artist to generate a creative outcome, they were also encouraged to identify aspects they would like to work on, such as confidence- or team-building skills, which could be transferred to other settings, such as work. Or, indeed, to help create spaces where young people can be critical about work and think about why and how we work. Students were also able to keep a journal in the form of a logbook of their work to showcase their contributions and capture their learning after each session. The first cohort took part in the forum from October to December 2015 and the group worked on producing a recording of a live radio show. The second cohort took place between January and March 2016 and the group produced a television show. The third cohort participated in the forum between March and April 2017 and the group wrote and created a live performance.

Gathering Feedback from Youth Forum Participants

For each cohort, the researcher attended for two full days. These visits were conducted at a mid-way point and also at the last session. On each day the researcher observed activities, had informal conversations with the participating young people, and captured this information in written field notes to be analysed at a later date. During the final visit she also carried out semi-structured interviews with young people to find out in more depth their experiences of the Youth Forum. Some of the young people were a little hesitant to be interviewed so it was suggested to them that they could be interviewed in pairs. This proved to be preferable for them and therefore this format was repeated with all the interviews carried out with the participating young people.

Young People's Views on the Youth Forum

The young people overwhelming enjoyed being part of each project and were able to articulate their learning and development as a result of taking part. The experience of working collectively with artists in particular offered many of the participants a new way of exploring their own development due largely to being taken out of their comfort zones. The discussion below compares the findings from the three cohorts and captures both the impact and any lessons learned which might be beneficial to those involved in using contemporary art practice as a way of working with young people.

Recruiting the Right Young People

It is clear from the interviews carried out with young people that certain skills can be developed by participating on the Youth Forum. These included: increasing confidence, learning to listen to others, finding your voice, working in teams and learning from peers. The young people all felt that these skills were transferable into the school setting and also further afield, including the world of work. Therefore, it makes sense that young people who need to develop in these areas would be ideal candidates for the Youth Forum.

The young people liked the idea of doing their placement with others rather than in isolation – and this, too, was a 'selling point', particularly for young people who felt quite anxious about the idea of going to do a placement in a company or retail outlet where they would be exposed to new people, either as colleagues or customers. Many young people were advised to go on the Youth Forum because they had no alternative placement lined up. An interesting suggestion made by a young person was for young people to do the Youth Forum before doing a different placement in the following term so that the skills acquired could be applied in the next placement setting with greater confidence and reduced anxiety:

> *I think this is a good start of this internship as it allows you to be more confident of the one you are going to do next. I am going to HSBC or maybe a pharmacy and maybe this will help me to be more open and confident. It really helps you out.*
>
> (Youth Forum participant)

There was a lot of confusion about the nature of the Youth Forum and particularly what the 'art' element would look like. Many participants were under the impression that they would be doing paintings or drawings, or helping out at a gallery.

> *I thought it was going to be a gallery like a proper gallery with art and pictures around and stuff. I thought it would be a museum or something like that.*
>
> (Youth Forum participant)

However, once they started to understand that each group would collaborate with an artist in order to generate the project as a whole, they realised why the Serpentine staff hadn't given too much information away in order to ensure participants were able to contribute to and shape what each project might look like. Perhaps the focus when advertising the placement opportunity to young people should be the skills they might gain from taking part – and matching these up to those young people who need to develop their confidence, communication and teamwork skills.

Having the Right Staff Team

The difference in the size of staff team varied considerably and this had an impact on the ratio of staff to students. Although the projects and group make-up were very different, the cohorts with the larger staff teams were able to complete the production of their art on time, culminating in two cohorts showcasing the live radio show recording and the live performance. The second cohort who worked on producing a TV show were unable to have the final edit ready for the planned showcase event. The young people did not seem bothered by this. However, the showcase event may have been possible if the staff team had been larger. This group, in particular, needed more support than the other cohorts and therefore having one or two more people available to get alongside individuals may have helped speed up the filming process. That said, the outcomes were on a par with the other two cohorts, with the young people identifying similar learning and outcomes. This shows how the young people were appreciative of the process just as much as the product and this had a lot to do with how the staff treated them:

> We are getting treated equally and fairly. I feel comfortable because we get to do what we want and share ideas and they don't say 'no, we don't like that' – they think about it and they agree with you. Even if they disliked it, they won't say it in a rude way.
> (Youth Forum participant)

For the third cohort there were four staff members leading on the Public Performance project, with 16 participating young people. This ratio worked well in terms of managing behaviour and supporting group dynamics. When potential conflict situations arose there were enough 'hands' to enable an individual staff member to take a young person aside and talk through any issues or concerns privately – leaving enough staff left to manage the rest of the group. It would seem that two artists and two curators is a number that works well for this size of group.

Managing Group Dynamics

Linked to the staff team size was the challenge of managing each group of young people. With the first two cohorts there was a lot of tiredness evident in the young people at the start of each session and the staff teams worked hard at motivating the groups, offering them encouragement and creating a sense of fun. The second cohort with the least number of staff members (three) had to work harder than the other cohorts. The third cohort seemed to have more momentum, as the group was meeting daily over two weeks. The young people in all cohorts appreciated the individual attention they received, particularly for those who lacked confidence. For many, English was not their first language, so they had additional barriers to overcome in understanding some of the tasks given to them. However, arts-based programmes have shown that linguistic barriers can be overcome when projects are delivered ethically by prioritising relational development rather than technical linguistic ability (Frimberger, 2016). The staff teams did well in building rapport and making time for feedback so that any issues or concerns could be addressed:

> *We always have time to reflect on everyone's ideas about what we did and it's really good because, it's just like you didn't move on to something new quickly, you actually thoroughly talked about what you've just done.*
>
> (Youth Forum participant)

All of the activities and input from staff were bespoke – they had been designed based on the work carried out in previous sessions. Although this approach is time-consuming for staff, it paid off as it helped the young people to feel heard and valued. There were a few time constraints with the third cohort as the two-week delivery time meant there was less time available to tweak and change the programme. That said, staff were often in touch via email during the evenings to ensure that changes could be discussed and managed by the next morning.

The Serpentine Gallery commissioned some group-work training for staff and artists between cohorts two and three and you could visibly see improved confidence and skills in managing conflict by the third cohort. There were a couple of incidents which could have escalated and hijacked progress – but staff were able to intervene quickly and de-escalate situations before things got out of hand.

Product vs. Process

Ultimately, the young people did not talk very much about the outputs they were all involved in creating. They were much more eager to talk about aspects of their own learning and development which had resulted from their involvement in the creative process. This was profoundly evident in the interviews that were carried out with the young people. Whilst they were clearly excited and proud about their achievement with each production, they were more consciously aware of the things they had got out of the process. Confidence was a particularly recurring theme – without the artists taking them out of their comfort zones, they might not have truly recognised the journeys they had been on where increased confidence was needed in order to overcome any fears:

> *It has been different from what we thought. It has been in groups, more like group work, discussing, acting, like confidence basically. Being on your own and developing ideas together.*
>
> (Youth Forum participant)

There were some concerns amongst staff that the process element was at risk of being lost through the change in format to a two-week intensive period of working. However, whilst there was a cost involved for staff members working more intensively, the outcomes for the young people participating were not compromised. Findings from the interviews showed that the same outcomes were evident in both formats – but behaviour management was made easier by improved relationship building where the young people and staff team saw each other every weekday for two weeks.

> *It is better than being once a week because we kind of get more used to them being around us and we build a relationship with everyone there. If it is once a week you are going to forget what you've done and it is not convenient.*
>
> (Youth Forum participant)

The relationship element was key in allowing young people to be the drivers of each project rather than artist-led. Collaborative processes can then enable each participant to discuss their creative contribution using analysis, interpretation and synthesis of ideas (Eckhoff, 2012).

Capturing Learning

Two-way feedback was evident in both cohorts as a continuous way of assessing how each group was getting on. In the second cohort in particular, many discussions were had about the young people's personal learning journals, which they were encouraged to complete at the end of each session. Looking through some of these, there were many creative elements included in the journal and one young woman in particular asked to take it home with her as she wanted to work on it in her own time. They enjoyed 'logging' the things they had done each week and the journal served as an important piece of memorabilia, capturing their learning in a very personal way.

In the third cohort, reflective skills were enhanced by debriefing sessions where young people were encouraged to express themselves honestly. Any feedback which mimicked previous reflections was discouraged by asking young people to use their own words, encouraging them to find their own voice. This was particularly powerful in helping young people learn how to develop their thinking and critiquing skills and use language to clearly articulate and communicate these opinions to the wider group, whilst respecting the views and beliefs of others. Research has shown that creativity in particular can be the key to unlocking critical thinking:

> *The ability to think critically is closely related to creativity because it involves making connections, seeing things from different perspectives, generating and developing ideas, making choices, solving problems, reviewing and refining work.*
>
> (Anderson and Chung, 2012: 264)

Recommendations for Future Development of the Youth Forum Project

Evaluating the Youth Forum project has highlighted ways in which arts-based programmes can help support community-based youth work programmes seeking to help young people consider the world of work. Often work experience placements can be formal and daunting for young people. Using the creative arts as a placement framework can help alleviate some of these pressures and allow youth workers and community educators the opportunity to help young people think about issues that could come up in the workplace. In order for programmes to be managed effectively, it is important that young people's expectations are managed when they are deciding whether or not to participate. A one-to-one informal interview can help manage expectations and talk through any fears. In order to effectively manage group dynamics, it is important that there are enough staff on board to help facilitate sessions. A clearer understanding amongst staff team members and participants of the potential sanctions that might be used if young people demonstrate a lack of commitment to the project needs to be communicated from the outset so that there is a common agreement. This should be reflected in the roles and responsibilities which differ between senior school staff, curators and artists.

Staff teams need to be aware of practice that supports equality and collaborative ways of working as this is hugely beneficial to participating young people. The format and regularity of sessions is also important so that momentum is not lost when young people are working collaboratively to create something. Whilst the young people didn't reflect so much on the art pieces they co-created, they were aware of how the use of art enabled them to do things like express themselves and share their opinions whilst also respecting the opinions of others. They also got to build relationships with young people in their school community whom they had not had the opportunity previously to get to know. The Youth Forum provided them with experiences that enabled them to go back into their school community feeling part of something bigger. If young people are going to find their place and thrive in their local communities, they will need opportunities like the Youth Forum to start to question and understand those around them in informed ways. Art can be powerful in helping some of these conversations happen.

Further Study

We suggest looking back through the book to further explore these specific issues from the case study:

- *Freire and popular education*
- *Group work*
- *Capacity and capability building*
- *Personal and collective empowerment*
- *Monitoring and evaluation*

References

Anderson, J. and Chung, Y. (2012) 'Community Languages, The Arts and Transformative Pedagogy: Developing Active Citizenship for the Twenty-first Century', *Citizenship Teaching & Learning*, 7(3), 259–271.

Eckhoff, A. (2012) 'Conversational Pedagogy: Exploring Interactions between a Teaching Artist and Young Learners During Visual Arts Experiences', *Early Childhood Education Journal*, 41, 365–372.

Frimberger, K. (2016) 'Towards a Well-Being Focussed Language Pedagogy: Enabling Arts-based, Multilingual Learning Spaces for Young People with Refugee Backgrounds', *Pedagogy, Culture & Society*, 24(2), 285–299.

Westminster Academy. Available at: www.westminsteracademy.org.uk.

Case Study 5.8

The 'JOY' Project

Clive Sealey, Ruth Jones, Joanne Lewis and Danny Gregory

Introduction

The JOY Project is 'a women only community project which provides support to enable women to gain a variety of skills, enhance their confidence and empower them to make their own informed decisions' (WCT, 2018a). It does this through the provision of activities, including skills such as sewing, cooking, courses to gain qualifications, that is, functional skills (literacy and numeracy), arts and crafts and drop-ins/coffee mornings. Participants are supported both individually and in group settings. A total of 158 service users enrolled on the JOY Project up to July 2018. Service-user data shows that the majority of service users self-referred. However, signposting or referral to 'JOY' is made by a range of organisations and agencies reflecting multi-agency working by staff. The target beneficiaries of JOY include women who are disabled, of diverse ethnic backgrounds, religions and differing sexualities.

The JOY Project evolved from the work of another project, the Asha Women's Centre, which supported women in Worcester for 20 years but closed in January 2017 due to lack of funding. The Asha Centre initially developed from work with women offenders and, in its heyday, attracted attention from the Department of Health who cited it as a good practice model in 2003. Baroness Corston (2007) identified it as a model of best practice in her Home Office report on vulnerable women in the criminal justice system. The Asha centre expanded its work to incorporate supporting any women from the local community who needed any kind of support but in its latter years stopped self-referrals and charged referring agencies for support given to the women they referred. Austerity measures introduced by the Coalition government in 2010 and since continued by the Conservative governments elected in 2015 and 2017 cut funding to the referring organisations and agencies, reducing available funds to pay Asha for referrals. This played some part in Asha's closure.

In the light of concern over what would happen to the women who were service users after the closure of Asha, the JOY Project was launched in April 2017. The Worcester County Council (WCoC) 'Domestic Abuse and Violence Needs Assessment' (WCoC, 2016: 16) highlighted that the 'numbers of victims appear to be increasing' in Worcestershire. Overall, numbers of victims in Worcestershire, according to police data, increased from 2,772 in 2014 to 4,762 in 2015, though this might be down to increased reporting (74 per cent of victims were women, with the most common age range of 35 to 44 years). The report identified a high volume of children being involved (mostly witnessing), and apparent links between victims living in areas of high deprivation and the use of alcohol by both victims and perpetrators. This led to a successful Big Lottery Fund bid by Worcester Community Trust in February 2017 for a 'Moving on Project' as a follow on. In the context of the austerity cuts to local authority funding, WCT was set up in 2010 to join together three charities and take on the management of community centres and youth and community work owned by both Worcester City Council and Worcester County Council. The work of WCT is funded through income generated by letting out the community centres and from grants, charitable funds and contracts (WCT, 2018b).

Social and Economic Context of Case Study Area

According to the most recent Worcestershire Health and Well-being Board Joint Strategic Needs Assessment (2016), Worcestershire is less deprived on average than England but in Worcester city, there are significant pockets of deprivation, such as in postcodes WR1 and WR5. Most service users of the group are from the WR4 and WR5 postcode areas, which is unsurprising given the location of WCT hubs where JOY activities take place. JOY Project service users are most commonly in the age groups spanning the most common age group for domestic abuse in Worcestershire and WCT hubs where JOY activities take place, the most common postcodes for reported domestic abuse. JOY Project service users had multiple support needs when they first started attending JOY but the majority cited issues related to 'confidence (57.9 per cent) and loneliness (47.4 per cent), and issues such as mental health and domestic abuse (34 per cent).

Model of Work

The theoretical underpinning of the JOY Project is feminist, in that it is a woman-only project that aims to empower women. As such it is part of the important legacy of second wave feminists, who created safe, women-only spaces where women could live (refuges for abused women), disclose sexual violence (Rape Crisis Centres), get support, socialise and learn (women's centres). Through the 1970s and 1980s, these became a vital part of the voluntary and community sector, providing much needed support to women (Women's Resource Centre, 2015).

In addition, it recognises that empowerment must begin from women's own experiences and the importance of the social, economic and environmental structures that shape women's lives (Carr, 2003). Lee (2001: 12) tells us that empowerment is an essential element of feminist theory, which seeks to increase the personal, interpersonal and political power of oppressed and marginalised populations for individual and collective transformation. As such empowerment is both a theory and a process (Carr, 2003; Carroll, 2004), Almaseb and Julia (2007) believe that empowerment is best viewed as a theoretical framework which helps women to have more control over their lives and develop a sense of self-efficacy, self-esteem and self-confidence, and this is evident in the work of the JOY Project.

In terms of a community setting this method of working represents Keith Popple's (2000) community develop model. The strategy underpinning this model encompasses the active participation of the women, with community workers acting as 'facilitators, enablers and Neighbourhood Workers', who support the women to 'develop the confidence and skills to improve their quality of life' (Popple, 2000:56). The main focus of the work is to work alongside the women within this community. They do this by enabling individuals to develop the ability and confidence to take control of their lives by taking part in a variety of activities and learning, which are designed to build both a skill set and self-esteem of the individual or the group. Twelvetrees, in his book Community Work, felt that this approach to working reflected the 'uniqueness of community work' (1991: 60).

The Age, Ethnicity and Social Status of JOY Participants

The target beneficiaries are women aged 16+. There is no maximum age limit. Demographically, women in Worcester in 2011 were mostly in the 40–49 and 70+ age categories. JOY Project service users on the other hand, are most commonly aged 30–49 years. The number of women aged 60+ attending JOY is low in comparison; as is the number of younger women.

Most service users were not in employment for a range of reasons including being full time parents or carers, including age-, disability- and childcare-related issues that make it difficult for service users to enter employment. Most service users also predominantly lived in Housing Association or council accommodation.

The priority is to support women who live in the city of Worcester, but JOY can support women out of area for group work. The majority of service users enrolled to date are, and have been, 'White British'. However, a much lower proportion of service users were 'White English' than was expected, according to the target set for the funder, and a lower number of women form 'other' white backgrounds. A higher number of Pakistani women attend the project than the estimated target set for the funder but a low number of Bangladeshi women.

Survey data shows that the majority of service users need help with issues that can impact negatively on community and employment participation, and on health. 57.9 per cent needed support with their confidence levels, for example, and just under half (47.4 per cent) cited loneliness, wanting to make friends and wanting to get involved with community as reasons for first attending JOY. Some 44.7 per cent said they needed support in relation to their motivation, 39.5 per cent needed support with social skills and mental health issues and 13.2 per cent needed support due to domestic abuse. Substance use and sexual abuse were the issues that fewest women said they needed support with though these issues are notoriously difficult to disclose (Elkins, 2008; Ullman et al., 2010). Fewer respondents said they attended JOY for 'hard outcomes' such as gaining educational qualifications (23.7 per cent) or help with gaining employment (15.7 per cent), though 39.5 per cent said they needed help with finances/debt. This correlates with responses given by questionnaire respondents, when asked about the activities they participated in (backed up by the JOY database: 2018), and what they hoped to achieve by attending JOY.

Survey data also shows that JOY service users have multiple issues that they needed support with, as seen in the graph below.

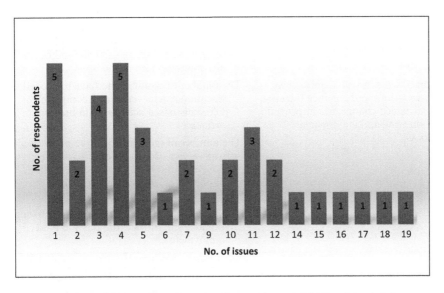

Figure 5.2 Number of Issues Questionnaire Respondents Said They Needed Support with when They First Attended JOY

Around 34.2 per cent of respondents highlighted ten or more issues (see Figure 5.2). Of these (53.8 per cent) were aged 40–49 years and predominantly lived in postcode areas WR4 and WR5 (two lived in the WR3 area, and two did not give their postcode). This is to be expected given that the majority of respondents were from these areas. The fact that only one service user from the WR1 area participated in the questionnaire means that information is missing about the needs of women in that area which is one of the most deprived. All issues listed are related to the ONS (2011) 'Dimensions of Deprivation', based on employment, education, housing and health and disability, which are discussed below.

The Planned Outputs and Outcomes

In identifying the need for a service to replace the closed Asha service, emerging from a concern over what would happen to the women who were service users of this closed service, WCT consulted with stakeholders (including Asha service users and potential referring agencies) to develop the project's structure and governance and recruit and train staff and volunteers, including a service-user steering group. All members of the steering group are current service users and their role is to represent other women who attend JOY and suggest activities. Though the project answers to the funders in terms of meeting set outcomes, it can be argued then that it is service user-led, in terms of what activities take place to meet the outcomes. This is supported by regular service-user consultations and evidenced by forms requesting women to state what activities they would like to do each term. The specific outcomes for the project are shown below:

OUTCOMES	*INDICATORS*
1. Disadvantaged women will have improved motivation, confidence and social skills leading to reduced isolation and increased community participation	The number of women who demonstrate increased self-confidence, motivation and improved social skills by actively participating in project and community
	The number of women who self-report improved and sustained self-confidence and interpersonal skills via activity and course questionnaires and evaluation
	The number of women who self-report improved and sustained self-confidence and interpersonal skills via activity and course questionnaires and evaluation
2. Disadvantaged women will acquire new skills and aspirations and enhance learning, leading to sustained change and improved future volunteering and employment opportunities	The number of women who have improved educational achievement by completing a JOY skills-based activity and obtained a certificate
	The number of women who have progressed from service user to become a volunteer or mentor and have provided mentoring support to at least two other women
	The number of women progressing to external opportunities including mentoring, volunteering, further training and paid employment

Targets are set by the funder in order to measure if the outcomes are being met, and it is clear that the funders require positive change to be measured quantitatively.

Activities are facilitated by project staff, volunteers, wider WCT staff, freelance tutors and external bodies such as the Heart of Worcestershire College (HOW). With support, each woman is directed to suitable activities during the one to one discussion when they first attend the project (though referrals from probation may be more directive) and they choose activities thereafter (Heywood, 2018). WCT states that 'each woman will access a journey tailored to their specific needs and abilities' (2018b: 3). Timetables of group activities are produced each term. There is no limit to how many activities women can attend.

What Happened?

An evaluation of the JOY Project outcomes was completed in September 2018 by the University of Worcester (Jones et al., 2018). This evaluation provided evidence that the vast majority of service users show increased levels of positive change in a wide range of areas including social, educational, volunteering, community participation and employment as a result of engaging with the JOY Project. This shows that JOY is effective in enabling service users to improve their personal and social circumstances. Informal, leisure activities result in a range of important 'soft outcomes' that should not be underestimated in terms of service-user health and well-being. The JOY Project has also had a massive impact on the mental health of service users, far exceeding what was expected by staff. One of the biggest additional outcomes is the important friendships women make, highly relevant in the context of the recent emphasis from government on 'social well-being' (Department for Digital, Culture, Media and Sport, 2018). Staff and service users said friendship should be an outcome in its own right. Service users are active in volunteer and mentor work at JOY and externally. It is also evident that JOY is identifying hidden and unmet needs of service users in terms of basic literacy and/or numeracy skills.

The project has a positive impact on the relationships of service users and on community participation. The project benefits local communities by having community hubs, via internal and external volunteering and mentoring, and entry into employment. For example, 29 service users moved into external opportunities (volunteering, education and paid employment), since the project launch in February 2018. This exceeds the 'Big Lottery Fund' target. Representatives from partner agencies state that it is highly unlikely that without accessing the JOY Project, some service users would have had the impetus to move on to external training and employment. The money that the local council saves by not having to spend on supporting the service users must be astronomical.

Additionally, JOY also enables the integration of women from a range of ethnicities and social/educational backgrounds and abilities, who would not normally come together and interact in the way that they did.

A significant feature that the evaluation identified as important to the project's success is the fact that activities are service user-led, as in line with the project's theoretical underpinning. In practice, this means that as service users constitute the project's steering group, they initiate and are consulted about what activities they want to do. The timetable is then agreed upon, in consultation with staff. The evaluation highlighted how the organisation and function of the steering group in this way is an important aspect of the success of the project to service users and staff, as a consequence of it being representative of the service users and being advocates for women in the wider community. The relevance of this is identified as ensuring attendance and retention, and the completing of courses and gaining certification. As a consequence of this, the WCT now have JOY steering group members on the WCT Board, and vice versa.

What was Learned?

An important aspect of the JOY Project is that it historically developed from an identified need within the community, by the community. This means that without the initial and continuing hard work of members of the community in which it operates, it is highly unlikely that the JOY Project would exist. As an example of this, it is important to note that the staff are not academically or professionally trained as community workers but are 'experts by experience, having lived through a variety of traumatic events themselves, and this means that the staff consistently stated that what they did felt intuitively right (Jones et al., 2018). It is evident that they are part of the community first and foremost and their role as JOY members of staff is a secondary consideration in the relationship they have developed with the women.

Operating projects in this way can produce a number of positive benefits. For example, the workers know exactly what the women needed and how to engage with them, developing strong bonds and high levels of trust both with individuals and groups. The underlying feeling from the workers is that they had received similar support in their lives and understood the impact and benefit of engaging in mutually supportive relationships. It can bring benefits such as a greater sense of community cohesion, ownership of the project, a sense of belonging and a shared understanding of protection and security for the women.

However, it can also act as a barrier to the progression of either individuals or the project. For example, it can impact negatively when it comes to supporting transitions within the lives of the women involved in the project. There is potential for this issue to occur when discussing how the women would cope if the project were to close, with many suggesting that they recognised how dependent they were on the project and could not envisage being able to deal with this concept (Jones et al., 2018).

It can also have a negative impact on the project when seeking to make the community more inclusive or when recognising the importance of exploring more sustainable methods of funding for the project. This was evident in an Evaluation Study (Jones et al., 2018), which identified that there were 'gaps' in the provision of service, particular in the 16 to 25 age group but this was not identified by either the staff team or the women as they felt that the programme of activities catered for their (own) needs. There is a danger that the women involved in the project would cease to operate as a community and instead would become a 'closed shop', valuing the exclusivity rather that the potential for inclusivity of the project. These were all issues highlighted to the group in the Evaluation Report.

Literature Underpinning the Development of this Work and the Analysis of it?

The outcomes from the JOY Project underlie the significance of two overarching aims and objectives for the success of community development projects, as outlined below.

The first significant point relates to the overarching aim of community development as 'to transform reality through the involvement and actions of people as their own agents of change (McArdle, 2014: 12). What this means is that community development cannot be done on people, it has to be done with people, with the problems or issues of focus first identified by the relevant community. Practically, this involves drawing on the skills and expertise that already exist within the community, as a method to meet the identified needs (Walker, 2016). Significantly, this relates not only to the way the project is designed, but also to the outcomes of any project, wherein:

> the intended outcomes from community development have to be linked to the concerns of communities themselves, linked to their agendas as defined in their own terms.

The issues that communities themselves are concerned with and want to change are the defined outcomes that those concerned with community development must look towards,

(McArdle, 2014: 12)

Often, the protagonists for community development live in the community in which they work, and this provides the opportunity for the authentic legitimacy and enduring legacy of community development (McCrea, 2017). The composition and function of the JOY steering group is a good example of how this can function in practice, and also how it can have beneficial outcomes for the project.

A second, linked, overarching aim is that the desired outcomes from community development occur at the collective rather than the individual level (Crickley, 2014). What this means is that community development works with and develops communities, not individuals. The significance of the previous point to this cannot be overlooked, but just as importantly is the emphasis on the long term rather than the short term in community development, which implicitly acknowledges that change is a process, and not an output (Stuart, 2018). The implication of this is perhaps best exemplified by contrasting the outcomes from social work, which is a practice located in the individual and so has outcomes located in the individual, and the wider implications that community development can have on a community (Crickley, 2014). Another linked differentiation from social work is community development's inherently political nature, meaning a focus not just on the management of a problem, but a commitment to social justice and social inclusion in its outcomes.

Arguably, the success of the JOY Project has been built out of the fact that it has these two significant features of community development at its core. In relation to the JOY Project, the emphasis on such community outcomes is evident in a number of ways. For example, the JOY Project has added a positive impact on service users' community participation through, for example, increased volunteering, education and paid employment. Additionally, the money that JOY saves the local council by not having to spend on supporting the service users provides a financial benefit to the community which reinforces the wider collective benefit of the project.

These reinforce the importance of ensuring that community development projects are grounded in the community, for the community, by the community.

Further Study

We suggest looking back through the book to further explore these specific issues from the case study:

- *Anti-discriminatory practice*
- *Empowerment*
- *Freire and popular education*
- *Slum Dwellers International and women-led development*
- *Monitoring and evaluation*

References

Almaseb, H. and Julia, M. (2007) 'Muslim Women Achieving Control over their Lives: Factors Supporting Empowerment', *International Consortium for Social Development*, 29(1), 81–99.

Carr, E.E. (2003) 'Rethinking Empowerment Theory using a Feminist Lens: The Importance of Process', *Affilia*, 18(8), 8–20.

Carroll, M.A. (2004) 'Empowerment Theory: Philosophical and Practical Difficulties', *Canadian Psychology*, 35(4), 376–381.

Corston, J. (2007) *The Corston Report: A Report by Baroness Jean Corston of a Review of Women with Particular Vulnerabilities in the Criminal Justice System*. London: Home Office.

Crickley, A. (2014) 'Introductory Remarks', in *Community Development in Europe: Towards a Common Framework and Understanding*, European Community Development Network, 5–8, [online]. Available at: www.scdc.org.uk/media/resources/documents/2014%2024%2009%20 EuCDN%20Publication%20-%20FINAL.pdf, accessed 2 November 2018.

Department for Digital, Culture, Media and Sport (2018) *A Connected Society: A Strategy for Tackling Loneliness – Laying the Foundations for Change*. London: HM Government.

Elkins, C. (2008) 'Barriers to Substance Abuse Treatment' [online]. Available at: www.drugrehab. com/treatment/barriers-in-seeking-treatment, accessed 2 November 2018.

Heywood, R. (2018) Interview with Research Team, 20 March 2018.

Jones, R., Lewis, J., Sealey, C., and Gregory, D. (2018) *An Impact Evaluation of the JOY Project*. Worcester: University of Worcester. Available at: https://eprints.worc.ac.uk/id/eprint/7173, accessed 3 November 2018.

Lee, J.A.B (2001) *The Empowerment Approach to Social Work Practice*. New York: Columbia University Press.

McArdle, O. (2014) 'Community Development in Europe: Shared Language, Shared Purpose, Collective Impact', *in Community Development in Europe: Towards a Common Framework and Understanding*. Brussels: European Community Development Network, 11–14. Available at: www.scdc.org.uk/media/resources/documents/2014%2024%2009%20EuCDN%20 Publication%20-%20FINAL.pdf, accessed 2 November 2018.

McCrea, N. (2017) 'Practising Solidarity: Challenges for Community Development and Social Movements in the 21st Century', *Community Development Journal*, 52 (3), 379–384.

ONS (2011) *2011 Census* [online]. Available at: www.ons.gov.uk/census/2011census, accessed 2 November 2018.

Popple, K. (2000) *Analysing Community Work: Its Theory and Practice*. Maidenhead: Open University Press.

Stuart, G. (2018) *Reflections on Community Development vs. Community Work*. [online]. Available at: https://sustainingcommunity.wordpress.com/2018/02/12/community-development-vs-community-work/, accessed 2 November 2018.

Twelvetrees, A. (1991) *Community Work*, 2nd edn. London: Macmillan.

Ullman, S.E., Ming-Foynes, M., and Tang, S. (2010) 'Benefits and Barriers to Disclosing Sexual Trauma: A Contextual Approach', *Journal of Trauma & Dissociation*, 11(2), 127–133.

Walker, P. (2016) 'Social Work and Community Development', *Community Development Journal*, 51(3), 452–454.

WCoC (2016) 'Domestic Abuse and Violence Needs Assessment'. Available at: www.worcestershire. gov.uk/jsna.

Women's Resource Centre (2015) 'Women's Organisations: The Net Beneath the Net' [online]. Available at: www.thewomensresourcecentre.org.uk/resources/womens, accessed 1 November 2018.

Worcester Community Trust (2018a) 'Welcome to Worcester Community Trust' [online]. Available at: www.worcestercommunitytrust.org.uk, accessed 3 November 2018.

Worcester Community Trust (2018b) 'WCT Update'. Issue 1, Summer [online]. Available at: www. worcestercommunitytrust.org.uk/wp-content/uploads/2018/, accessed 1 November 2018.

Case Study 5.9
Show Racism the Red Card

Luke Campbell and Nicola Hay

Context and Purpose

Established by Ged Grebby in Tyneside in 1996, Show Racism the Red Card (SRtRC) work to combat racism through blending the mass appeal of football and footballing role models within anti-racism education practice. In support of their stated aims of (i) 'producing educational resources'; (ii) 'developing activities to encourage people, including young people, to challenge racism'; and (iii) 'challenging racism in the game of football and other sports' (SRtRC, n.d.), the charity delivers anti-racism education via interventions in schools, additional support for learning units, youth work groups, and workplaces, as well as grass-roots and professional sporting clubs (SRtRC, 2017a). With financial support from, amongst others, Scottish Government, Big Lottery Fund, Youthlink, The Robertson Trust, Rowanbank Financial Consultants, First Scottish, Friends Legal, The Education Institute of Scotland, Unite the Union, the G.M.B., and Thompson Solicitors (see SRtRC, 2009a, 2011a, 2017b, 2017c, 2018a), SRtRC Scotland are able to provide year round education sessions designed to combat and reduce forms of prejudice and discrimination.

Developmental History

Founded in North Tyneside (England) in January 1996 by Grebby, SRtRC were initially born out of the Youth against Racism in Europe (Y.R.E.) movement (Dixon et al., 2014; F.I.M.U., n.d.). Part of the Committee for a Workers' International – an international network of Militant members across several European nations – Y.R.E. members worked with schools in the UK to create anti-racism educational resource packs (Y.R.E., n.d.). These educational packs were widely distributed, with Shaka Hislop (now a retired international goalkeeper from Trinidad and Tobago) pledging to support the anti-racist activists through a donation of circa £50 after receiving a copy (SRtRC, 2009b). Hislop (2011), currently Honorary President of SRtRC, cited his own distress when subjected to 'kids [...] shouting racist abuse [before] they came over looking for autographs' as a core motivation for his support for the earliest incarnations of SRtRC.

Since its inception, the charity has grown in both reputation and stature, establishing new offices in Southend-on-sea (Southern England Office), as well as in Wales (SRtRC Wales), and Scotland (SRtRC Scotland). Further bodies adopting the same educational model currently operate in the Republic of Ireland (also known as 'Show Racism the Red Card'), Finland (Punainen kortti rasismille), Denmark (Giv Rasismen det Rode Kort), Sweden (Ge Rasismen Rött Kort), Germany (Zeig-Rassismus-Die-Rote-Karte), and Norway (Gi Rasisme Rødt Kort). Established in 2003, SRtRC Scotland has worked with diverse communities in a variety of settings – ranging from Her Majesty's Young Offenders Institution

Polmont to trade union conferences (see SRtRC, 2010, 2013a). Historically, SRtRC's education provision was based on delivering one-off anti-racism workshops in order to educate young people on the implications of racism, with a limited number of workshops focusing on Islamophobia and anti-Gypsyism (SRtRC, 2011b, 2013b, 2017d). Employing visual, auditory and kinaesthetic activities (Kingett et al., 2017), the educational works are normally delivered by an education worker with support from an ex-professional footballer. Activities often involve small group work, with class discussion and age-adapted learning activities. However, as research and knowledge on 'good practice' and 'what works to reduce prejudice' emerged from the likes of McBride (2015), the educational outcomes and output from the Scottish office were redeveloped and further underpinned by academic theory and policy.

Impact and Engagement

The European Commission (2008) argues that 'the sports movement has a greater influence than any other social movement', further claiming that 'sports is the largest social activity in Europe, interesting citizens from all member states'. Statistical data gathered by S.P.F.L. Insider (2018) has consistently demonstrated that despite having the 24th largest population of the 55 national association members of U.E.F.A. (the Union of European Football Associations), within men's top tier professional football, Scotland is the highest attended national league. In 2016, this meant that an average of 1.15 per cent of the adult population in Scotland attended a men's professional football match, which as noted by Campbell and Hay (2018: 7) is 'higher than northern European neighbours Norway (1.07%), Denmark (0.47%), and Finland (0.14%) – each of which has a comparable population [to Scotland] at 5.233 million, 5.731 million, and 5.495, respectively'. In addition, the 2016 average attendance was 'more than double those in Germany (0.47%) and almost triple those in England (0.40%)'. Changes in top flight teams via promotion and relegation has meant that in 2018, this average attendance figure has increased to 1.78 per cent in Scotland (with England at 0.72 per cent, Spain at 0.59 per cent and Russia at 0.08 per cent). In this sense, association football serves as what Henri and Pudelko (2003) and Willmott (1989) describe as communities of interest ('people assembled around a topic of common interest'). Hoggett (1997) suggested such communities are not limited to place-based setting, and thus association football as a sport, but also supporter bases for any given club, can serve as the mutual interest. Within Scotland, at least, this may justify the use of association football as the medium for educational engagement.

As detailed in, amongst others, Kingett et al. (2017), Clark et al. (2018) and Campbell and Hay (2018), the work of SRtRC has historically fallen into the short-term equality and diversity training category. However, evidence from McBride (2015) suggests that a programme of sustained education over an extended period is more likely to change prejudicial attitudes. Understanding the significance of this work from McBride (2015), but also Allport (1954), the Scottish SRtRC office re-designed their prejudice reduction education content to allow participants additional time to explore multiple forms of contemporary racisms and their developmental learning trajectories across several sessions (Campbell and Hay, 2018). Much of this redesigned programme aims to support learners to develop the necessary skills required to challenge hate crime generally and racism specifically when witnessed. Doing so has meant however, that the anti-racism educational model employed in Scotland has differed from that of other divisions of the organisation in, for example, England and Wales. In acknowledging the importance of sustained learning programmes, SRtRC Scotland's educational interventions became increasingly grounded in theory.

Contemporary anti-racist educational theory contends that contact with one's 'out-group' – see the 'the out-group homogeneity principle' in, for example, Linville and Jones (1980) or Park and Rothbart (1982) – can counteract negative perceptions and promote cross-group friendships (Allport, 1954; Pettigrew and Tropp, 2006). Scottish Government policy has thus centred around integration and social inclusion (see Farrington and Farrington, 2005; Mulvey, 2018; Pierson, 2009; Riddell, 2009) whilst also placing community involvement in the third sector as vital to positive community relations can aid in social integration and community cohesion. To that end, SRtRC Scotland has sought to develop and deliver their anti-racist educational content to a broad range of communities including schools, youth groups, and as noted above, trade union conferences. For example, the *Lighthouse Refugee Integration* project (first trialled in circa 2017 was developed and continues to be co-delivered by a refugee who shares his personal experiences of escaping from Zimbabwe in the 1980s. His experiences of integration and social inclusion (or conversely of struggling against forms of marginalisation and prejudice) are delivered based on the same research from Ager and Strang (2008) that underpins current Scottish Government policies such as the New Scots document.

In a similar manner, SRtRC Scotland developed and continues to co-deliver their *Tackling Gypsy, Roma and Traveller Bullying* (see SRtRC, 2017e, 2017f) education programme with both members of Scottish Traveller communities and with Article 12 in Scotland (SC02771). Allport's (1954) understanding of 'contact theory' within educational practice is therefore a crucial element of SRtRC Scotland's current educational process as it supports participants to learn about the experiences of marginalised communities such as Gypsy, Roma, Traveller and refugee populations, which, based on evidence on exposure to 'out-groups' can increase empathy (Allport, 1954). Whilst these programmes (the *Lighthouse Refugee Integration* project and *Tackling Gypsy, Roma and Traveller Bullying*) are informed by contact theory, due to funding constraints SRtRC Scotland are unable to act on the paradigm of sustained education. This, Campbell and Hay (2018) warn may limit impact.

Finally, SRtRC's UK-wide *Fortnight of Action* is perhaps the organisation's highest visibility activity. Designed for maximum public engagement over a short period, the Fortnight of Action 'is a general awareness raising initiative targeted specifically at football fans of the Scottish Professional League, Scottish Women's Football, Scottish Junior Football and Grassroots Community football clubs' (Campbell and Hay, 2018: 12). Traditionally taking place each October, the two-week period involves sustained action *en mass*, utilising traditional media forms including posters, notes in match day programmes, and press interviews. McBride (2015) notes that such campaigns are targeted at a specific audience (football supporters, players and staff) and include public awareness-raising initiatives designed to educate members of the public on how to report a hate crime. Illustrating the extent of public engagement achieved through the Fortnight of Action, in 2017 around 115,000 football fans witnessed or engaged with STtRC's activities (SRtRC, 2017g). A note of caution, however, as there will be significant overlap with many supporters attending multiple matches during the campaigning period. Furthermore, as noted by Abrams (2010) there is limited existing academic research on the impact of effectiveness of this form on the public campaign initiative. Furthermore, there is currently no research evidencing the effectiveness of SRtRC's Fortnight of Action.

Outcomes and Output

Davidson et al. (2018) cite an 'intellectual dishonesty' over the common myth that 'Scots are in some sense different from the English' in terms of openness and inclusivity of non-majority cultures, religions and languages ('out-groups'). A diverse body of academic and organisational research, including from the Scottish Government (2015) repeatedly indicates that a significant proportion of minority communities in Scotland have experienced some form of racism. Taking Meer's (2018) findings as one of the most recent examples, respondents stated that upwards of 33.7 per cent of men from minority ethnic communities in Scotland had experienced some form of discrimination in the last five years. SRtRC Scotland have therefore ensured to produce a diverse set of educational resources addressing the specific racism and discriminations that many minority communities in Scotland (and beyond) face. Current resources include *Tackling Contemporary Racism*; *Tackling Gypsy, Roma and Traveller Bullying Education*; *Refugee Inclusion Education*; *Tackling LGBTQI Bullying Education*; and the *Young Volunteers Empowerment Programme* – which the organisation suggests support 'young people [...] to develop and deliver their own prejudice reduction education (SRtRC, 2017b).

Historically, educational materials have included a DVD featuring contributions from several internationally celebrated male football players. Early examples include the DVD *Show Racism the RED Card*, which featured interviews with Thierry Henry (France), Ryan Giggs (Wales), Samuel Eto'o (Cameroon), Didier Drogba (Ivory Coast), and Mustapha Hadji (Morocco). The 2009 DVD *A Safe Place*, sought to address prejudice and discrimination towards asylum seekers, with a significant proportion of the educational content centred on anti-Muslim hatred (Islamophobia). Provided as part of a larger education pack, the resource also contains activity guides for educators to use beyond the one-off interventions generally undertaken by SRtRC's Education Worker.

Current education packs available from the SRtRC online shop include *Homophobia: Let's Tackle It* (2012) which contained two films, a 49-page learning booklet, and a range of supplementary materials; as well as the *No Place for Hate*, which educates viewers on effective methods for challenging the political far-right in the twenty-first century. The resources are priced at £30 and £15, respectively. These educational resources move beyond just utilising football players and feature actors (e.g. Kieron Richardson), comedians (Rhona Cameron), and other sports players (e.g. Ben Cohen [rugby]). This perhaps demonstrates attempts by SRtRC to broaden their appeal. Beyond their initial remit, other current educational materials include the *Out of Site* pack, priced at £5, which educates learners on the specific forms of racism towards Gypsy, Roma and Traveller groups; and the anti-sectarian *Rivals Not Enemies*, which forms part of the Show Bigotry the Red Card campaign (SRtRC, 2018). The latter resource was designed with guidance from the Scottish Government's Curriculum for Excellence (SRtRC, n.d.).

Given limited funding and therefore tight capacity for contact with learners, the charity also organises an annual creative competition during which young people attending a school or further education college in Scotland have the opportunity to engage with anti-racism education through creative arts, including artwork, poetry, short stories, music composition, multimedia presentation, dance, drama performance, conducting a research project or producing a t-shirt design (SRtRC, 2018d: 5). This affords the organisation a wider reach than their current budget would normally allow – for example, 19,485 young people participated in the 2017 SRtRC Creative Competition on either an individual or group basis (SRtRC, 2017g: 17).

Limitations

Despite research and policy on what works demonstrating that best practice in anti-racist education requires sustained periods of contact time with learners (Allport, 1954), the short-term nature of modern funding streams in the Third Sector enable only partial implementation of contact theory. There thus have to be trade-offs between absolute best practice and widest reach. Where funding was obtained to implement a sustained programme, this has often not allowed for the co-development and co-delivery of educational content with community members from the out-groups. This paradox may best be illustrated through SRtRC Scotland's *Tackling LGBT Bullying* programme wherein, over a number of weeks, participants learned about terminology, rights to inclusion and how best to challenge LGBTI+ bullying, but funding constraints did not allow for the co-delivery of education with a member of the LGBT community. Despite the aforementioned financial constraints, the combined SRtRC's UK divisions deliver anti-racism education to upwards of 50,000 people annually, whilst SRtRC Scotland specifically worked with more than 4,209 young people and 111 adults (SRtRC, 2017g). Football is, however, only one of many sports commonly engaged in by communities in Scotland. There is an existing body of research into racism in others sports, including rugby (e.g. Jarvie, 2003; Maguire, 1991) and cricket (e.g. Burton, 2003).

Campbell and Hay (2018: 6) chart history of racism in men's professional football in Scotland, ranging from 'Indian-born ex-Celtic midfielder Paul Wilson endur[ing] racial slurs (mid-1970s)' through to 'Clyde Football Club's Ally Love [being] served a five game ban by the SFA following allegations of racist comments against Annan Athletic Football's Rabin Omar' (BBC, 2018). With the concept of utilising the public profile of association football players as role models constituting a core dimension of SRtRC Scotland's work, issues of a racist or discriminatory nature within professional sport impact on the organisation's public profile. As such, the organisation has a duty to respond publicly to issues as and when they arise. Examples in 2018 alone include calling upon the Scottish Football Association (SFA) and the Scottish Professional Football League (SPFL) to investigate claims of racially motivated abuse from Celtic FC fans towards Aberdeen FC player Shay Logan (BBC, 2018; SRtRC, 2018c); and the SRtRC issuing a joint statement with the Professional Footballers' Association of Ireland on anti-Irish racism[1] (SRtRC, 2018b).

Commentary

SRtRC Scotland are not unique in understanding the potential reach of association football as a medium for enabling *en masse* education. As noted by Campbell and Hay (2018), many other organisations have centred their learning activities on social issues also apparent with association football. Amongst them are Heart of Midlothian Football Club's Big Hearts Community Trust (SC037311) and Hibernian Football Club's 'Game Changer' initiative, both of which demonstrate understanding of the social responsibilities of large sporting organisations. Both programmes engage large fan bases in the Scottish capital (Edinburgh) based on, for example, kinship care (Big Hearts, 2018) and homelessness (EEN, 2016; EVOC, 2018; TFN, 2018). Other organisations such as Football Memories and the Adult Learning Project's (SC007226) football literacies initiative have addressed specific issues including Alzheimer's disease (Ramsay and Ramsay, 2014; Schofield and Tolson, 2010) and low-level adult literacy (Ledwith, 2011; Player, 2013). What, arguably, makes SRtRC Scotland distinct from their peers is their legacy of anti-racism education spanning more than two decades in the UK and 15 years in Scotland; their efforts to maintain relationships with key educational stakeholders including football clubs, the SFA, schools, youth clubs, trade unions, and the Scottish Government; and also the breadth of initiatives they undertake to challenge hate crime and discrimination in all its forms (e.g. racism, bigotry, Islamophobia, anti-Gypsyism and LGBTI+ hate).

1 The call for an investigation into anti-Irish hate came after Hibernian FC manager Neil Lennon was targeted during an Edinburgh derby match on Wednesday 31 October 2018 (see Evening Echo, 2018).

With a population of around 5.4 million people (National Records of Scotland, n.d.), 91.8 per cent of whom identified as 'White British' in the 2011 Scottish Census, individuals from minority ethnic communities in Scotland have – contrary to popular belief – consistently faced, and continue to experience, discrimination based on religion (e.g. Flint, 2008; Meer, 2018; Waiton, 2018; Walls and Williams, 2006); language (e.g. Powney et al., 1998); and culture (e.g. Bradley, 2006; Clayton, 2006; Hashagen et al., 2018; Liinpää, 2018). The Office for National Statistics (2015) notes that the most significant minority populations in Scotland come from Poland (ca.76,000), India (ca.26,000), the Republic of Ireland (ca.20,000), Germany (ca.19,000), Pakistan (ca.18,000). The aforementioned Davidson et al. (2018) research highlighted barriers to the social integration of minority communities, therein challenging the positive narrative surrounding the Scottish Government's 'New Scots' concept. Meer (2018) further confronts the myth of no racism occurring in Scotland by arguing that 'hyphenated Scots' (e.g. African-Scots, Black-Scots, and Asian-Scots) remain 'somehow not quite Scottish'. The work SRtRC Scotland undertake is therefore vital in promoting understanding of diversity in its broadest sense.

By undertaking what Clark et al. (2018: 118) described as an 'intersectional approach to unpacking power, privilege and justice', SRtRC Scotland work to educate a range of communities in Scotland on issues of discrimination and prejudice across a broad range of equalities issues. Given association football's mass global appeal, particularly in countries like Scotland where, as SPFL Insider (2018) demonstrated, almost 1 in 50 attend a top-flight men's football game in an average weekend, organisations such as Show Racism the Red Card Scotland – who are privileged with support from the Scottish Football Association (SFA) and its member clubs – are well placed to design and deliver anti-racist educational interventions with broad appeal. In addition, it is important to note the *Fortnight of Action* activities involves not only men's professional football clubs, but also Scottish Women's Football, Scottish Junior Football, and Grassroots Community football clubs in this co-ordinated period of focused activity. However, as is perhaps symptomatic of the contemporary Third Sector, funding cuts and strict budgets limit SRtRC Scotland's capacity to engage Scottish communities in anti-racism education to the extent advocated by Allport (1954) and McBride (2015).

Further Study

We suggest looking back through the book to further explore these specific issues from the case study:

- *Values and purposes of community development*
- *Hegemony and culture*
- *Anti-discriminatory practice*
- *Freire and popular education*

Note: Show Racism the Red Card Scotland are available via their website at: www.theredcard.org/contact/; on Twitter @SRtRCScotland; and on Facebook at *Show Racism the Red Card Scotland*.

References

Abrams, D. (2010) 'Processes of Prejudice: Theory, Evidence and Intervention', *Equality and Human Rights Commission*. Research Report 56.

Ager, A. and Strang, A. (2008) 'Understanding Integration: A Conceptual Framework', *Journal of Refugee Studies*, 21(2), 166–191.

Allport, G.W. (1954) *The Nature of Prejudice*. Cambridge, MA: Addison-Wesley.

BBC (2018) 'Shay Logan: Charity calls on SPFL to investigate claims of racist abuse by Celtic fans'. Available at: www.bbc.co.uk/sport/football/44785875, accessed 7 November 2018.

Big Hearts. (2018) 'Big Hearts Celebrate 3 Years of Support to Kinship Care Families'. Available at: www.bighearts.org.uk/news/fourth-kinship-family-day/, accessed 8 November 2018.

Bradley, J. (2006) 'Sport and the Contestation of Ethnic Identity: Football and Irishness in Scotland', *Journal of Ethnic and Migration Studies*, 32(7), 1189–1208.

Burton, M. (2003) *Cricket: Derrick: Matt for England*, 1st edn. Cardiff: MGN Ltd.

Campbell, L. and Hay, N. (2018) 'A Critical Examination of Anti-Racist Initiatives Taking Place among Young Adult and Adult Association Football Fans in Contemporary Scotland'. Available at: www.morayhouse.education.ed.ac.uk/conferences/esrea2018/papers/paper%20campbell_hay.pdf, accessed 16 October 2018.

Clark, C., Matthew, D. and Burns, V. (2018) 'Power, Privilege and Justice: Intersectionality as Human Rights', *The International Journal of Human Rights*, 22(1), 108–126.

Clayton, T. (2006) 'Diasporic Otherness': Racism, Sectarianism and "National Exteriority" in Modern Scotland', *Social & Cultural Geography*, 6(1), 99–116.

Davidson, N., Liinpää, M., McBride, M., and Virdee, S. (2018) *No Problem Here: Understanding Racism in Scotland*. Edinburgh: Luath Press.

Dixon, K., Lowes, J., and Gibbons, T. (2014) 'Show Racism The Red Card: Potential Barriers to the Effective Implementation of the Anti-racist Message', *Soccer & Society*, 17(1), 140–154.

Edinburgh Evening News (2016) 'Hibs will open stadium to homeless on Christmas Day'. Available at: www.edinburghnews.scotsman.com/sport/football/hibs/hibs-will-open-stadium-to-homeless-on-christmas-day-1-4309198, accessed 8 November 2018.

European Commission (2007) *White Paper on Sport*. Brussels: Directorate-General Education and Culture.

Evening Echo (2018) 'Online threats targeted at James McClean revealed by wife Erin'. Available at: www.eveningecho.ie/nationalsport/Online-threats-targeted-at-James-McClean-revealed-by-wife-Erin-6cc18bfe-eab5-4a55-a829-099959fef7a1-ds, accessed 7 November 2018.

EVOC (2018) *GameChanger Wellbeing Centre*. Available at: www.evoc.org.uk/noticeboard/notices/gamechanger-wellbeing-centre/, accessed 7 November 2018.

Farrington, J. and Farrington, C. (2005) 'Rural Accessibility, Social Inclusion and Social Justice: Towards Conceptualisation', *Journal of Transport Geography*, 13(1), 1–12.

FIMU (Suomen Monikulttuurinen Liikuntaliitto FIMU ry) (n.d.) *Show Racism the Red Card*. Available at: www.fimu.org/in-english/projects-and-campaigns/show-racism-the-red-card/, accessed 7 November 2018.

Flint, J. (2008) 'Governing Sectarianism in Scotland', *Scottish Affairs*, 63(1), 120–137.

Hashagen, S., Doyle, M., and Keenan, B. (2018) 'Cultural Identity, Migration and Community Development in Glasgow', in G. Craig (ed.), *Community Organising Against Racism*. Bristol: Policy Press.

Henri, F. and Pudelko, B. (2003) 'Understanding and Analysing Activity and Learning in Virtual Communities', *Journal of Computer Assisted Learning*, 19(4), 474–487.

Hislop, S. (2011) 'In SRtRC'. *Interview: Shaka Hislop, Honorary President, Show Racism the Red Card*. Available at: www.theredcard.org/news/2011/09/15/interview-shaka-hislop-honorary-president-show-racism-the-red-card, accessed 7 November 2018.

Jarvie, G. (2003) *Sport, Racism and Ethnicity*. London: Routledge.

Kingett, J., Abrams, D., and Purewal, K. (2017) *Show Racism the Red Card: Evaluating the Impact of Anti-Racism Educational Interventions on the Attitudes of Young People in Secondary School Education*. Glasgow: Equality and Human Rights Commission.

Ledwith, M. (2011) *Community Development: A Critical Approach* (2nd edn). Bristol: Policy Press.

Liinpää, M. (2018) 'Nationalism and Scotland's Imperial Past', in N. Davidson, M. Liinpää, M. McBride, and S. Virdee (eds), *No Problem Here: Understanding Racism in Scotland*. Edinburgh: Luath Press.

Linville, P.W. and Jones, E.E. (1980) 'Polarized Appraisals of Out-group Members', *Journal of Personality and Social Psychology*, 38(5), 689–703.

Maguire, J. (1991) 'Sport, Racism and British Society: A Sociological Study of England's Elite Male Afro/Caribbean Soccer and Rugby Union Players', in G. Jarvie (ed.), *Sport, Racism, and Ethnicity*. Bristol: Falmer Press.

McBride, M. (2015) *What Works to Reduce Prejudice and Discrimination? A Review of the Evidence*. Edinburgh: Scottish Government.

Meer, N. (2018) 'What do we know about BAME Self-reported Racial Discrimination in Scotland?', in N. Davidson, M. Liinpää, M. McBride, and S. Virdee (eds), *No Problem Here: Understanding Racism in Scotland*. Edinburgh: Luath Press.

Mulvey, G. (2018) 'Social Citizenship, Social Policy and Refugee Integration: a Case of Policy Divergence in Scotland', *Journal of Social Policy*, 47(1), 161–178.

National Records of Scotland Web Team (n.d.) 'National Records of Scotland', Available at: www.nrscotland.gov.uk/news/2018/scotlands-population-2017.

Office of National Statistics (2015) Scotland's Population 2015: The Registrar General's Annual Review of Demographic Trends – 161st edn: SG Paper 86 216, 2016.

Park, B. and Rothbart, M. (1982) 'Perception of Out-group Homogeneity and Levels of Social Categorization: Memory for the Subordinate Attributes of In-group and Out-group Members', *Journal of Personality and Social Psychology*, 42(6), 1051–1068.

Pettigrew, T.F. and Tropp, L. (2006) 'A Meta-analytic Test of Intergroup Contact Theory', *Journal of Personality and Social Psychology*, 90(5), 751–783.

Pierson, J. (2009) *Tackling Social Exclusion*. Cambridge: Routledge.

Player, J. (2013) 'Critical Discourse Analysis, Adult Education and "Fitba"', *Studies in the Education of Adults*, 45(1), 57–66.

Powney, J., McPake, J., Hall, S., and Lyall, L. (1998) 'Education of Minority Ethnic Groups in Scotland: A Review of Research', *SCRE Research Report Series*, 88.

Ramsay, S. and Ramsay, M. (2014) 'A Football Reminiscence Group for People with Dementia: The Forfar, Kirriemuir and South West Angus Experience', *Mental Health Nursing*, 34(5), 32–33.

Riddell, S. (2009) 'Social Justice, Equality and Inclusion in Scottish Education', *Discourse: Studies in the Cultural Politics of Education*, 30(3), 283–296.

Schofield, I. and Tolson, D. (2010) *Scottish Football Museum Reminiscence Pilot Project for People with Dementia: A Realistic Evaluation*. Glasgow: Glasgow Caledonian University.

Scottish Government (2015) 'Racist Incidents Recorded by the Police in Scotland, 2013–14'. Available at: www2.gov.scot/Resource/0048/00489644.pdf, accessed 7 November 2018.

SPFL Insider (2018) Twitter, 10 June 2018. Available at: https://twitter.com/AgentScotland/status/1005893424879472642, accessed 7 November 2018.

SRtRC (Show Racism the Red Card) (n.d.) 'ABOUT US'. Available at: www.theredcard.org/about/, accessed 7 November 2018.

SRtRC (2009a) 'Promoting racial equality in schools'. Available at: www.theredcard.org/news/2009/05/01/promoting-racial-equality-in-schools?rq=scotland%20funding, accessed 7 November 2018.

SRtRC (2009b) *Fact Sheet 1: Sport and Racism*. Available at: https://web.archive.org/web/20090405090222/www.theredcard.ie:80/fs/factsheet1.html, accessed 7 November 2018.

SRtRC (2010) 'Scottish TUC Black Workers' Conference'. Available at: www.theredcard.org/news/2010/10/06/scottish-tuc-black-workers-conference?rq=conference%20scotland, accessed 7 November 2018.

SRtRC (2011a) 'Scottish Government to continue funding Show Racism/Bigotry the Red Card in Scotland'. Available at: www.theredcard.org/news/2011/03/09/scottish-government-to-continue-funding-show-racism-bigotry-the-red-card-in-scotland?rq=scotland%20funding, accessed 7 November 2018.

SRtRC (2011b) 'Support for Baroness Warsi'. Available at: www.theredcard.org/news/2011/01/20/support-for-baroness-warsi?rq=Islamophobia%20scotland, accessed 7 November 2018.

SRtRC (2013a) 'Scottish TUC Annual Conference hosts SRtRC Scotland fringe meeting'. Available at: www.theredcard.org/news/2013/05/08/scottish-tuc-annual-conference-hosts-srtrc-scotland-fringe-meeting?rq=conference%20scotland, accessed 7 November 2018.

SRtRC (2013b) 'Event for Roma young people in Govanhill'. Available at: www.theredcard.org/news/2013/03/01/event-for-roma-young-people-in-govanhill?rq=roma, accessed 7 November 2018.

SRtRC (2017a) 'PFA Scotland sponsor Fortnight of Action 2017'. Available at: www.theredcard.org/news/2017/9/11/pfa-scotland-sponsor-fortnight-of-action-2017?rq=2017%20scotland, accessed 5 November 2018.

SRtRC (2017b) 'Show Racism the Red Card receives a generous donation from Rowanbank Financial Consultants'. Available at: www.theredcard.org/news/2017/12/1/show-racism-the-red-card-receives-a-generous-donation-from-rowanbank-financial-constultants?rq=scotland%20funding, accessed 5 November 2018.

SRtRC (2017c) 'Show Racism the Red Card Scotland receives generous donation from Friends Legal'. Available at: www.theredcard.org/news/2017/9/7/show-racism-the-red-card-scotland-receives-generous-donation-from-friends-legal?rq=scotland%20funding, accessed 7 November 2018.

SRtRC (2017d) 'SRtRC Scotland, Scottish Government Equality Unit and Police Scotland tackle contemporary racism'. Available at: www.theredcard.org/news/2017/4/7/srtrc-scotland-scottish-government-equality-unit-and-police-scotland-tackle-contemporary-racism?rq=Islamophobia%20scotland, accessed 7 November 2018.

SRtRC (2017e) 'SRtRC responds to Daily Record article ahead of Rangers FC and Celtic FC meeting'. Available at: www.theredcard.org/news/2017/9/23/srtrc-responds-to-daily-record-article-ahead-of-rangers-fc-and-celtic-fc-meeting?rq=Tackling%20Gypsy%2C%20Roma%20and%20Traveller%20Bullying, accessed 7 November 2018.

SRtRC (2017f) 'Show Racism the Red Card responds to Tory MP's divisive comments about Gypsy and Traveller Communities'. Available at: www.theredcard.org/news/2017/8/24/show-racism-the-red-card-responds-to-tory-mps-divisive-comments-about-gypsy-and-traveller-communities?rq=Tackling%20Gypsy%2C%20Roma%20and%20Traveller%20Bullying, accessed 7 November 2018.

SRtRC (2017g) *Annual Review*. Accessed from https://static1.squarespace.com/static/574451fe37013bd0515647ac/t/5a54b40124a6947246d5d68b/1515500734071/SRtRC+Annual+Review+2017.pdf.

SRtRC (2018c) 'SRtRC Scotland statement – Shay Logan'. Available at: www.theredcard.org/news/2018/7/10/srtrc-scotland-statement-shay-logan, accessed 3 November 2018.

SRtRC (2018a) 'Show Racism the Red Card Scotland receives generous donation from First Scottish'. Available at: www.theredcard.org/news/2018/7/16/show-racism-the-red-card-scotland-receives-generous-donation-from-first-scottish?rq=scotland%20funding, accessed 3 November 2018.

SRtRC (2018d) *Creative Competition 2019*. Available at: https://static1.squarespace.com/static/574451fe37013bd0515647ac/t/5b9a3dcb4ae23743aef0d148/1536835039622/Creative+Comp+2019+Info+Booklet.pdf, accessed 3 November 2018.

SRtRC (2018b) 'Football Associations must respond with investigations of anti Irish racism'. Available at: www.theredcard.org/news/2018/11/6/football-associations-must-respond-with-investigations-of-anti-irish-racism, accessed 3 November 2018.

Third Force News (2018) 'Homeless charity's Hibs hook-up is a real game changer'. Available at: http://thirdforcenews.org.uk/tfn-news/homeless-charitys-hibs-hook-up-is-a-real-game-changer#TCzvjKXSzFEX9jmm.99, accessed 2 November 2018.

Waiton, S. (2018) 'Criminalizing Songs and Symbols in Scottish Football: How Anti-sectarian Legislation has Created a New "Sectarian" Divide in Scotland', *Soccer & Society*, 19(2).

Walls, P. and Williams, R. (2006) 'Religious Discrimination in Scotland: A Rebuttal of Bruce et al.'s Claim that Sectarianism is a Myth', *Ethnic and Racial Studies*, 28(4).

Youth against Racism in Europe (n.d.) *What the YRE is*. Available at: www.yre.org.uk/history.html, accessed 3 November 2018.

Case Study 5.10

The Bengali Women's Programme 2011–2014

Rick Gwilt and Rehana Begum

Background

Social and Economic Context

Hyde is one of several post-industrial towns that together form the Metropolitan Borough of Tameside, one of the ten districts of Greater Manchester. It is between Oldham to the north and Stockport to the south. It has traditionally been a solidly Labour-led borough, featuring a high level of local authority in-house provision and a largely undeveloped voluntary sector, consisting mainly of small unpaid community groups.

Tameside hosts a major concentration of people of Bangladeshi heritage, specifically in Hyde, as well as significant Pakistani, Indian, African and Eastern European communities. Bangladeshi women experience a triple disadvantage arising from gender, ethnicity and locality. Demographic evidence (ONS, 2011; DCLG, 2010) shows it at the foot of key equality league tables, with illness rates persistently 10 per cent higher than those for White women and economic activity rates at only 40 per cent, compared with around 80 per cent for White women and 90 per cent for both Bangladeshi and White males. 'Non-proficiency in English' impacts very heavily on women, with employment rates dropping to only 34 per cent. Our local neighbourhood ranks within the bottom thousand for multiple deprivation.

Cultural traditions mean that young women from rural Sylhet continue to arrive in this country to take part in arranged marriages. They usually speak little or no English and are reluctant to travel outside their own areas where language is the key underlying barrier.

Most local public services recognise their own difficulty in reaching the Bengali community. They have very few Bengali-speaking staff and have tended to welcome the opportunity to work with us.

Hyde Community Action (HCA)

HCA was formed as an independent charity to address health inequalities in marginalised groups in Tameside.

Between 2003 and 2011, using community development principles, we worked on engaging Bengali women as community assets – informants and advocates – becoming architects of improved community health. Women hitherto regarded as 'hard-to-reach' by public services, started to do the reaching for themselves: engaging friends, neighbours and relatives through word of mouth and attending social activities to raise awareness around health-related issues.

With our approach of 'growing your own leadership' we achieved high levels of engagement from Bengali women, as service users, volunteers and trustees of the charity. The work highlighted problems of social exclusion, which extended well beyond traditional notions of health. This led to a three-year bid to the Big Lottery Fund (Reaching Communities) for an ambitious programme aimed at Bengali women in Hyde.

How the Work Evolved

The new programme aimed to:

- Further develop the work around health and well-being;
- Develop a greater focus on skills, knowledge and employability;
- Improve access to public services and increase community cohesion;
- Increase levels of influence and participation.

The Programme started in Autumn 2011 with the recruitment of two full-time staff members: a Project Co-ordinator (a British-Bangladeshi public-sector administrator) and a Community Development Trainee (a Bangladeshi-born and –educated volunteer who carried out voluntary work with HCA after moving to Hyde). As a pair they closely fitted the twin demographics of Bangladeshi women locally.

Over the next three years they developed a programme of activities as set out below.

Outcome 1: Mental Health and Well-being

Through consultations with service users and volunteers we identified social isolation as a key underlying issue. Consequently, a programme of activities was developed with the following outcomes in mind: social interaction through community events, visits, arts activities, trips, walking buses to activities and intergenerational work.

Outcome 2: Knowledge, Skills and Employability

Having also identified a lack of basic skills and responsibility for childcare as key underlying issues, we focused on creating a wide range of training and volunteering opportunities, with childcare and interpreter support.

Training included non-accredited and accredited learning, covering areas like: Conversational English, computing, confidence, first aid, food hygiene and nutrition, craft skills, horticulture, health walk and physical exercise leadership, interpreting, counselling, community research and enterprise.

Volunteer roles included: administrative support, course facilitator and session helper, health walk leader and helper, event helper, researchers, outreach and community engagement work, and trustee and language support.

Outcome 3: Access to Services and Community Cohesion

Tackling social isolation was a theme that cut across the programme. A key activity here was the 'Travel training', which supported women in using public transport to travel beyond their neighbourhood. Work centred on auditing patterns of service access and development of significant partnerships with organisations from all sectors.

Outcome 4: Increased Influence and Participation

The themes under this outcome covered a spectrum not unlike the classic Arnstein ladder of participation, that is, ranging from giving information, through various forms of indirect influence, to positions of direct control:

- confidence-building training in public speaking etc.;
- more specific training in being a community representative or organiser (using the School of Participation model);
- training in community research (participatory appraisal model);
- attending a devolved spending forum for small grants;
- visiting the local authority's district assembly;
- making a public art (wood carving) contribution to the town centre re-launch;
- participating in public service ambassador roles on issues ranging from tobacco-chewing to alley-gating;
- encouraging self-directed activity, e.g. first aid, arts workshops, event steering group, planning trips.

Supporting Activity: Translation and Interpretation

We provided interpreters for training sessions (except ESOL), but not for group activity, where an informal mix of Bengali and English was used.

There was little call for translation of written materials, as participants generally either read English or did not read at all.

Supporting Activity: Childcare

We had identified from early on that many service-users had young children and that childcare responsibilities were a potential barrier to participation.

We attempted several different approaches to childcare:

- employing our own crèche workers;
- negotiating places with a local commercial day nursery;
- encouraging participants to make their own child-minding arrangements.

What Worked, What Didn't and What We Learned

Performance Evaluation

Survey sample: 141, representing a minimum of 61 per cent of service users.

Outcome 1: Mental Health and Well-being

By the end of year three 200 Bangladeshi women reported that their mental health and well-being had improved as a direct result of the project.

Actual number of beneficiaries	230
Project reach against target	115 per cent
Sample mean performance against outcome measures	100 per cent

This result was expected as we always knew that our target group was seeking an escape from social isolation.

Outcome 2: Knowledge, Skills and Employability

By the end of the project 200 Bangladeshi women reported an increase in knowledge and skills and employability as a result of the volunteering and educational placements provided by the project.

Actual number of beneficiaries	216
Project reach against target	108 per cent
Measure 1: increase in knowledge and skills	99 per cent
Measure 2: more able to find or apply for jobs	73 per cent
Measure 3: able to access further training	64 per cent

This remained one area of underachievement. We reviewed the possible reasons for this at a small focus group made up of service users reporting negative outcomes in this area. There was a unanimous view that:

- Bengali women do want to undertake further training and find paid work;
- a lack of language skills is the most significant barrier; and
- cultural inhibitions about working in a mixed-gender environment are *not* a significant barrier to entry into the jobs market, although there may be unchallenged assumptions about women's domestic roles.

Our subsequent reflections as a team were that:

- We needed to retain our commitment to addressing this issue, but we also needed a clearer theory of change, linking outcomes, targets and activities.
- We had set a high target for this outcome, identical with Outcome 1. Outcomes around vocational progression were always likely to be much more challenging with our target group, and we should have set a lower target.
- We should prioritise ESOL progression, external volunteering and other less formal opportunities for English conversation practice.

Outcome 3: Access to Services, Community Cohesion

Over the life of the project, 85 per cent of Bangladeshi women reported improved access to mainstream services resulting in reduced isolation and improved relationships with people from different backgrounds.

Measure 1: improved access to services	91 per cent
Measure 2: reduced isolation	97 per cent
Measure 3: diversity of contacts	91 per cent

One of our greatest achievements was probably to extend the local horizons of our service users beyond their immediate neighbourhoods. Prior to this Programme, although they had probably flown at least once between the UK and Bangladesh, they had made little use of local public transport.

Outcome 4: Increased Influence and Participation

Each year of the project 20 (60 over the three years) Bangladeshi women reported increased confidence leading to an increase in their influence and participation over decisions that affect their lives.

Actual number of beneficiaries	144
Level of achievement: project reach	240 per cent
Measure 1: greater involvement in local area	96 per cent
Measure 2: increased influence on local issues	83 per cent
Number of beneficiaries within sample with positive outcome	129
Minimum success rate against original target	215 per cent

We were slightly underwhelmed by our visits to the local authority's district assembly and wondered if we had created a hostage to fortune in trying to empower people within structures where the real power remains so stubbornly centralised. However, we realised we did have the power to cut to more direct forms of engagement with people working directly on local issues through voluntary action and community governance roles. Making steady advances in this area allowed us to start exploring the potential to influence health policy through Healthwatch and Patient Participation Groups.

Unplanned Outcomes: Community Research and Cultural Awareness

Although in the end we made limited use of Participatory Appraisal techniques for evaluation purposes, the skills we acquired gave us added capacity to conduct future community research.

We also piloted the delivery of cultural awareness training to staff and volunteers at Mind (Tameside, Oldham and Glossop), identifying this as a potential area for development, given that:

- the key issues for services seeking to engage with the Bengali community are, on the whole, better understood in cultural rather than religious terms;
- most awareness courses tend to be driven from a religious perspective, which can be a barrier to objectivity.

Process Evaluation: Organisational Learning

Service-User Engagement

The Programme was working close to capacity from its early weeks and our building was regularly buzzing with activity. Our most effective publicity methods were word of mouth, volunteer phone-rounds, and monthly poster and leaflet drops.

By adopting the five key community development values (Social justice and equality, Anti-discrimination, Community empowerment, Collective action, Working and Learning together), we engaged and found that service users were always ready to enter discussions around how the programme might develop, and informal focus groups were our favoured method to consult, evaluate and review.

Organising Activity

This was never a problem area, except in the sense of trying to meet the level of demand with the staffing resources available. Where possible we used our own Centre – a place that Bengali women had already placed their stamp on. But our Centre was sometimes too small or booked up, so we regularly used other venues including schools, medical centres and the local fire station.

Partnership Working

Agencies were eager to enter into informal partnerships with us to reach a target group that they found hard to reach. Sometimes we encountered resistance to formal partnership agreements, but this did not present a practical problem.

Engaging stakeholders in end-of-project evaluation was largely unsuccessful, perhaps due to poor timing: the public sector was at the time engaging in a major staff reduction exercise. We also noted that other agencies had started to incentivise consultation feedback through small raffle prizes, for example, a free meal in the charity's café. Given that we don't have equivalent in-house incentives, a potential solution might be to seek, for example, gift vouchers from local retailers that we could use in a similar way.

Volunteer Management

Whilst we feel we developed some very good practice in this area, the level of demand meant there was always a sense of tension between numbers of volunteers and quality of support. Ideally we would have liked to include an element of supported volunteering for those furthest from readiness to work, but staffing resources did not permit this.

Childcare

Around 20 per cent of our service users registered childcare needs, and we attempted several different approaches:

1. employing our own crèche workers – a useful learning experience, but a heavy drain on staff time and quite an inflexible tool for meeting unpredictable levels of demand;
2. negotiating places with a local commercial day nursery – a potential saving on staff time, but it also proved to be an unsuitable arrangement for dealing with unpredictable demand;
3. encouraging participants to make their own child-minding arrangements (often through family members) and reclaim the costs – this worked well until it was queried by our internal examiners.

The solution we ended up with was a mixture of the third option (with a more formal accounting process) and the use of mainstream childminders; however, we remained unconvinced that this gave us the strongest basis for reaching out to parents with young children, given the underlying issues we had identified:

- An initial reluctance on the part of new service users to make use of childcare provided by strangers.
- A continuing preference for childcare either provided directly or arranged by HCA – and perceived as having the HCA stamp of approval.
- Arising from this we identified closer collaboration with local children's centres as a way forward that would not only support our activities but would also help break down these barriers and encourage a more open attitude to childcare options.

Monitoring and Evaluation

Year 2 highlighted the challenge of measuring individual outcomes for over 200 beneficiaries, most of whom would probably not be literate in either English or Bengali. We decided that belated introduction of the Warwick-Edinburgh scale, as originally envisaged, would be too big a distraction at this stage.

Having said that, we arguably created our own distraction by trying to create a volunteer-led community research team. Rather than investing in external evaluation consultants we entered into partnership with Manchester Metropolitan University to deliver a major training programme in participatory appraisal techniques. Whilst the course was valuable for those who took part, it turned out to be of debatable value in relation to our specific purpose. The course became a project within itself, absorbing large amounts of staff time.

Our other practical problem was in trying to use the customer relations management database that was promoted by our sub-regional infrastructure body. We concluded this was unfit for our purposes, and it was only in Year 3 that we appointed a staff member with the necessary skills and established a generic database to crunch the numbers of our statistics and outcomes.

We also concluded that we had set some rather woolly outcomes, possibly because we had started with too many and ended up compositing them. This was not a problem, and our use of different outcome measures proved very informative (see Outcome 2 results, above). We decided we would keep our future outcomes clear, simple and unambiguous, favouring the use of recognised measurement tools but only where they offered an appropriate match.

By the final six months of the programme we knew we could contact all the beneficiaries to gather feedback, and agreed with our funder to use sample monitoring of about two-thirds.

We also identified other 'lost opportunities' as a result of our belated mastery of evaluation processes:

- We might have built in some in-depth tracking of our service users' experience;
- We might have attempted a more ambitious overall evaluation exercise, including some form of benchmarking against practice elsewhere and some formal attempt to quantify social impact.

Financial Resources

With hindsight, we got the balance wrong between staffing and non-staffing costs in our original bid. Staff members were constantly working to capacity and beyond to meet the demands, whilst we were underspending on non-staffing costs. Some of the reasons for this were:

- whilst childcare can be expensive, take-up levels are always hard to predict and, in practice, take-up was lower than expected;
- our partnership approach frequently leads to opportunities for co-delivery of training where we are not paying for the tutor;
- we found that our service users tended to be literate either in both English and Bengali or in neither language, so there was little demand for translation of written materials;
- nearly all our volunteers turned out to live within walking distance of our Centre, which reduced volunteer costs;
- we did not appoint external evaluation consultants as originally planned.

Paid Staff

The Programme benefited strongly from our pre-existing 'grow your own' approach to community leadership. Our Programme Co-ordinator further developed her skills through a combination of management courses and with a fearless approach to 'learning by doing', essential in a programme that is breaking new ground. Similarly, our Community Development Trainee quickly became so proficient in working independently that we promoted her to Community Development Worker in Year 3.

Volunteering

One of the Programme's biggest successes was the response to opportunities created for volunteering. We engaged 45 active volunteers during the Programme.

External volunteering opportunities proved difficult and ultimately beyond our control. We were constrained by our staffing capacity to support volunteers within our own work, and the constant pressure to meet demand in this area meant that at times we felt like victims of our own success, even though we tried to maintain a strong focus on progression routes. One thing we learned is that our volunteers have differing expectations in terms of the preferred levels of formality within their volunteering roles, so we cannot try to implement a one-size-fits-all system.

Volunteers that have been through our participatory appraisal and school of participation programmes took on key roles such as public service ambassador, advice surgery triage, health walk leader, event organiser and Board member. Approximately over 2000 volunteering hours annually was dedicated to the programme giving an annual value of around £22000.

During Year 2 (2013), we received a Pride of Tameside award for our work involving volunteers.

Premises

Our premises, the Hyde Healthy Living Centre, proved to be a key asset. Bengali women have made the centre their own, filling it with their voices, their food, their children, their crafts and above all their aspirations. In other local community and faith centres where Bengali is spoken, Bengali women are either barred from entry or accustomed to sitting at the back of the room. This building has played a unique role in their lives.

Planning for Sustainability

As the end of the funded project approached, our focus turned increasingly to the sustainability of the work. At activity level we supported:

- volunteers leading arts and crafts and social group activity;
- volunteers taking up operational roles within our other programmes;
- volunteers taking up operational roles externally, for example, as public service ambassadors (Council and Fire Service) or as advice assistants (various);
- service users taking up representational roles within other structures (Healthwatch, Patient Participation Groups);
- volunteers taking over responsibility for community events;
- We also gave our service users details of other local training providers.

At programme level we:

- never subscribed to the *Big Society* myth – the idea that community volunteering can be self-sustaining without some continued financial investment. We hoped that a strategic shift in favour of preventive and asset-based work would result in a public-sector market for the sort of work we do. In the climate of public-sector cuts, this proved slow to materialize;
- We rejected two notional options as inappropriate: (1) loan-financed social enterprise development; and (2) payment-by-results-funded work around employment.

By Year 3, it was clear to us that we were going to need further grant funding to sustain our programme and build on what we had learned.

We also uncovered significant interest in co-operative working, in the form of either a marketing co-operative or a full workers' co-operative.

How this Learning Impacted on Our Future Plans

This learning influenced our direction of travel in a number of key respects:

- We moved slightly away from the idea of finding external volunteering opportunities through partner agencies, as this was looking less and less promising. Instead, we started to focus on the potential for direct service delivery through volunteers, partly as a way of addressing other community needs but partly as a way of finding roles for volunteers and obtaining dedicated funding for managing those volunteers. We also knew that significant staff time would be needed to manage and support those volunteers, and that we should not allow wishful thinking to land us with an inadequate project budget. Once our local consultations had identified mental distress and domestic abuse as key areas of need, this led directly to the planning of our new Peer Mentoring Programme.
- We immediately looked for opportunities to deliver skills-based work with more tightly defined (but still realistic) objectives, and this led directly to the planning of our Community Learning Programme.
- We started to look for opportunities to continue the work around self-employment and co-operative working. However, the models we looked at seemed to have yielded little more than contributions to group funds, so any follow-up work was likely to be breaking new ground. We concluded that this would be a very high-risk activity to undertake based on loan finance, and significant grant investment would be essential.

Further Study

We suggest looking back through the book to further explore these specific issues from the case study:

- *Slum Dwellers International work with women*
- *Models of community organising*
- *Identifying local assets*
- *Participation*
- *Building social capital and local networks*

- *Building capacity and capability*
- *Building local leadership*
- *Personal and collective empowerment*
- *Setting objectives, monitoring and evaluation*

References

DCLG (Department of Communities and Local Government) (2011) 'English IMD 2010 data'. Available at: www.communities.gov.uk/publications/corporate/statistics/indices2010.

ONS (Office for National Statistics) (2011) '2001 Census aggregate data (May)', UK Data Service. Available at: http://dx.doi.org/10.5257/census/aggregate-2001-2.

Case Study 5.11

Developing a New Generation of BAME Community-based Leaders: Lessons from an Ongoing Journey

Yvonne Field

- *Personal narrative*
- *Black and Feminist perspectives*
- *Anti-racist practice*
- *Concept and practice of Ubuntu*
- *Impact of gentrification on urban communities*
- *Concepts of Leadership*

This case study offers insights into evolving community-leadership-based practice by a new African Diaspora-led social enterprise which is illuminated by the autoethnographical reflections of its founder.

It examines some of the ways in which older experienced Black community leaders, social change practitioners, community activists, organisational development consultants and social entrepreneurs are supporting a new generation of young Black, Asian and Ethnic Minority (BAME) change agents in the design and implementation of creative ideas. The emerging story is one that begins to shed light on interventions that might help sustain communities experiencing urban gentrification. A particular theme is how community leadership might be shared and then passed between older (over 50 years) and younger (18–35 years) people.

The Ubele Initiative, which is at the centre of this case study, was registered in 2014. Its mission is to contribute to the sustainability of the African Diaspora community in the UK and to help build a better future. It has since expanded its remit to support work with a range of BAME communities and those working directly with BAME communities although its current core leadership is from the African Diaspora.

Elements of Ubele's founder, Yvonne Field's, personal and professional journey are also included in this case study. The development of Ubele and the story of her life's work are deeply interconnected. Adopting an autoethnographical lens encourages researchers to draw from historical moments that have impacted on their lives using material drawn from journals, blog-writing, newspaper cuttings and audio recordings. The ability to centralise and validate researcher's differing worldviews, speech, writing, values and beliefs resonates deeply with the founder as a Black British woman of Jamaican parentage. It allows her to bring her Black feminist voice and a critical race theory lens to her writing (Delany, 2004; Didion, 2005; Goodall, 2006; Herrmann, 2005, all taken from Ellis et al., 2011).

This case study introduces and authenticates what Heron and Reason (2008) suggest are different ways of knowing, thereby validating life experience and practical as well as propositional knowledge. They go on to argue

... that all knowing is based in the experiential presence of persons in their world. Any form of inquiry that fails to honour experiential presence – through premature abstraction, conceptualization and measurement, or through a political bias which values the experience only of socially dominant or like-minded groups – ignores the fundamental grounding of all knowing.

(Heron and Reason, 2008: 367)

The Personal is Political – Part I

Yvonne Writes:

I was inducted into the idea of an individual's as well as a community's ability to lead and facilitate effective social change at the tender age of 11 years by my mother. The story of her Black educational activism and state resistance has been captured in a short biography I produced following her death in 2011.

Such documents, originally designed to be family heirlooms, challenge the ideas of 'epistemological violence that lands heavily on minority women' (Kelbert, 2018: 7). Kelbert argues in her review of Bassel and Emejulu's recent book on minority women and activism, for the need for a form of 'epistemic justice' by minority women producing knowledge for and about themselves (Bassel and Emejulu, 2017). There is also evidence in my life of a positive association between parent and child influence and political and civic engagement (Andolina et al., 2003; Beck and Jennings, 1982) as I feel that my mother's single act of defiance was formative in my own life-long quest for social justice.

My mothers' actions can be described as 'voicing educational needs, ideas, and concerns related to youth in their communities and strategizing to promote educational improvement while countering oppressive organizational, instructional, and political dynamics', Wilson and Johnson (2015: 13), saw her lead a small community campaign in 1971 against the then local education authority.

Johnson (2013) suggests that that there is a history of Black families and communities across the African Diaspora who have used activism and protest politics to improve educational opportunities and outcomes for Black children and young people.

After three months of home schooling by a group of Black teachers in training, use of the local print media and a series of letters back and forth to the local education authority with support of our local Council for Race Relations Council, led to me being offered a place at a local grammar school.

My mother's actions support research findings that suggest ... 'activists' racial consciousness and their acute understanding of how race influences micro-to-macro level educational injustice, [motivates] their political resistance' (Wilson and Johnson, 2015: 13).

A Creative Response to Austerity, Urban Gentrification and Continuing Social Exclusion

This single act of defiance by my mother, supported by members of Deptford's Black community, led to four decades of dedicated professional work designing and implement social justice, equality and diversity strategies, programmes, activities and campaigns. Yvonne's work (within and mostly working alongside individuals, groups and organisations) aimed to influence policy and practice for and with members of marginalised communities: individuals and groups of ethnic minority communities, young people and women. Her local, national and international work includes more than 20 years of independent consultancy and training.

The origins of The Ubele Initiative stemmed from Yvonne's rising personal curiosity about the sustainability of Black African Diaspora communities in the UK as the Windrush 70th anniversary loomed. Towards the end of 2010, she wrote an article, entitled 'My Big Question', which acted as a catalyst for a new community-based initiative called Ubele, a Swahili expression meaning 'The Future'.

The article posed a fundamental question about the future, as the majority of the Windrush generation (including her own parents) did not realise their dreams of 'returning home' after several decades of living in the UK. It asked the community to consider the types of community strategies that might be needed, to ensure the continuation of their communities. The article suggested the need for a more proactive, collaborative and socially innovative approach instead of waiting for central and local government to react to identified needs – often after the actual events.

Yvonne Reflects:

It challenged us to visualise our future through creating new solutions rather than simply replicating the past. At its core, the Ubele Initiative asks us to reflect on some of the next big social, economic and political challenges facing our community and how we might create new ways of addressing them. This curiosity set the stage for me organising and facilitating a series of informal 'community conversations' in South London over a period of three years, which attracted a broad group of people who were involved in varying aspects of community development.

We were primarily 'elder leaders' (people between 45 and 65 years) already involved in delivering a wide range of community-based initiatives in culturally diverse communities including health and social care provision, formal and informal education provision including youth services, political activities, campaigns and advocacy, creative arts practice, and small business owners. All of us identified as members of the Black African Diaspora community.

The emerging Ubele community was also concerned about how they might consciously create the next generation of community-based leaders, given that many people who championed community causes from the 1950s onwards had retired from public service, returned 'home', were ill or had actually passed away. Some of the conversations centred on what appeared to be a widening gap between generations, rather than a conscious power-sharing and eventual 'passing of the baton' and the need for mutual and open dialogue.

Intergenerational practice can be defined as bringing 'people together in purposeful, mutually beneficial activities promoting greater understanding and respect between generations and contributing to building more cohesive communities' (Beth Johnson Foundation, 2011). However much of the intergenerational practice that has occurred has not been recorded in the UK (Granville, 2002) and it appears that businesses are becoming increasingly worried about the lack of effective strategies for creating the next generation of leaders to support business growth, which in part is seen to be due to a lack of appropriate mentorship (Holst-Knudsen, 2014).

Yvonne Reflects:

During our community conversations, the elders surfaced some profound insights including the unattended needs of our young people (who now view England as 'home'); the unmet needs of an increasing population of elders (who could not or did not want to go 'home') and a growing sense of 'loss' of community 'assets', i.e. individual community anchors and advocates ageing and/or passing away, as well as the closure or redistribution of iconic community-based spaces. We also began to express dismay at the changing nature of local communities due to gentrification.

Hubbard (2016) argues that relatively few studies that focus on gentrification in UK cities include race, and if mentioned at all, do little to critically examine or analyse the impact of race and gentrification. Attempts have been made by Lees et al. (2008), Lees et al. (2016) and Kirkland (2008) to examine this issue from a UK perspective, but it still leaves considerable scope for further research and critique. There is a real and somewhat urgent need for research to help us better understand current community-led leadership development, social activism, and/or collective entrepreneurial approaches by BAME communities which seek to challenge and intervene in local development plans that marginalise communities and often lead to claims of social and ethnic cleansing.

Emergence of Ubele's Strategy

A small group of Ubele members approached Locality in 2014. The conversation sought to explore levels of BAME engagement in the national Localism agenda. Locality supports groups to transform their local community through, for example, neighbourhood planning and securing community assets from local authorities.

An acknowledgement that there was a dearth of such groups, led to seed funding and an invitation to work in partnership with Locality on specific local projects. As a result of this support, Ubele created a team of 15 volunteers via a partnership between Just Space and University College London Bartlett School of Planning. This was the beginning of Project Mali, a national research project into African Diaspora community assets – important community spaces and community leaders.

The subsequent report entitled A Place to Call Home (Field et al., 2015) included digital and audio maps of community assets and stories about them. It found significant evidence of lost community spaces (multi-purpose community centres, sports facilities and shop fronts) with spaces being taken back by local authorities as leases ran out and, in some cases, sold to private developers (Locality, 2018). Furthermore, the research found that:

- those that remain in their original 'ownership' are seriously struggling to survive, given the lack of local government support;
- there was an urgent need to create a new generation of community leaders to ensure the future sustainability of spaces and to develop new models to support them;
- African Diaspora females have been occupying unrecognised leadership positions in Black communities and some of the assets that had been secured for future generations are currently under female leadership.

The Personal is Political – Part II

In 2004, I enrolled on a part time postgraduate degree programme in change agency skills and strategies as I felt I needed to integrate new models into my professional toolkit. I was also becoming restless and started to explore professional opportunities and personal relationships in South Africa. This programme transformed my practice. It enabled me to develop new framing for many of my practices, which had resulted from previous professional development, learning from colleagues as well as from deep instinct. As a result of this transformative personal and professional experience, I eventually closed my consultancy practice. I immersed myself back in the 'field', aiming to find new people to 'play with' and more creative concepts to integrate into my practice.

Between 2006 and 2015, I spent increasing amounts of time in South Africa and neighbouring countries. I had a 40-year relationship with the country (over 20 of them at a distance) and with people who had returned home post apartheid. I increasingly became interested in the African concept of Ubuntu and how its principles influence African everyday values and community life, and its potential application to community development and leadership practice in the UK.

Ubuntu helps us understand what it means to be human and '*... emphasises the interconnectedness of self within society and the extension of humanness within shared community*' (Brubaker, 2013: 96, emphasis added). It does not say, '*I think therefore I am.*' It says, rather, '*I am human because I participate. I share*' (Archbishop Desmond Tutu, taken from Bojer et al., 2008, emphasis added).

Malunga (2006) suggests that Ubuntu values are built on the following five interrelated principles:

- sharing and collective ownership, responsibilities and challenges – an example of this is collective responsibility for child-rearing (your friend's child is viewed as your own). This can include discipline or payment of school fees and other expenses, which can be undertaken by several adults and is demonstrated through the well-versed adage, 'It takes a village to raise a child'.
- the importance of people and relationships over things – relationships are given high priority, with fathers and uncles, mothers and aunts ranked the same, with cousins being brothers and sisters. Marriage is viewed as between two clans rather than individuals, with respect of elders being paramount.
- participatory decision-making and leadership – although to some, indigenous African leadership might appear autocratic and automatic, legitimacy of a newly elected leader is critical, even for those born into royal lineage. Because there might be many possible candidates for leadership, strict criteria are applied. Decisions about who should lead are often approved by the people. Several areas of leadership competency must be demonstrated: understanding people, human relationships, managing conflict, diplomacy and relationships with other kingdoms, and strategic thinking.
- patriotism – survival of the kingdom over individual interests is paramount. It is important not to forget the source of the clan and to understand the need to create a common bond of security and promote pride in one's clan.
- reconciliation as a goal of conflict management – emphasis on the values of trust, fairness and reconciliation and the importance of relationships. The chief and council play a critical role in conflict mediation and maintenance of relationships.

The participatory decision-making processes of Nelson Mandela's Thembu tribe (of which his grandfather was a chief), had a profound effect on him. He describes it as '...democracy in its purest sense. There may have been a hierarchy of importance amongst speakers, but everyone was heard ... no conclusion was forced on those who disagreed'.

Some of the criticisms of Ubuntu include the potential for tribalism; leaders not wanting to leave office; excess wealth accumulation; that respect for elders could lead to outdated ideas still being supported; and that a desire for continuity may lead to resistance to much-needed change.

Yvonne Reflects:

Whilst visiting and at times working in South Africa, I was introduced to powerful African ways of problem solving through the convening of 'legotla', 'imbizo' and 'indadba's' – *African circles for dialogue and conversations within which all voices are heard. As effective communication is central to good leadership practice, I readily embraced these new concepts. This allows me to name processes which deeply resonated with ways of working with and being 'in community', which I instinctively understood.*

Mille Boyer and Colleen Magner, Reos Partners colleagues of mine with whom I worked in Europe and in South Africa, describe them as '...living conversations'; a way of life which not only use direct verbal communication, but also art, drama, drumming and song, with '.....women in particular.'. using '....song to communicate what is going on for them'.

(Bojer et al., 2008: 136, emphasis added)

Malunga (2006) argues that '... most leadership development initiatives emphasise developing oneself and not one's community or country' (Malunga, 2006: 7) and advocates for African models especially, but not exclusively, in Africa.

Using Ancient Paradigms to Inform Future Community Leadership Practice

The creation of the Ubele community of change agents, has been a slow, intentional 'bottom-up' approach. It first involved the gathering of a new intergenerational group of 20 exceptionally creative African Diaspora volunteers, ranging from people in their 20s to those over 60. Most have deep connections with continental Africa and/or the Caribbean, through direct family ties, other relationships, work and/or travel. They are active in the African Diaspora community in the fields of arts and heritage, education, health, land practices, social care, women's development, community and business development and transformative social change. Because of our diversity of backgrounds in terms of culture, professions, experience and knowledge, members bring a rich variety of perspectives, a unique microcosm of who we are as Africans in the Diaspora. Our shared mission to facilitate social innovation and change within that community is the platform from which areas of mutual interest have emerged.

The initiative is intentionally intergenerational, in line with Ubuntu's principle of collective ownership. It enables us to create a 'family' system where younger leaders are encouraged and mentored. Even though Ubele is still an emerging community, our diverse group of individuals has been fiercely loyal in supporting its evolution.

An intergenerational dialogue facilitated in September 2013 engaged more than twenty of our community members operating in three different teams, taking responsibility for design and delivery of the conversation. Even though each group had a nominated leader, responsibility was shared. Everyone collaborated, taking responsibility for delivering a seamless and successful African-centred event for more than 70 participants.

Malunga (2006) suggests the use of proverbs, rituals and ceremonies as part of leadership development. To publicise the community dialogue, we used the African proverb, *Every journey of a thousand miles starts with a single step.*

Yvonne Reflects:

We acknowledged and embraced our African heritage in several ways. We transformed the plain sports hall into an inviting and welcoming space with African cloth and artefacts, and African music playing to welcome our community to the gathering. We observed the ritual of acknowledging our Ancestors, thanking them for guiding us thus far and inviting them to join us in the dialogue. We listened deeply to the stories of nine experienced change agents from areas including community activism, visual arts and multi-media, the criminal justice system, Black education and training, health and the media. We shared our own experiences, creating a highly engaging and thought-provoking event for our community.

Growing a New African Diaspora-led Organisation

Further dialogue sessions, member meetings and listening to ideas led to the eventual identification of specific priorities, objectives and activities.

Four key strategic objectives now provide the focus for their work:

- Building resilient and sustainable communities,
- Generating Learning and Knowledge,
- Strategic Partnerships to influence policy and practice, and
- Global Diaspora Connections.

The majority of projects and activities are intergenerational in nature and provide opportunities for co-learning, mentoring (between younger and older members and vice versa) as well as space for co-creation. All of Ubele's participants are over 18 years of age.

Funding is secured through a mix of local, national and European Union grants as well as consultancy assignments and commissions from local and national organisations. However, Ubele has not secured core funding and still primarily operates on a part-time basis. There is one full-time staff member and short-term teams that deliver specific projects. Experience suggests that some of the traditional funders are not keen to support BAME-led groups with such a strong sense of self-determination.

Since 2011, Ubele has engaged more than 1300 people, with over 90 per cent from BAME communities. It has delivered 22 local projects (for its own members as well as providing capacity-building support to other organisations), two regional projects, four national projects and 11 international projects, having sent 175 people to 17 different countries in mainland Europe, Africa and Indonesia. It is currently in the process of assessing its social impact and looking forward to celebrating its 5th official anniversary.

Yvonne Reflects:

A small intergenerational group of Directors helps guide our overall strategic development. I am currently on the board. However, over the next two years a transformational change will take place, with the elders shifting out of the way and Ubele being led by young emerging leaders in a co-operative system which will ensure the process of sharing and that the eventual passing of the baton is complete. This will help us to, '... address the ["age"] challenges the organisation is facing through meaningful participation' [of the next generation], so that they '... also own and commit to the identified solutions' (Malunga, 2006: 9).

Some examples of Ubele's recent work include:

- **Wise Women on Wheels** – a local intergenerational health and well-being programme which explored health issues and saw younger women from BAME communities teaching older women to cycle and to being to explore health issues;
- **PatHERways London** which focused on BAME young women's empowerment (linked to a two-year international programme of the same name with seven countries including Cape Verde, Mozambique and Peru). PatHERways offered participants

aged between 18 and 30 change agency skills, project development support, a weekend retreat, and capturing their own stories and those from older women change agents and putting them on a digital map.

- *Identifying the mental health and well-being needs of children and young people after the Grenfell Fire* – this included identifying the mental health services and support that was available and finding gaps in provision. This also included the production of a digital map and a directory of services in the Royal Borough of Kensington and Chelsea.
- *Leading Routes and Black in Academia* – An Incubation Project which aimed to support Black young people into Russell Group universities as well as to increase the pipeline of Black academics. This initiative is being designed and led by a younger leader who is being coached, mentored and provided practical resources such as infrastructure support and access to free venue space. Leading Routes will eventually become an independent organisation.
- *Working on Our Power* (WOOP) – A Europe-wide leadership development programme for women and transgender people of colour.

The Ubele Initiative was recently invited to become a member of a consortium which grows and distributes food, provides healthy-eating education and a range of community-based activities. The Wolves Lane Consortium is based on a 3.5 acre former London Borough of Haringey horticultural centre site, which has a large glass-house growing space, a Palm House, allotments, woodlands, a café, and a suite of offices. Ubele is now based there and will be contributing community enterprise and community development support.

Yvonne Reflects:

Ubele is still emerging in an organic way and with unconventional support mechanisms, yet it is clearly growing to create a new cadre of creative community development practitioners and social change agents from BAME communities. We feel it is quite unique.

Our seemingly random, yet interconnected process of learning through doing, professional and personal development opportunities, and creating a safe space for reflection is already having a significant impact.

A number of participants comment on the benefits of being part of the Ubele community. In addition to the building of skills, networks and accessing opportunities, some suggest that not having to explain who you are in terms of cultural or racial identity and not being viewed as a 'minority' are important factors. There is a deep sense of comfort, of individual and group strength, that can emerge from being in community with people who reflect and implicitly understand who you are.

Maathai (2001) unapologetically challenges us to consider that, 'without culture, a community loses its self-awareness and guidance and grows weak and vulnerable. It disintegrates from within as it suffers a lack of identity, self-respect' (Maathai, 2001: 23).

Our community leadership development practice continues to be emergent and yet some key features can already be identified:

- *the building and nurturing of relationships – individual, inter- and intra-group;*
- *creating partnerships with organisations with similar social change and equality missions;*
- *identifying common areas of interest, skills and experience to co-design and collaborate on new projects and ideas;*

- *'hands on' opportunities for community leadership practice through initiating and/or co-leading projects and activities;*
- *creating as well as accessing local, regional and international capacity-building opportunities;*
- *increasing members' knowledge and competence in the use of social change and community development methodologies;*
- *fusing new learning with traditional models and strategies that reflect African principles and practices such as Constellations, Ubuntu and Sankofa;*
- *creating support for and interest in Ubele through accessing professional networks and new social media platforms;*
- *the continual surfacing of compelling questions for the community and designing and testing new ideas and interventions which seek to address them.*

Ubele's model is also slowly being informed by African ways of being and should ultimately create a new community leadership model that is 'home grown', reflecting the UK Africa Diaspora experience, the basic principles of which should be applicable to a wide diversity of local, national and international communities. It could also interrupt a tendency to import and try to apply lessons, theories and models from the USA without often considering the relevance or 'fit'.

Malunga (2006: 2) suggests that, '… the trend towards globalisation implicitly foregrounds Northern values and can give the sense that indigenous values and practices are somehow inferior'.

Yvonne Concludes:

I feel it is important to recognise and appreciate that much of what is currently taught globally as Western leadership theory and practice has its roots in African and/or Asian cultural norms, a fact often conveniently overlooked, ignored or simply unknown.

I plan to research into Ubuntu and other African concepts such as Sankofa (the Ghanian Akan Adinkra symbol which is a mythical bird often depicted retrieving the 'gems' or knowledge of the past upon which wisdom is based; it also signifies the generation to come that would benefit from that wisdom) supported through a doctoral research process.

Despite organisational development challenges, which are in part due to systemic issues that often impact negatively on BAME-led organisations, Ubele has engaged some 3000 (elder and emerging) community leaders and facilitated partnerships with more than 23 countries. We recently co-created a unique home though a consortium arrangement within which we adopt a leadership role as stewards for a horticultural centre in North London. We support food growing, healthy eating, volunteering opportunities, social enterprise development and creative community-based activities that actively reflect the cultural diversity of our borough.

References

Andolina, M., Keeter, S., Zukin, C., & Jenkins, K. (2003) *A Guide to the Index of Civic and Political Engagement*. College Park, MD: The Center for Information & Research on Civic Learning & Engagement.

Bassel, L. and Emejulu, A. (2017) *Minority Women and Activism: Survival and Resistance in France and Britain*. Bristol: The Policy Press.

Beck, P.A. and Jennings, M.K. (1982) 'Pathways to Participation', *The American Political Science Review*, 76(1), 94–108.

Beth Johnson Foundation (2011) *A Guide to Intergenerational Practice*. Stoe-on-Trent: Beth Johnson Foundation.

Bojer, M., Roehl, H., Knuth, M., and Magner, C. (2008) *Mapping Dialogue, Essential Tools for Social Change*. Chagrin Falls, OH: Taos Institute.

Brubaker, T.A. (2013) 'Servant Leadership, Ubuntu and Leadership Effectiveness in Rwanda', *Emerging Leadership Journeys*, 6(1), 95–131.

Ellis, C., Adams, T.E., and Bochner, A.P. (2011) 'Autoethnography: An Overview', *Forum: Qualitative Social Research*, 12(1, January).

Field, Y., Murray, K., and Chilangwa Farmer, D. (2015) *A Place to Call Home*. London: Locality.

Granville, G. (2002) *A Review of Intergenerational Practice in the UK*. Stoke-on-Trent: Beth Johnson Foundation.

Heron, J. and Reason, P. (2008) 'Extending Epistemology within a Co-operative Inquiry', in P. Reason and H. Bradbury (eds), *Handbook of Action Research*, 2nd edn. London: Sage Publications.

Hubbard, P. (2016) 'Hipsters on Our High Streets: Consuming the Gentrification Frontier', *Sociological Research Online*, 21(3), 106–111. Available at: https://doi.org/10.5153/sro.3962.

Johnson, L. (2013) 'Segregation or "Thinking Black"? Community Activism and the Development of Black-focused Schools in Toronto and London, 1968–2008', *Teachers College Record*, 115(11), 1–2.

Kelbert, A.W. (2018) 'Taking Minority Women's Activism Seriously as Epistemic Justice', *Ethnic and Racial Studies*, 41(13), 2310–2317.

Kirkland, E. (2008) 'What's Race Got to Do With It? Looking for the Racial Dimensions of Gentrification', *The Western Journal of Black Studies*, 32(2), 18–30.

Locality (2018) *The Great British Sell Off: How We're Losing our Vital Publicly Owned Buildings and Spaces. Forever*. London: Locality.

Maathai, W. (2001) 'The Mirror Cracked', *Resurgence*, 227, n.p.

Malunga, C. (2006) *Learning Leadership Development from African Cultures: A Personal Perspective*. Praxis Note No 25. Oxford: International NGO Training and Research Centre (INTRAC).

Wilson, C. and Johnson, L. (2015) 'Black Educational Activism for Community Empowerment: International Leadership Perspectives', *International Journal of Multicultural Education*, [S.l.], 17(1, January), 102–120. ISSN 1934-5267. Available at: www.ijme-journal.org/index.php/ijme/article/view/963.

Case Study 5.12

'Peas & Love'. A Case Study in Kindness and the Power of Small Actions: Incredible Edible, Todmorden

Martin Purcell

Introducing Incredible Edible Todmorden

Celebrating their tenth anniversary in 2018, Incredible Edible Todmorden (IET) evolved out of radical, grass-roots community activity, which they characterise as food activism promoting community resilience. Underpinning IET's approach to 'radical community building in action' is a commitment to kindness, inclusion and mutuality, as they focus on growing food to share, running festivals and cooking demos, and supporting businesses and other local groups; all with no paid staff, no buildings, and no public funding.

A way of working that has been incorporated into over 700 communities worldwide, Incredible Edible started as a seed of an idea that germinated during a discussion between friends and activists sitting round a kitchen table, discussing social and environmental problems facing the local and global community. The consensus around the table that night was that 'there was no point waiting for governments to do something about it: we would have to stop being victims and just do it: we could make a kinder, safer and more sustainable environment for ourselves and our grandchildren'.

Committed to working in an inclusive and non-hierarchical manner, this small group of passionate people called a public meeting to explore the extent to which other local residents shared their perspective. Fifty-nine people attended that first meeting, and since then over 1,000 people have participated in IET activities, whilst the group's membership has grown exponentially; possibly reflecting the fact that their membership criteria state simply that 'if you eat, you're in!'.

The group operates under a simple stated aim, which is to 'work together for a world where all share responsibility for the future well-being of our planet and ourselves'. IET aims to provide access to good local food for all, through:

- working together
- learning – from cradle to grave
- supporting local business

Incredible Edible Todmorden is registered (Under the Co-operative & Community Benefit Societies Act 2014) as a Community Benefit Society, reflecting the fact that everything they do is undertaken by unpaid volunteers 'doing our best for our town', and relying entirely on donations for funding. The stated object of IET is to 'carry on any business for the benefit of the community' by (amongst other things):

1. Building a strong local community by developing and offering volunteer opportunities and skills development;

2. Developing and capitalising upon opportunities to reclaim unused land and grow food to share;
3. Protecting and enhancing local biodiversity;
4. Offering workshops and materials to local residents to develop skills in growing food;
5. Offering workshops and demonstrations to local residents to develop skills in cooking tasty nutritional food on a budget;
6. Encouraging reuse, up-cycling and repurposing of goods and thereby reducing landfill;
7. Organising and supporting events to unite and/or strengthen and/or support the local community.

About Todmorden

Todmorden is a market town and former mill town situated at the confluence of three valleys in the heart of the South Pennine Hills, on the historic border of Yorkshire and Lancashire. Although subsumed into the local authority district of Calderdale in West Yorkshire (dominated by the administrative centre in Halifax), Todmorden retains a strong sense of identity, and people characterise themselves as being fiercely independent. The town and its extensive rural hinterland has a population of around 15,500, the age profile of which is similar to England: 18 per cent are under 16 years of age, 9 per cent are aged 16–24, 54 per cent are aged 25–64, 16 per cent are aged 65–84 and 3 per cent are aged 85 and over. There is only limited ethnic diversity in the community, with over 92 per cent of the population identifying as white. Nevertheless, there is a small but significant population of people of South Asian heritage, many of whom live in a tight community in the heart of the town.

Although home ownership in the town is slightly higher than national and district averages, and educational attainment rates at level 4 and above are slightly higher than the national average, a significant proportion of the population experience poverty. Official figures (IMD, 2015) show that 17.5 per cent of the population is income deprived, 22.9 per cent of children aged 0–15 live in families that are income deprived, and 18.7 per cent of people aged 60 or over are income deprived (compared with 14.6 per cent, 19.9 per cent and 16.2 per cent respectively for England). Health and care indicators (Census, 2011) for Todmorden's resident population suggest that rates of bad/very bad general health and limiting long-term illness or disability are significantly higher than the English rates.

Much of this deprivation – which places up to three-eighths of Todmorden's housing amongst the 10 per cent most deprived areas in the country – is experienced by people living in private rented accommodation in the town centre and in peripheral social housing estates. The proximity of high levels of deprivation alongside affluent areas is not uncommon for rural areas; nevertheless, it can exaggerate the experience of deprivation for those people living in the poorer parts of town.

The characteristics of the population summarised here have informed IET's key priorities. The emphasis on kindness, inclusion and mutual support has arisen from their recognition that – like the UK as a whole and in relation to global comparisons – social, health and economic inequalities persist in the town. When meeting with volunteers, it is evident that they come from all parts of the community, for example reflecting the disparate ethnic backgrounds of residents as well as including people of all ages, abilities and socio-economic status. This inclusivity has been achieved through deliberate, persistent and genuine attempts to reach out to all parts of the community, making people from all backgrounds feel welcome and treating all members and volunteers with equal respect and dignity. This has even extended to providing food for one particular local 'character': a neo-Nazi online activist who promulgates hatred between different parts of society, and refuses to accept state benefits to which they are entitled. Kindness extends in this way to everyone in the community, in the hope that they will feel included and maybe learn to be kinder to one another.

Radical Community Building in Action

In the early days, members of the evolving IET (and other community activists) engaged in 'guerrilla planting', taking the initiative to smarten up derelict pieces of land, as they felt these had been neglected for long enough by the authorities and landowners. Where the IET actions differed from the guerrilla tactics of other environmental campaigners was that they ensured that their planting – as well as enhancing the appearance of the target sites – would generate edible produce that they could make available to members of the community. Hence, cherry trees, fruit bushes, rhubarb crowns, herbs and other produce were planted in a number of sites across the town, and the local newspaper ran articles promoting the IET agenda and letting local residents know that the food was there for them to harvest as and when it ripened.

As more people joined the group, it became clear that IET needed to become more organised in its approach, so as to maximise their impact on the town's environment and to ensure that everybody who wanted to had a role to play in the process. IET began formalising the structure of the group (which led ultimately to its registration as a Community Benefit Society) and allocated roles and tasks within the structure to suitably qualified and experienced individuals. For instance, people with experience in managing finances became involved in fundraising; people who had previously organised community events worked together with others with experience of delivering training to develop events that would appeal to and inform members of the wider community about issues relating to local food production, sustainability and healthy eating; and people keen to get their hands dirty were invited to attend regular planting and gardening maintenance days.

Heightened awareness around the town of IET's aims and *modus operandi* was achieved very quickly, as members were active from the start in promoting their ambitions, both to generate understanding and support and to secure more engagement in their activities. Every informal education opportunity was taken to engage people in discussions around IET's reason for being active, to raise awareness and encourage people to grow and buy locally produced food. As part of this work, IET members developed relationships with local food shops, supporting them in promoting the 'buy local' message, both as a means of reducing the environmental impact of transporting food long distances and to ensure that money spent on food in Todmorden was circulated through the local economy, to everyone's benefit.

Other partnerships have forged with local community organisations, landowners and businesses/agencies with properties in the town centre. These relationships have been nurtured through honest dialogue and respect, resulting in partners either coming forward to offer, or acquiescing to requests for permission to plant on their land, thereby creating more formal opportunities for planting. High profile planting and maintenance has taken place in this way in raised beds in front of the police station and the railway station, in and around several schools throughout the town, around the recently-opened health centre (where IET have planted an Apothecary's Garden), outside the local volunteer-run theatre and on a high-profile site 'land-banked' by a supermarket chain for a number of years. These sites are in evidence throughout the town, and are seen by the whole population of Todmorden – and visitors to the town – on an almost daily basis. Not only has this resulted in the townscape environment being improved, people are also regularly harvesting herbs, fruit and other seasonal produce as a matter of course.

Having been successful in securing funds through their own endeavours, IET has been able to pay for and implement other environmental improvements throughout the town. For instance, creative volunteers have painted murals at various sites, complementing the planting and brightening up the town through the fallow seasons. Information boards – promoting a deeper understanding of issues relating to diet and food production and transportation – have been erected at different points throughout the town. All of these bear the Incredible Edible name and logo, and encourage local people to become involved; 'if you eat, you're in' translated into action every day. IET has also secured wide support (from the Town Council, local traders and residents) for key public areas in the town to be nominated as Assets of Community Value, thereby ensuring their continued contribution to the health of the town and its environment.

ˉThis model of community-generated activism has sustained the engagement of large numbers of community members in voluntary activity over an extended period. The fortnightly planting and gardening sessions attract in excess of 40 participants, and draw people from all parts of the community. Everyone who attends is allocated a role, and care is taken to ensure that these roles are commensurate with the abilities and interests of participants. In this way, IET has been particularly successful in facilitating the participation of local people who may be learning disabled; experiencing mental health problems; recently-arrived and/or migrants; speakers of other languages; or exhibiting the characteristics of other traditionally excluded groups. One participant commented that:

> We've seen the power of mundane actions: for instance washing up is a long rigmarole, but people love it ... and people you might think would never speak together queue up to take dirty dishes, and work and talk together. It's exactly the same with weeding and litter picking.

What makes the group's activities so successful is their commitment to sharing a free meal made entirely from local produce with all volunteers at the end of these sessions, embedding kindness and a sense of belonging and community in everything the group does. The Chair of the group characterises this as follows

> The primitive notion, the tribal thing of eating together, knowing you belong to that tribe ... nothing is nicer than a huge table full of folk chatting and eating after a morning's graft. Looking down that table and listening to the conversations: between teachers and people with Downs syndrome; between alcoholics and solicitors ... that's why people come here ... not for gardening ... it's for food and community.

Impact and Outcomes

As well as the evident impact on the townscape and environment in Todmorden. IET claims to have had a positive impact in all three of the broad areas on which it focuses: community, business and learning. A recently conducted evaluation (Morley et al., 2017) explored, amongst other things, why people have become, and remain, involved in IET's activities. Some of the main reasons cited correspond with the group's community-building aspirations, with participants emphasising the positive impact of their involvement in IET on their health and well-being, as well as their enhanced understanding of a range of issues. In particular, and corresponding with the characterisation above, IET members and volunteers highlighted the positive impact of their participation on their sense of belonging to a community and friendship. Whilst IET is clear about its broad aims, it steers clear of setting targets, or working towards outcomes framed by external stakeholders:

> *Kindness isn't outcome-driven. It's not three years funding. It's embedded. It grows.*

This explains why they avoid applying for or accepting funding from public sector bodies, as this invariably comes with conditions that typically do not correspond with the group's ethos of kindness and collaboration.

The evaluation found that IET has had a broadly positive impact on, and is supported by, local business, although it identified concerns expressed by some local traders that the notion of providing free food runs counter to their economic interests. This demonstrates the complexity of balancing the aspirations of grass-roots-led action with the competing demands of a wide range of stakeholders.

Similarly, the extent to which IET has had an impact on local people's learning or awareness about the issues that triggered its formation ten years ago is hard to quantify. Undoubtedly, the group can claim to have succeeded in providing learning opportunities for large numbers of people, hundreds having attended growing and cooking classes, and participated in a range of events designed to raise awareness of the way in which food is produced, transported and marketed. A recent four-day *Festival of Ideas* drew on the contributions of experts and local people to accommodate a range of ideas about place-making and making resilient communities (resilient in relation to the environment, the people, and the infrastructure). Unsurprisingly, this event concluded with:

> *an incredible fabulous feast, bringing all sorts of people together to make connections, exploring the power of small actions ... seeing how far can we push collaboration and kindness, using kindness as our currency.*

> (IET volunteer)

Whilst participation in these formal and informal learning opportunities can be assumed to have had an impact, it is difficult to measure their impact. Similarly, positive outcomes might be ascribed to the involvement of children in IET-led initiatives at schools throughout the town. As well as running growing projects in school grounds, IET has helped schools to develop the curriculum to build on pupils' practical learning.

Discussion and Analysis

IET's approach embraces a range of community development processes. Their work values the local knowledge and culture of their members, and builds on the assets within the community, reflecting social justice, ecological and asset-based approaches (Ife and Tosoriero, 2006). The IET model demonstrates that the pursuit of an 'abundant community' is possible, taking responsibility for local and global environmental issues and offering a way of working that acknowledges the centrality of community to individual and group health and well-being (McKnight and Block, 2015).

Explaining the centrality of kindness in their work, IET's Chairperson acknowledges the extent to which this form of practice reflects Freire's (1970) characterisation of education as an 'act of love', behaving towards all those with whom they come into contact in a 'humanising' manner. The act of eating and talking together at the end of group activities to acknowledge individuals' contribution and as a means of strengthening community facilitates interactions at a respectful, human level, exemplifying Freire's (1993) call for love to feature as the 'foundation for dialogue'. The title of this case study is formed from something one of the volunteers said during a recent talk: 'we are all about peas and love … the food is a means to developing a loving and resilient community'.

The group talks openly about power in all their deliberations. In the first instance, the decision to proceed was conceived as an act of the community seizing power from statutory agencies that were deemed too slow or lacking commitment to the changes sought by activists. Inasmuch as IET has managed to take responsibility for implementing their own decisions – often in spite of opposition from traditional power structures – their approach reflects (at a local level at least) the view that power lies in the ability to produce intended effects (Hague and Harrop, 2013). The group has undoubtedly been impactful, and has demonstrated the effectiveness of not waiting until (more powerful) others grant permission for actions to bring about change; and has managed to challenge and change the policies and practices of local decision makers along the way.

Furthermore, IET has developed considerably the individual and collective capabilities of its members, thereby creating new forms of community or commons (Negri and Hardt, 2009). IET's creative application of power has resulted in the reclaiming by local people of the public realm of Todmorden, and has built on a counter-cultural tradition to strengthen local people's 'just do it' attitude, thereby contributing to both place-making and place-keeping (Dobson, 2014).

Assessing the distribution of power within the group highlights the challenges of working in a co-operative manner, where the views of all members are given credence in the decision-making process. Undoubtedly, the success of IET in sustaining the involvement of large numbers of people is testament to this, and they are the embodiment of people power, in terms of internal decision-making as well as activity (such as 'guerrilla planting'). The recent evaluation of IET highlighted, however, the importance of the drive and dynamism of a small number of 'charismatic, inspirational and entrepreneurial champions', or change agents, highlighting concern about what might happen when they are less involved or leave the group. IET's ethos reflects the passionate commitment of the original activists, one of whom leads the group in their role as chairperson; should a differently inspired personality seek to lead the group, it is possible this way of working would be diluted.

Other factors illuminated by the group's work include the impact on their success of resistance to change, scepticism and divergence. Whilst the group can legitimately claim to be inclusive, some members of the community remain to be convinced of their arguments and – whether through scepticism or an unwillingness to embrace IET's approach – have not engaged in their activities. Likewise, differences in opinion of committed members have tested the robustness of the group, and some of the original members have broken away to implement projects that reflect more closely their own interpretation of the group's original vision. To date, these schisms have not been destructive, reflecting the personalities and values of key personnel; but the destructive potential of such upheavals cannot be ignored.

As already alluded to, the success of IET's commitment to kindness, inclusion and mutuality has garnered interest from around the world. Their approach has been replicated in over 700 communities across the globe, and IET regularly plays host to international visitors keen to learn from their approach to radical community building. Without being prescriptive about how others should work, IET has given their support to these other initiatives, allowing them to use their branding and developing a support network. This demonstrates the power of small actions to change the conversation and bring about change, all based on one small word, which ends this description by a volunteer of the atmosphere at IET's most recent AGM:

> *I can't tell you how much good was in the room, how much creativity and collaboration and kindness*

In the words of Lao Tzu:

> *Kindness in words creates confidence. Kindness in thinking creates profoundness. Kindness in giving creates love.*

Further Study

We suggest looking back through the book to further explore these specific issues from the case study

- *Values of community development*
- *Understanding power*
- *Identifying local assets*
- *Building resilience*
- *Freire and Popular Education strategies*
- *Group-building*
- *Building Capability*

References

Census (2011) London: Office for National Statistics.

Dobson, J. (2014) 'Achieving Food Equity: Access to Good Local Food For All', *Journal of Urban Regeneration and Renewal*, 8(2), 124–134.

Freire, P. (1970) *Pedagogy of the Oppressed*. New York: Continuum.

Freire, P. (1993) *Pedagogy of the City*. New York: Continuum.

Hague, R. and Harrop, M. (2013) *Contemporary Government and Politics: An Introduction*. Houndmills: Palgrave Macmillan.

Ife, J. and Tosoriero, F. (2006) *Community Development: Community-based Alternatives in an Age of Globalization*. Frenchs Forest, NSW: Pearson Education.

Index of Multiple Deprivation (2015) London: Ministry of Housing, Communities and Local Government.

McKnight, J. and Block, P. (2015) *The Abundant Community*. Oakland, CA: Berrett-Koelher.

Morley, A., Farrier, A., and Dooris, M. (2017) *Propagating Success? The Incredible Edible Model*. Manchester and Preston: MMU and UCLAN.

Negri, A. and Hardt, M. (2009) *Commonwealth*. Harvard, MA: Harvard University Press.

Section 6
Summing Up

6.1 What Community Development Can Achieve

To conclude this book, we wish to make a few statements on what community development is for, and where it may be going and needs to go (which is not always the same thing).

Working in and with communities covers a broad range of activity. The purpose of such activity can be influenced by explicit or implicit goals, ideologies and motivations. To be effective in what you do, it is important to know and be clear about what you are trying to achieve, why you are trying to achieve it, and how this might best be achieved.

In the book we have adopted a clear position on these issues. Of course you, the reader, may or may not agree with what we write, but our purpose is to stimulate thought, discussion and changes in practice, which hopefully leads to better outcomes for the communities in which we work.

From our perspective, community development is underpinned by clear values that prioritise challenging oppression, working for social justice and for broader social change. At the micro level this is about people taking more power over both their own lives and collectively within their communities, and as part of wider macro social movements.

To do this we need some theoretical insights: about how the world works (and dysfunctions), the nature of power, and how change can be promoted at various levels. These theories should underpin a toolkit of models that inform and guide how practice may be effectively applied in different contexts.

The practice studies in the book provide snapshots of the diversity of practice. One of the key things the studies tell us is that we need to be open-minded, creative and flexible. What has worked before is a good starting point, but we also need to be adaptable to changing circumstances. Crucially, we always need to work with local people in assisting them to identify their needs and their way forward. Community development workers are one of the assets in the change process, but we are never the 'expert' with the answers.

6.2   The Journey of Community Development

Community development is a social product, and as such it evolves as society, culture and the economy changes. How all this works out is also dependent upon which society we are working in. For example, practice in the USA developed from a unique set of conditions and has since taken a different route compared to that of the UK. Each country will have its own road, separate from, and yet influenced to various degrees by, the experience of other countries. This following discussion focuses on the UK, and each country will have their own version of this narrative.

In the UK, community development as a defined activity comes from nineteenth-century roots based on a Christian ethos of helping the poor. Over the following hundred years or so, community development slowly developed an unequal symbiotic relationship with public policy. It has highlighted social needs, influenced social reform, and in turn has been shaped by government legislation. Sometimes government has promoted community development, and other times it has ignored it. In the later years of the twentieth century, government incorporated community development into its own agenda (it is open to debate whether this was to help promote community development or to control it). Either way, community development has, in operational terms, become separated from its radical, oppositional strand. Broadly, it is now there to organise communities into partnerships with government. Many good things have come from this client status. However, many things have been lost, including the idea that the community can be its own power centre with its own agenda. If you examine community development in the UK from an SDI or Community Organising/ACORN perspective, it can look small scale, unambitious, and domesticated.

In these early years of the twenty-first century, community development in the UK is in decline. Its closeness to government has meant it has overrelied upon local authority funding. In a time of austerity budgets, community development activity has been seriously defunded. A legacy of all this is that people's experience of community development is centred around looking for grants, with projects being, in one way or another, dependent upon these funds. The idea of the community self-funding projects as practised in the USA is indeed a foreign concept.

Our view, and something that can be seen in several of the case studies, is that the old paradigm of community development practice is changing. The usefulness of values, theories and models (Freire, Community Organising, etc.) remain. What is required is a new way of funding and delivering practice.

Ideologically, many people are fixed on community development being closely connected to the state and state funding. Sometimes, this is because it is what people know, for others it is that the state should provide, and community development is really an arm of the state to do this. Whether we like it or not these days have most probably gone.

For community development to have a viable future it needs to reinvent how it organises itself. In our view a number of things need to happen. Community development needs to do the following:

- Remain committed to the values of CD, continue to explore the social theories that help explain the world, and further evolve the key practice models;
- See itself as independent from government, but willing to work collaboratively on an equal basis when this would be advantageous to the community;
- Operate on a larger scale and be more ambitious in what it wants to achieve in communities.

For this to happen, community development workers/organisations need to:

- Embrace creativity, flexibility and risk-taking and move away from the small-scale bureaucratic ways of working that hinders new thinking;
- Overcome austerity budgets and ties to government community development activity, which needs to be mostly self-funded;
- Achieve self-funding through operating as a social enterprise, or other nonprofit distributing models.

Whether community development can rise to these challenges remains to be seen. There is a danger that it may continue to decline with its best days behind it. Reinvention is never easy, but often that is the only way forward.

6.3 Statement of Hope

In the face of all the challenges, compromises and failures, and the missed opportunities, we remain hopeful.

We have been lucky enough to meet fellow practitioners in many parts of the world and are always amazed by their ability to see and work for a better future. People say 'I'll believe it when I see it' but people working for social change believe it first, work for it, and then see it.

We have seen people, who refuse to accept the lack of youth provision in their community in Belfast, set up a youth club in a tent in their back garden. People who give up lucrative careers with global charities to set up self-funded projects that work with marginalised communities in New Delhi. We have talked with the chairperson of the rag-pickers association in Mumbai, her eyes blazing with pride as she talked of all they had achieved, gaining a living for the people and recognition from the government. We have sat with people who were resisting the redevelopment of the ninth ward in New Orleans, taking on the developers and making a place for those displaced by hurricane Katrina to come home. We have witnessed the impact of education programmes embedded in the townships of South Africa, building a sense of identity and power.

We are hopeful because we see young people rejecting the top-down, controlling approaches of state-sponsored provision. Instead they are taking part-time jobs that fund them to do 'real' community work for the rest of the time. Recently we have seen school children go on strike from school to protest against climate change, despite the pressure from teachers and the threats of falling behind and missing out. For them, the bigger issue is worth the sacrifice.

We are hopeful because we see people who had been told they would amount to nothing, discovering their voice, their agency and are making a difference in their world. People who, despite all of the poverty and injustice that life has thrown at them, who have, as their overriding motivation, a desire to give something back to their community, to use what they have suffered and what they have learned through their suffering to make the world a better place.

Finally, we are hopeful because we 'trust the process'. If you bring people together in a supportive environment and talk with them, think with them and work with them, something good will always come out of it. People are able to make sense of their world and develop solutions to issues they face as they gain a sense of collective strength and support. Let's all move forward together.

Dave Beck, Rod Purcell – Glasgow, January 2020

Index

Note: Page numbers in *italics* refer to figures

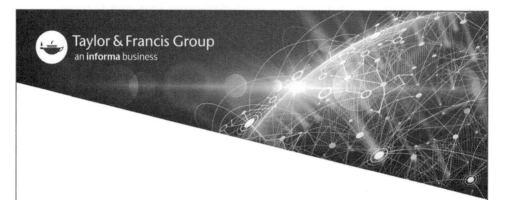